CAN YOU DIG IT

2085 Rockspr... VIDEO GAME

257 VIDEO GAME

208

48
93
94 "'60 sheydogs"
95 C1 "HOMICIDE
Incorporated"

11B

176
(178 sheets)

242
(feb 1974)

CAN YOU DIG IT

THE PHENOMENON OF

SEAN EGAN

Foreword by Michael Beck

BearManor Media

2021

Can You Dig It: The Phenomenon of The Warriors

© 2021 Sean Egan

Published in the United States of America by:

BearManor Media
1317 Edgewater Dr #110
Orlando FL 32804
bearmanormedia.com

Printed in the United States.

ISBN—978-1-62933-805-7

CONTENTS

FOREWORD

BY MICHAEL BECK

FOR ALL YOU BOPPERS OUT THERE, this is the book you've been
waiting decades for.

In *Can You Dig It*, Sean Egan—not unlike Xenophon in his relaying
of the March of the Ten Thousand—takes the reader on a heroic trek,
fraught with skirmishes, retreats, assaults, and defeats, but which
ultimately leads to a homecoming filled with vindication. He ushers us
from a used bookstore in the late 1970s, where a savvy producer grabs a
"good idea" for a film from a paperback novel synopsis, to a movie-house
retrospective showing of that finished picture four decades later, where a
renowned writer-director smiles to himself as a raucous audience shouts
his well-known lines to the characters on the screen.

Through extensive research and in-depth interviews, Egan
orchestrates disparate voices—two Hollywood producers, an A-list
writer-director, a dozen or so cast members (as well as a son and a sister
of deceased actor participants), a proactive stunt coordinator, a gifted
costume designer, a cutting-edge soundtrack composer, and the skeptical
author of a nearly forgotten novel that started it all—into a Greek chorus
that collectively tells the full, frank story of a remarkable piece of cinema.
Egan's journalism is first rate. He fleshes out each person he interviews
with background biography which, filtered through his droll British wit,
gives the reader a sense of who that person is, was, or might have been. He
elicits threads of remembrance from numerous sources that oftentimes

vii

don't agree, and he leaves their frayed ends hanging for you to weave together into your own mental tapestry of the events on the set on any given day.

An informative and fun read, *Can You Dig It* is a book for any cinephile seeking greater understanding of *The Warriors'* status as a cult classic. It provides answers to questions you've always had and discovers things you've never thought or heard of before. *I* learned new things— and I played the film's Swan, for crying out loud! And as that War Chief himself might have said, "Sean Egan's story of *The Warriors* is the Best."

INTRODUCTION

"**IT WAS A SURPRISE** the entire way. I had fantasies, then I was just skeptical, then I was exhilarated, then my dreams were dashed. And now it's this timeless, amazing fable that just goes on and on and on."

Deborah Van Valkenburgh, the actress who played the female lead in *The Warriors*, is recalling the remarkable ride that the film has constituted for her and the rest of its cast and crew. The joy of obtaining a potentially life-changing role, followed by dismay and incredulity at the innovativeness-cum-strangeness of what was being filmed; then the euphoria engendered by unimaginable commercial success, followed in turn by dismay at the irresponsible, even evil, status that the picture abruptly and unexpectedly acquired; and finally the vindication and joy that came with the film's subsequent steady cultural and artistic rehabilitation into cult classic status.

The 1979 Walter Hill-directed Paramount motion picture *The Warriors* told the tale of a Coney Island street gang making a perilous journey back to home turf across rivals' terrain after a conclave at which they are framed for murder. The film overcame a low budget, an absence of marquee names, and minimal promotion to lead the box office. Within weeks, though, this glory was tarnished when deaths at and around screenings of the film created an unparalleled controversy about on-screen violence and the potential for its imitation among the cinema-going public. The picture never recovered commercial momentum. However, it never lost the critical kudos it picked up at the same time: some of the era's most esteemed film writers weighed in on its side.

The Warriors started life in 1965 as a novel by Sol Yurick, who hit upon the idea of grafting New York gangs onto the storyline of the Greek

1

classic *The Anabasis*, which true-life narrative by Xenophon depicted an army of 10,000 men embarking on a heroic homeward trek across enemy territory. Producer Lawrence Gordon, ever alert for good movie ideas, happened upon a precis of the plot of Yurick's novel on a bookstore discount spinner and was immediately taken by the concept.

After commissioning a script from David Shaber, Gordon hired Walter Hill to direct, with Hill also reworking Shaber's screenplay to his own specifications. Social realism was not on the moviemakers' agenda. With the sheer nastiness of the gang in the book out of the question, the film adaptation began moving almost as a matter of course towards a surreal take on inner-city street life, something assisted by the fact that this was a New York picture being made by Californians unfamiliar with the Big Apple's manners, customs, layout, and ambience. Even so, some of the singular scuzziness of Seventies New York City informed the finished film, preserving it for posterity long after reform and gentrification consigned it to history.

For a movie with such narrow parameters (it all occurs within a 24-hour period in an urban area whose furthest extremes are no greater than a subway ride away), *The Warriors'* shoot was attended by an extraordinary degree of strife, even chaos. Everything that could go wrong did go wrong. The filming was always going to be arduous work by virtue of the picture's chase-driven and nocturnal nature. On top of that, though, the project quickly fell behind schedule and went over-budget, causing the always dubious Paramount to make noises about closing the production down. Then there was the problem of real-life gang members loitering around the sets, bringing with them blackmail and disruption. In addition were the multiple injuries sustained to Van Valkenburgh. The biggest disturbance, though, was the drastic decision taken seven weeks into shooting by Hill and Gordon to fire their leading man, Thomas Waites, dictating a rewriting job that was no less substantial for it being necessarily hasty. Perhaps it's little surprise that the studio could barely conceal its skepticism about the product that Hill turned in.

Others, however, were entranced. Whereas the milieu of *The Warriors* was one normally only depicted in motion pictures as an examination of a social problem, this movie portrayed life from the street gang's point of view. It was an obvious but revolutionary approach that struck a chord with the urban working class, especially its adolescent sub-set. The quasi-balletic action set-pieces and the hypnotic luminescence of the film's optics added further layers of fascination, as did some fine performances, particularly that of Roger Hill as gang leader Cyrus, whose conclave speech—replete with insurrectionary refrain "Can you dig it!"— was like gutter-level Shakespeare. The cherry on the cake derived from the spurning of the traditional classical or jazz score for a cutting-edge doomy synthesizer soundtrack.

In the second week of February 1979, lines began forming around blocks where the movie was playing. As Hill notes, "From out of nowhere we were the number one box-office film." Yet the appeal of *The Warriors* went further than the paying public. Respected reviewers like the *New Yorker's* notoriously hard-to-please Pauline Kael perceived beauty in a picture some were quick to dismiss as exploitative trash.

However, there followed a precipitous fall from grace. Within a week of the film's release, there had been three allegedly *Warriors*-associated deaths. Some cinemas dropped the picture, while others took up a nervous Paramount's offer to pay for security at screenings. Many who saw the film wondered what the fuss was about. Although the movie had been advertised with an incendiary poster, the violence in *The Warriors* was tame even by the standards of the era. Yet though the controversy might have been a bum rap, the harsh spotlight shone on Paramount ultimately made the studio lose its nerve and—according to whom you speak—either pull the film's advertising or withdraw the picture from circulation altogether. Either way, *The Warriors'* unlikely domination of the American box-office came to an abrupt end less than a month after its release.

The always limited circulation of *The Warriors*—whether it be by dint of the fall-out from the scandal or simply the fact of its "R" rating—caused it to be enveloped in myth. This in turn gave it an aura of dread: people who knew it only second-hand felt it to epitomize the plagues of the 1970s, where screen violence, youth unrest, social decay, and economic decline seemed to be combining to create a perfect storm that would inevitably lead to the end of everything that decent citizens held dear. For that reason, it will always be as culturally fascinating as it is artistically compelling.

The Warriors has now risen above both its original notoriety and its subsequent period-piece status. As well as enjoying the standing of a cinematic and cultural landmark, it is an industry, having spun off video games, action figures, comic books, and a director's-cut DVD. The cast are constantly in demand for "conclaves"—conventions with Q&As and signing sessions.

Can You Dig It tells the full story of *The Warriors*, from high-minded original novel to multiple screenplay drafts to rushed, chaotic film shoot to paradoxically polished and stylish final movie. It also comprehensively explores the ups and downs of fortune subsequently experienced by those associated with it. A full array of participants—director, producers, actors, crew—have provided their memories and insights to explain one motion picture's remarkable rollercoaster journey.

THE SOURCE

THE WARRIORS was originally an insurance policy.

In the early 1960s, Sol Yurick was having trouble selling his first novel, *Fertig*. Its narrative depicts a man systematically murdering those he holds responsible for the death of his son after the latter is refused admission to hospital. The titular father actually desires a trial because he sees it as a means to obtain a platform for a denunciation of a system that kills people. He is up against an establishment judge who detests everything Fertig represents. Equidistant between the two—morally and motivationally—is Fertig's lawyer, Bleakie. Once published, the book was hailed as a powerful contemporary satire. However, prior to this the route to its publication seemed impassable. "*Fertig* was being circulated and being rejected 38 times," the late Yurick told this author in a 2009 interview. (All Yurick quotes in this book are from that conversation unless otherwise stated.) "So I thought, 'Well, while I'm waiting for it to happen or not, hadn't I better write something else?'" That something else was *The Warriors*. It would make Yurick's name and kickstart his career, but he admitted that without the initial failure of *Fertig*, "I might not have actually sat down to write the book."

Solomon Yurick was born in the Bronx in 1925. His father was a milliner. Yurick's parents were both Jewish immigrants and he didn't speak English for the first five years of his life. After high school, Yurick enlisted in the army, where he trained as a surgical technician and served in World War II. Following cessation of hostilities, he took advantage of the GI Bill to enlist at New York University, where he obtained a bachelor's degree, majoring in literature.

5

Following graduation, he became what is generically known as a social worker but was specifically termed by New York City's Department of Welfare a "social investigator." Yurick's first creative writing could be said to be the "intimate journals" he began keeping in 1956, but writing with the specific aim of publication was something Yurick defrayed, his journals finding him wondering if he could "muster enough anger to write anything meaningful." *Fertig* broke that dam psychologically, while *The Warriors* made writing a commercial proposition. The impetus for the *Warriors* story came from Yurick's social work. The children of some of his clients were what were then called juvenile delinquents and some of them belonged to fighting gangs. "I had been doing a lot of reading, both in literature and in sociology, especially the classics," he said. "Durkheim and people like that." In a comment emblematic of a rationalism that was sometimes rarefied to the point of impenetrability, he added, "Which is elementary forms of religious life." More comprehensibly, Yurick explained that he felt he could utilize "actual practical experience in seeing life as it was, and not agreeing with what I read in social workers and people who were talking about *Rebel Without a Cause*, that kind of thing." The latter is a reference not to the famous James Dean motion picture but to the 1944 book-length study by psychiatrist Robert M. Lindner subtitled *The Hypnoanalysis of a Criminal Psychopath.*

While sociology told Yurick what he *didn't* want to write, literature provided him with templates for what should be in his book. He cited three main inspirations. One was the *Outlaws Of The Marsh*, perhaps better known as *The Water Margin*, a sort of Ancient-Chinese *Dirty Dozen*. "I love the work," he said. "One of Mao's most favorite books, which I didn't know at the time." Another—"oddly enough," Yurick admitted—was John Milton's epic, blank-verse 17th-century religious poem *Paradise Lost*. Pointed out Yurick of the explicit influence of this work on *The Warriors*, "All the gangs have the same names as the division in heaven: Thrones, Dominations..." However, the primary literary influence for *The Warriors* was *The Anabasis*. Yurick recalled mentioning to a friend in the 1950s, almost as a joke, the idea of a fighting gang based on the story of Xenophon's most well-known work. "The idea occurred to me really when I was in college, when I first read *The Anabasis*," Yurick reflected. "All of this came together bit by bit. We're talking from the late Forties all the way into the early Sixties. I wrote the book in, I guess, '63. It formed in my mind and it took me three weeks to write."

Xenophon, born in approximately 431 BC, was both a soldier and a writer. He was an active participant in the March of the Ten Thousand, whose other common title—Anabasis—means a march into the heart of a foreign country. This particular 401 BC expedition was predicated on a quest by an army of Greek mercenaries retained by Cyrus the Younger for the purpose of seizing Persia from his brother, Artaxerxes II. Despite initial victory, the quest became moot when Cyrus was killed in action. With the army now stranded in enemy territory, Xenophon exhorted the demoralized and bewildered ten thousand to begin the long journey home. Their tenacity and bravery when faced with perilous conditions and hostile forces not only secured them a safe return to the Black Sea, but a place in legend—with a little help from Xenophon's not-exactly-impartial written account of the proceedings. Yurick's retelling replaced Cyrus' Greek mercenaries with a contemporary New York City street gang, the Dominators, and the trek across 1,766 miles through the Persian Empire to the Black Sea with a fifteen-mile journey from the Bronx to Coney Island, Brooklyn.

Although Yurick's writing process may have taken less than a month, it was preceded by extensive research. He traced his projected route for his gang, timing it and ascertaining its plausibility. After an abortive period spent interviewing gang members—he concluded that they were telling him what they thought he wanted to hear—he began spying on them instead, using a hired panel truck with holes punched in the sides, which he would park on their turf. Yurick said this turf was, at that period in time, the entire world for New York street gangs, who kept to their own neighborhood, not least because they didn't have access to cars. At the same time, these kids had more in material terms than the ones with whom he had worked. "By that time, they were changing... To an extent I was looking really at the gangs of the late Forties and Fifties. The American gangs at that point had absolutely no economic function. In the Sixties, they began to have an economic function as they branched into drugs and things like that."

Yurick rejected the criticism that he was inappropriately projecting onto these insalubrious characters noble and heroic precedents. "What were the ten thousand warriors? They were like surplus population and they were essentially mercenaries," he reasoned. "So I had no feelings of nobility about Greek culture whatsoever. To me, they're just as bad as any other culture I can think of. Remembering too that the Greeks, working through their city states, were essentially expansionist. They were imperial. Especially Athens. Xenophon was an Athenian who later betrayed Athens itself." However, he did accept that his protagonists were thoroughly nasty pieces of work. "There's a gang rape in the book and there's a kind of ritualized killing. What I was trying to portray was the kind of frenzy that happens in a mass action when you're excited and you're scared and what have you." He had little sympathy for these excited and scared youths. "The only sympathy I had is that these people had an absolutely lost life. The movie hints at the possibility of redemption or hope in some way. The book does not. It's all downhill. They have to lose in the long run... I'm not particularly ennobling them but look at people who get caught up in certain social situations for which there is no way out. That does elicit, to me, a little bit of sorrow." Incidentally, readers would be mistaken if they inferred contempt from the insulting sobriquets Yurick conferred on his characters ("Lunkface," "Bimbo"). "These kinds of names were the kind of names they gave each other," he said.

Gang members, of course, possess a certain stature, even if one largely illusory. Although inconsequential in wider society, within such a set-up they have power and allure—until the physical prowess that gave them this stature atrophies and they are overtaken by the younger members. Asked whether he felt that the doomed trajectories of gang members are akin to a Greek tragedy, Yurick said, "Well, in a sense what is Greek tragedy about but a kind of nobly written soap opera? You look at what Oedipus had to do to get the power and his fall and it's a dynastic struggle within that. And the tragedy that's expressed, for example, in the British play, especially Shakespeare, is the same thing. You have what are essentially thugs struggling for power who've been given noble words by writers, but who obviously in real life rarely talk like that. So my view is pretty cynical about all that."

There was no ideology behind *The Warriors*. "At that point I was not political," Yurick said. Though he stated, "I grew up in a communist family," he himself became disillusioned with politics at a tender age. "I had stopped being political when I was fourteen in August 1939—the Hitler-Stalin pact—and remained apolitical 'til about maybe a year after *The Warriors* came out." However, he also acknowledged that his hinterland seeped into him whether he knew it or wanted it, as he found out when he was touting around the manuscript. "One of the editors said, 'I can't believe a gang leader who talks like a Marxist.' That kind of shocked me because that's not what I had consciously intended. So you grow up and some stuff goes into your unconscious, and not in the way Freud ever thought about." When, post-*Warriors*, Yurick rediscovered his political passion, he found that he did in fact view the world through Marxist eyes.

He maintained that perspective for most of his life, although by 2009 was noting, "I'm beginning to pass it. I'm becoming a combination Marxist and Darwinian. I can give you a biological basis for the accumulation of surplus value that starts right from the beginning of someone's life."

Yurick said that some of the characters in *The Warriors* were based on people he'd met as a young man or as a social worker or both. He hadn't run into any of those people subsequently, but did say, "After the book came out, my wife and I started to work with street kids in our neighborhood in Brooklyn in Park Slope. Most of them just went down and went nowhere." In a remarkable addendum he noted, "One became a policeman."

As to his book's historical, literary, and sociological references, Yurick insisted that his aim was to keep them hidden. "If you saw them, fine; if you didn't, okay. I didn't want these things to get in the way. I didn't want them to operate in such a way as a writer might be saying, 'Look how smart I am' or 'Look at how many references I can throw in.'" Even so, the character Junior keeps himself amused on the Dominators' travels by reading a comic book about "ancient soldiers, Greeks, heroes who had to fight their way home through many obstacles, but in the end they made it." Moreover, the first edition of *The Warriors* contained on its first page the following quote:

> "Soldiers, you must not be downhearted because of recent events.
>
> "I can assure you that there are as many advantages as disadvantages in what has happened.
>
> "My friends, these people whom you see are the last obstacle which stops us from being where we have so long struggled to be. We ought, if we could, to eat them up alive."
>
> – from *Anabasis* by Xenophon

The narrative of *The Warriors* takes place within one non-calendar day, starting at 3 p.m. on July 4th and ending on July 5th at 6 a.m. The book opens with a scene in the clubhouse of the Delancey Thrones, a gang led by a charismatic Puerto Rican named Ismael Rivera. Although Ismael is reluctant to give up the lifestyle of a "Presidente," his social worker Mannie has introduced him to "the better things of life—interest in a job, books, a future..." (One gets the feeling that this fleetingly seen social worker is, at least in part, Yurick.) The social worker knows that something is going down and is trying to find out what, but to little avail. What's cooking is not a "bop" (also referred to as a "rumble" or a "jap") but an assembly or Big Meeting, to which Ismael has invited every gang in the city, including the book's central ensemble, the Coney Island Dominators.

The Dominators actually refer to themselves far less often by this name than they do "the Family," a term partly devised by leader Arnold in defiance of a subway poster that declares, "Where family life stops, delinquency begins." The gang has ranks based on familial roles: father (Arnold), uncles, sons, daughters, cousins, etc. Although scornful to a degree, the appropriation of the term "family" also buys into the notion of its benefits, and the cachet that the notion of family possesses is made more understandable by the youth of the ranks: all gang-member ages mentioned are between fourteen and seventeen.

The Dominators have a uniform of short neck-buttoning jackets, blue paisley print button-down collar shirts, tight black chino trousers, ankle-high elastic sided boots, and high-crowned narrow-brimmed straw hats. This is, of course, very Sixties attire. The narrative is explicitly contemporaneous to publication, for instance referencing the Beatles. Into the hats are inserted the Dominators sign: Mercedes-Benz hub-cap ornaments pulled off parked cars and affixed via safety pins soldered in school workshops. The Mercedes-Benz' status as a car well beyond the means of the common man was underlined six years after the publication of Yurick's novel by a half-mocking, half-yearning Janis Joplin song about owning one. The pin is, according to the thoughts of Hinton—a "brother" in the outfit—a source of pride: "Everyone saw you belonged, had something, were something…" However, the insignia also creates danger, being "a come-on, a cause to fight." It makes the Dominators' enemies angry: "They wanted to take it from you and make you the way they were."

Seven Dominator "plenipos" are selected by Arnold to attend the assembly with him. The word seems to come from "plenipotentiary," Latin for ambassador. If it seems implausible phraseology for the milieu, it should be remembered that "pleb" is a common insult in Britain among people who are completely unaware of its origin as an abbreviation of "plebian." The pleinpos are:

- Hector. A pretty boy, thought of by a supporting character as having "a beautiful face and blond, wavy hair."

- Lunkface: A Puerto Rican who is short-tempered, unpredictable, stupid, and frequently inebriated. However, he is useful for strength, being six foot one, broad, and strong.

- Dewey (described by Yurick as both sixteen and seventeen) is a reliable, long-term Family member. He wears thick-rimmed glasses.

- The Junior (actual name: Junior) is aged fourteen. He is a sort of mascot, although recognized to be in possession of "heart."

- Bimbo is cool, unimaginative, steady; a good man to have by your side in any bop/jap/rumble. His role is "bearer," him charged with the responsibility of holding the subway tokens.

- Hinton will emerge as the book's main character. A kid with gray eyes and skin like chocolate, his talent for caricature and fancy lettering has made him the Family's resident artist. This being slightly before the era of aerosol paint cans, the means by which he leaves the Dominators' sign is merely a Magic Marker. Despite his artistry, he has a certain psychotic tendency: when he gets the fighting madness, even Lunkface fears him a little. This is a piece of manipulation on Hinton's part, bravado disguising the fact that he knows he doesn't have "the strength or the heart." He has only been in the gang a short while (eight months).

At Ismael's instruction, the thousand-strong delegates from the city's various gangs congregate in the Bronx's Van Cortlandt Park. They are referred to by the authorial voice as "warriors." So too is the protagonist gang, but only once does one of the protagonist gang themselves refer to the Dominators as warriors. In the park, Ismael reveals the purpose of the assembly. After warming up the crowd by pointing out the bleakness of their lives and prospects, he tells them that—including the affiliates, the unorganized but ready to fight, and women—the warriors are a hundred-thousand strong. In contrast, there are only about twenty thousand New York City "fuzz." "One gang could, in time, run the city... they would tax the city and tax the crime syndicates..." For a moment, he has them all convinced, but his dreams of unity are quickly shattered and for the most petty of reasons: "Someone slapped at a mosquito; a jumpy warrior misinterpreted the sign and struck back. A fight broke out. Groups began to bop in the darkness." When police cars arrive, in the fractious atmosphere those prepared to believe the worst about Ismael assume it is he who betrayed them. Guns are produced and two bullets fatally reach him.

In the resulting melee, the Dominators get separated from Arnold, who is presumed by them to be in a police paddy wagon. "It takes about an hour, an hour and a half, depending on the subway service, to get from the top of the Bronx to Coney Island," states the text. "Coney Island is about fifteen miles away." This relatively short journey home, though, is now fraught with danger. The truce mounted to facilitate the assembly is now clearly over. Moreover, the Dominators are defenseless in enemy territory, as the only weapon they'd carried was a .22 pistol that Arnold had intended to give to Ismael as a "token".

In the absence of Arnold, Hector assumes the role of Father. He points out that the police (part of a capitalized "Other" that the authorial voice speaks of as the Family being in opposition to, willingly or otherwise) will "pick you up if you're between fourteen and twenty and look wrong. And tonight, everyone looks wrong."

They phone Wallie, their Youth Board Worker. Telling him they are in trouble, they ask him to drive over and pick them up. Wallie agrees. However, partly as a function of their youth, they begin spinning paranoid, inchoate fantasies about the Big Meeting being a way for the Other to get all the gang leaders at once. Accordingly, they decide not to wait for Wallie but to make their own way home.

The first train they take is stopped due to the track being out for repair. Unable to get a transfer because of the chaos caused by the timetable disruption, they go out into the street. An Hispanic gang immediately spot their insignia. Realizing that they are too exposed to hang around waiting for the replacement buses, the Dominators decide to parley for safe passage. The gang is the Borinquen Blazers, who wear plantation-owner straw hats. Hector feels racist contempt for them ("You could just tell... they were practically off the plane from the mother-island"). However, all the Family are impressed, at least physically, with a heavily made-up, bare midriffed Puerto Rican girl—not named—accompanying the Blazers. After the two gangs prove to each other their notoriety via clippings from the *Daily News* and *La Prensa*, Blazer leader Jesus Mendez gives the Dominators permission to cross the Blazers' turf. However, hostilities flare up after the girl is rebuffed by the Dominators when she demands one of their Mercedes-Benz pins. "Are you going to let them parade through our land wearing insignia?" she demands of Mendez. Although he knows he is being manipulated, Mendez also needs to show he is not chicken and imposes the condition that the Dominators remove their pins. ("You go through as civilians—all right. You go through as soldiers—no good.") The Dominators take some swigs from a whiskey bottle for courage, fling it at the Blazers, and march on, hoping that the other gang's reinforcements won't arrive before they've passed through their territory. They find themselves followed by the girl, who is still hankering for a pin and expresses contempt for "this land of the cuckoos and the capons."

When a passer-by glances at the girl, the Dominators decide to pick a fight with him. Egged on by the girl, they batter him, hit him with bottles, and stab him with a knife stolen from Mendez. With the man lying lifeless on the ground, their bloodlust is transformed into a different kind of lust and they turn their attentions to the girl, whom they gang-rape. They then abandon her and run for their train. The Family now have two additional reasons to avoid the authorities.

Although they board a waiting train, they have to hurriedly leave it when transit cops spot them. They get separated, with Hinton jumping off the end of the platform. Panic-stricken, he continues into the tunnel in front of him. The following chapter in which Hinton fearfully makes his way up the dark tracks to the next station is the first time the text has focused on an individual character's thought processes for any sustained length. (Perhaps significantly, Yurick had already written about Hinton in a short story.) It makes for a much better reading experience than anything hitherto, Yurick no longer flitting with irritating omniscience between different points of view. The fact that Hinton is spooked by his own footsteps in the paranoia-inducing gloom, him literally sobbing, emphasizes that these protagonists are—for all their bestial behavior—children.

Meanwhile, Lunkface, Hector, and Bimbo end up in a park where they are distracted by a drunk, overweight nurse sitting on a bench. She is sexually interested in Lunkface, but when Bimbo tries to steal her purse, starts screaming for help. A prowl car happens to be passing and the boys are arrested in no uncertain manner. The author notes, "And so they went down to the station house where it was going to be much worse."

The home straight of the novel once again focuses exclusively on Hinton and, like the tunnel chapter, is a superior piece of writing. Having made his way back to Times Square and finding no sign of the other Family members, Hinton wanders uncertainly around. He takes refuge from the cops in a women's lavatory, which turns out to have been co-opted by pimps. There, he has a joyless coupling with a white prostitute, although turns down drugs. Indeed, narcotics are the one thing about which the Family seems to be moralistic ("...he knew where that led. It meant to be out because the Family wouldn't tolerate addicts. How could you depend on somebody with a habit that could betray you?")

Hinton further passes the time by ravenously consuming junk food and exploring an amusement arcade. He plays the type of games that seemed impressive in the analog age, ones involving gripping mock gun stocks while firing at opponents represented by cut-outs and flashing lights. After playing a game with a Second World War vista, he moves on to one involving a shoot-out with a sheriff. He works out how to beat the system, realizing that he needs to fire while the sheriff is still mouthing his spiel ("This is a law-abidin' town and we aim to keep it that-a-way. Clear out, you polecat, or I'm-a-goin' to run you in").

In the flush of his victory, Hinton feels like a man, even possessing enough willpower to resist playing again despite the machine having awarded him a free game. Yet for all his manly status, he briefly toys with the idea of going off with one of the homosexuals who keep harassing him ("have a kick or two and then deck the fag and take his money").

Hinton, Dewey, and Junior reconnect in the station. As they don't know where the others are, Hinton decides that they will go home. On the train, two smartly dressed white couples—possibly fresh from a prom—sit opposite them. The males eye the Dominators with contempt. Their innocent-looking, pretty dates provoke a yearning in Hinton. "It would be nice to have a girl. It would be nice to cut out from the Family, to retire from bopping." It lasts only until the couples get off the train, and then his thoughts turn once more to violence ("He would remember that station and someday, just someday, he might lead the men and come down on a little raid around here, looking for them, because who were they to jive the Family?"). His thoughts turn to raiding again when, back in Coney Island, the Dominators have to cross the territory of rival gang the Colonial Lords. However, it's now dawn and the Dominators' yelled challenges from the playground of the Lords' housing project are met with silence. Hinton makes do by leaving some profane graffiti. Arriving at the beach, they are as overjoyed—just like the Greek soldiers in Junior's comic book had been at the sight of their own water-based objective.

Hinton's new status of Father evaporates as soon as they meet up with the gang's girlfriends, who inform them that Arnold made it back hours ago. Hinton disconsolately proceeds to the Prison, his term for his housing project. In its communal toilet, he is too tired to stick to his custom of keeping off the seat as he defecates. In his crowded, sleeping apartment, he finds his half-brother Alonso still awake, if possibly drugged up. Hinton tries to tell him about his adventures that night, but his unimpressed sibling advises him, "There is only one thing and that is the kick, the Now. Nothing else counts. Get yours. Get it because, you know, no one cares and they will always put you down in the end..." Hinton climbs onto the fire escape and goes to sleep with his thumb in his mouth.

Although not technically a first novel, *The Warriors* suffers from several naiveté-related flaws. Yurick keeps telling, not showing, especially with speech. (In fact, this shorthand style curiously makes the novel often read like a screen treatment, a simplified precursor to a screenplay.) This is a pity, as when he proffers dialogue rather than a summary of it, Yurick evinces a pleasing ear for colloquialism ("Man, did you see that Ismael? He's not so big now. Choom. Right through the eye"). Yurick's authorial voice includes an awkward combination of writerly prose and hipster stylization ("The pony-junkies noticed nothing. They were down, and drowned in the lose-gloom, and were getting those empty-pocket, come-down shakes"). However, the book is very unusual for the time in being a depiction of a world hidden from most of society, especially those sections of society populated by book lovers. It is also an uncommonly non-salacious and non-judgmental depiction of that world. The delicious frission that such literature sent up the spines of people otherwise insulated from the milieux it explored could cause them to overlook deficiencies. "When the book came out, it got a lot of good reviews all around the country," noted Yurick.

The Warriors appeared through the auspices of Holt, Rinehart & Winston on August 16, 1965 as a 189-page hardcover. Its front featured a design by Lawrence Ratzkin depicting a switchblade buried in a white surface that bore the red-scrawled title and author name. Adorning the front flap was an encomium by Warren Miller. Miller was at the time the trendiest of novelists, partly for his 1959 work *The Cool World*, a sort of black, working-class *Catcher in the Rye*. As its fourteen-year-old narrator Duke Custis is the War Lord of a Harlem gang, Miller was a natural choice for endorser. His blurb stated, "It seems to me the best novel of its kind I've read, an altogether perfect achievement. I'm sure that to many it will sound like sacrilege, but I have to say that I think it a better novel than *Lord of the Flies.*" The book's dustwrapper flaps offered a precis that ended with the observation, "Some readers will sympathize with these protagonists. Others will want to lynch them. No one who reads *The Warriors* can fail to be moved."

Kirkus Review seemed to agree. It wrote, "The 'Warriors,' spawn of the miasmic streets, form the modern tribes of the Shook-up Generation...the Gangs. A first novel, this is written powerfully enough to make you succumb to the distorted reality and values of these groups... Raw, intense and perversely readable..." Said review also made mention of *The Amboy Dukes*, a 1947 bestseller by Irving Shulman depicting restless, fornicating, criminal gangs in wartime Brooklyn.

Yurick's book secured a UK license in the form of a 1966 W. H. Allen "hardback" (in the local lingo). Its jacket featured a perplexing arbitrary Peter Pope design of splayed fingers holding a cigarette, although it did at least feature the apropos Mercedes-Benz symbol. The blurb on the front flap adapted the one from the American edition, but added a line designed to give these New Yorkers' adventures a resonance in "Blighty": "Readers have only to think of some of our own Mods and Rockers to realize that the behavior described in this book is far from being something that could not happen here." The book made it into paperback in the UK in 1967 through Panther. Its back cover quoted at length a *Sunday Citizen* review in which Alan Forrest wrote, "'It's *West Side Story* and then some, and nobody's singing I Feel Pretty...' This was adapted for a tagline on the 1972 reprint (or "strapline" as the UK-based designer would have more likely put it). The book was also published in Japan.

Despite the acclaim and the foreign editions, though, *The Warriors* did not enjoy the bestseller status of some of its infamous precedents, not even transferring to softcover in the USA until 1979. "The movie made it catch on," admitted Yurick.

THE ADAPTER

THE RAVE REVIEWS garnered by *The Warriors* would seem to have passed by film producer Lawrence "Larry" Gordon. He had never heard of the book when he by chance became cognizant of its plot via a synopsis. However, he was quickly enamored.

Born in 1936, Gordon was raised in Belzoni, Mississippi. After graduating from Tulane University, he attended law school at the University of Mississippi for a year, but Hollywood beckoned him to a more glamorous calling than attorney. His first screen-related job was working with Aaron Spelling, a man whose name had been a byword for televisual success since the early Sixties (not least because it was prominently displayed on his many productions). Starting work on *Burke's Law* as a $50-a-week gofer, Gordon eventually hauled his way up the ladder to the status of associate producer. He became head of West Coast Talent Development at the ABC television network but departed to become a Vice President of Screen Gems (later renamed Columbia Pictures Television). There, he developed new projects, among which numbered the critically acclaimed and widely watched *Brian's Song*, an ABC-TV movie-of-the-Week starring James Caan and Billy Dee Williams.

His next port of call was American-International Pictures, where he took up the post of Vice President in Charge of Worldwide Production. In his three years there, he was responsible for, among other successes, *Dillinger* and the cartoon *Heavy Traffic*. He resigned to form his own production company, an act presaged by him having served as executive producer on *Dillinger*.

Gordon's first non-executive production was *Hard Times*. A 1975 Charles Bronson vehicle about a bare-knuckle Depression-era fighter, it was written and directed by Walter Hill. This expression of faith in the idea of the writer as the creative force in motion pictures again had a precedent in *Dillinger*, which at Lawrence's instigation had seen John Milius film his own screenplay.

Gordon produced the violent 1977 Paul Schrader/Heywood Gould Vietnam-vet story *Rolling Thunder*. Black comedy *The End* (1978) wasn't critically well-received but, like just about any Seventies production in which Burt Reynolds took the central role, did more than respectable box office. *The Driver* (1978) was Gordon's second collaboration with Hill, the latter again directing from his own screenplay. In the same year, Gordon exec-produced *Hooper*, another Burt Reynolds picture, this one a tribute to stunt performers. The next Gordon project to see release was *The Warriors*.

Always on the look-out for ideas for motion pictures, Gordon happened upon this one when he was standing in a "used Hollywood bookstore." The story he has always told is that he found a paperback which gave a first-page synopsis of *The Warriors*. However, *The Warriors* was not yet in softcover and the US hardcover did not have a synopsis on the first page. Having gone into his *Warriors* archive, Gordon reports that the book he bought was "a ratty hardcover of *The Warriors* with the cover missing." He also offers, "I could've skimmed the book." Either way, what he read lived up to a filmmaker maxim. "I was taught by Aaron Spelling and also at AIP: it's two or three sentences. That's all it takes to know you have a good idea. Now that doesn't work for *Field of Dreams*. It doesn't work for certain movies. But for action movies, genre movies, that works. It was enough to just grab you like that. A simple premise… That's what I picked up on immediately. I still get chills thinking about it. They had one night to get across a very big and dangerous city with every gang in the city looking to get them… Simply put, it was a very good idea for a movie. It was a great idea for a chase film." He seems to have acquired the movie subsidiary rights before he read the book: he has recalled enquiring about them the morning after becoming aware of *The Warriors*. For the record, when he did read Yurick's novel he felt that "it wasn't a great book." Having "sparked to the idea," though, this didn't matter.

"I had no idea," Sol Yurick said when asked if he thought his novel would make a good movie. He admitted that his decision to allow Gordon to option the property was a hard-nosed one. "I had no faith whatsoever in the Hollywood system, but the point is I needed the money and to me what that meant is that the book would have a half-life thereafter and allow me to keep on writing more stuff." So hard-nosed was Yurick, in fact, that he quite brutally abandoned an independent filmmaker who had been courting him. Said unnamed filmmaker had promised that, in keeping with his love for the novel, he would film it almost exactly as written. The day before Yurick was due to sign with him, his agent received the offer from Gordon. Knowing Gordon was Hollywood as opposed to art-house and that Walter Hill (mentioned as putative director) was similarly mainstream, Yurick went with the more lucrative option. Having said that, Yurick and Gordon had interestingly contrasting viewpoints on how lucrative was the adaptation deal. "I made a very small option deal with Sol Yurick, 'cause I didn't have any money," says Gordon.

Of course, part of the compromise involved in allowing a book to be adapted for the screen is that the vast majority of the public will only know the filmed version. In many cases with cinema, "filmed" is synonymous with "traduced." "Well, there's really no choice about it," Yurick shrugged. "I'd recognized a certain system and operation long before I ever published anywhere because I had a friend whose parents had been Hollywood writers and he told me the way things worked. So there were no surprises. You make certain compromises. Not in my writing, but in relation to what secondary rights come out of it and the ability to make some money and keep on going."

Gordon, meanwhile, found that his enthusiasm about the project wasn't matched by studios. In 1979, he implied to David Bartholomew of *Film Bulletin* multiple knock-backs, with the reason given that the putative production "involved no major star roles." However, he ultimately found allies at Paramount and would publicly credit the company's chairman Barry Diller and president Michael Eisner for being prepared to take a chance on *The Warriors*.

With a development deal agreed, a script was needed. David Shaber was born in Cleveland, Ohio in 1929. He was a writer who straddled intellectually diverse entertainment worlds. He held a Master's Degree in Theater from the Yale University Drama School and had taught at Allegheny College and Smith College. He was co-producer of both a 1957 off-Broadway revival of Noel Coward's *Conversation Piece* and the 1962 Broadway production *A Gift of Time* written and directed by Garson Kanin and starring Henry Fonda and Olivia de Havilland. His screen work at the point Gordon engaged his services for *The Warriors* was scant, numbering merely the likes of a 1963 episode of *Channing*, a 1964 installment of *Mr. Broadway*, and an "adaptation" byline for the 1971 Otto Preminger movie *Such Good Friends*. He may have been prominent in Hollywood minds, though, through unproduced screenplays: Shaber's private notes show that, while he ultimately had eight motion-picture scripts go into production, he was actually responsible—fully or in part—for 39.

"I did not know him," says Gordon. "The studio wanted him, as I remember. They were hiring him for something he had written, and I can't remember what I read but he seemed okay. We went with him. Very nice guy. He was a very smart guy, very intellectual." That intellectualism, of course, could have counted against Shaber when it came to such a proletarian picture. Although Gordon says this didn't occur to him, he does admit, "After meeting with him and talking about it and so forth, I was kind of hoping against hope that he was going to get it. One of those situations."

Yurick said he neither received nor asked for input into the screenplay. "I didn't even bother. I knew it was pointless. If they wanted me in the first place, they would have asked me—and that would have led to all kinds of trouble... I was never particularly drawn to being a screenwriter or doing any of that stuff. Not unless I had the kind of control that you just don't get. I know story after story of writers who wrote books and asked to do the script and got swallowed up in the whole process."

Shaber's first draft of his adaptation of *The Warriors* broadly follows the architecture of Yurick's story but develops it and enriches it. At the same time, it betrays it by sanitizing it, even to the point of absurdity. This is something that would also apply to the finished film. At that point in Hollywood history, such a traducing was probably unavoidable.

Indeed, it's clear from the opening scene that this is intended to be a film with a rather different tone to the book. The Coney Island Dominators are not the kids of the novel but "rough young men in their early twenties." The scene finds seasoned Dominator Hinton—who is "resourceful, courageous"—initiating a younger member, a black boy of "sixteenish," an age which makes him the baby of the group and leads to his sarcastic handle of "Grandpa." Dodging transit guards, the pair leave the Dominators' gigantic sign on a subway train that has just emerged from a car wash. The scene clearly has its eyes on the zeitgeist: the comparatively new phenomenon of American public transport being plastered with the sort of elaborate graffiti recently made possible by aerosol paint cans was one of the issues of the day. (Shaber's research included a May 1977 *Esquire* magazine article by Norman Mailer titled "The Faith of Graffiti.")

Meanwhile, an interloper in the Coney Island neighborhood has been apprehended by fellow Dominators. When Crusher—"a mammoth kid with a barrel chest and a wild look in his eye"—releases his vise-like grip on the stranger's throat, the latter vouchsafes that he is an emissary from one Ismael, who has tasked him with informing the Dominators that they are to be at Van Cortlandt Park tomorrow evening at 8:30. Dominators leader the Fox—"something shrewd and Mediterranean in his face, a cruel line to his mouth"—tries to be offhand ("We'll think about it. We gotta take it up in Council"). The emissary is scornful: "You dudes lucky to be invited, and you know it. Your action has all been strictly Brooklyn, strictly local."

Ismael—a cool black dude in sunglasses—is holding court in the converted-ballroom clubhouse of his gang, the Delancey Thrones. In a scene very reminiscent of the opening chapter of Yurick's novel, an agitated social worker knows something major is going down and is vainly trying to extract from Ismael details as to what.

The next day, the Fox upbraids Crusher for drinking ("We all gotta be sharp tonight, man"). Similar moralizing occurs in Hinton's tenement apartment, where Hinton remonstrates with his older brother Arnold for stashing drugs in the hidey-hole where he keeps his spray cans. In turn, Arnold mocks Hinton for the futility of his gang associations. "I ain't really in the Dominators, anyway—not really in," Hinton responds. "I'm just... considering the idea." Asked why he is even considering it, Hinton reasons, "You gotta have something going for you out there, you know that, man. You gotta get yourself an edge to make it." Hinton primly disdains Arnold's suggestion that he deal for him. With this exchange, Shaber's clean-cut and even mealy-mouthed vision for *The Warriors* has been definitively set.

Shaber increases to nine the number of gang delegates chosen to attend the Van Cortlandt Park meeting. He also decides to have Fox call what Yurick termed only an "assembly" and "Big Meeting" a "conclave," as quasi-unconvincingly rarified a word as was Yurick's "plenipos." In addition to the Dominators already mentioned, the delegates are:

- Caesar, a cocky Puerto Rican stud.

- Coffee-colored lieutenant Hector.

- Tom-Tom, a stolid black man who is silent throughout.

- Frito, a chubby, good natured Puerto Rican.

- Dewey, a half-bored, simple-minded white boy looking for excitement.

As can be seen, this rainbow nation is very different to the restricted racial make-up depicted in the book, let alone found in real life gangs. However, the Dominators' uniform is pretty much as it was in Yurick's text, including the Mercedes-Benz hood ornament.

At the Dominators' headquarters—a derelict classroom—the Fox explains the importance of the journey to the unfamiliar reaches of the Bronx, where, on the instruction of Ismael, they will be unarmed. "This Ismael, he some kind of genius. I don't know what he's cookin', nobody knows. But he got delegations from every major gang comin' on a truce, like little goody-boys. And I been humpin' to play in that league for two years."

The Fox issues the instructions for the delegates' roles. Hector is second in command. As the "brotherhood artist," Hinton will leave the gang's mark with his spray cans. Caesar and Frito are scouts. Tom-Tom is the "bearer," tasked with carrying the booze and the money for the subway. Crusher and Dewey are vaguely assigned "soldiering in the middle." Grandpa is "reader," which turns out to mean the man whose job it is to decipher the confusing schematic maps lately to be found in New York subway cars, a slightly comical and resonant contemporary note for inhabitants of the Big Apple.

A montage shows the delegates of the other invited gangs—"one outlandish set of uniforms after another"—putting aside differences to determinedly converge on the Bronx. Bystanders expecting trouble are left gazing after them in confusion. The only exception to this peaceable vista is presented by the Rogues, roughnecks led by a murderous-faced man who is never named in dialogue but is termed in the script "Butcher-Boy." This gang make a din, don't pay their bus fares, and knock old men's hats off their heads, which in this particular narrative makes them hard asses.

When the gangs converge in a Van Cortlandt field, Ismael proceeds to tell them they are "suckers" who have been "shucked" into not realizing their strength in numbers. "A hundred thousand. They ain't but 20,000 police in the whole town. Can you dig it?... One gang could run this city... We could terrorize the whole place, nothing moves without we say 'go.' We could tax the crime syndicates, the mafia, even the police. Because we got the streets, suckers." The gang delegates are rapt at the powerful rhetoric. However, Butcher-Boy decides that he has "heard enough outta that black jigaboo ass," and—producing a gun he has smuggled into a sup-posedly clean conclave—shoots Ismael dead. The only person who sees him do it is Hinton, but before Butcher-Boy can waste the witness to his deed the cops arrive and the gang members are fleeing every which way.

The Fox is horror-struck by the sight of Ismael's corpse. To deflect suspicion from himself, Butcher-Boy jumps on him, shouting, "I got him! *I got the one.*" As the Fox is pounced on by vengeful Delancey Thrones, Butcher-Boy makes his escape. As the gang members are spreadeagled against cars by the police, the embittered whisper "Dominators" rustles through their ranks.

The remainder of the Dominators congregate in a graveyard. Hinton muses that the only thing to do now is go home. "Coney Island must be twenty miles away," Frito complains. "Maybe thirty." Caesar points out their perilous situation: "Every cop in the city looking to bust our heads and every gang waiting to come down on us." Hector takes charge, saying, "All we gotta do is find a subway stop, grab a train to Times Square, and change for Coney Island." Crusher challenges this assumption of power ("Who named you leader?"). At that point, Hinton—from his vantage point on a mausoleum—announces that he has spotted the nearest sub-way. The distraction comes as some relief to Hector, who is secretly un-sure of his fighting prowess.

As the Dominators make their way nervously to the subway, the Rogues are invading a candy store minded by an old man. Butcher-Boy enters the shop's phone booth and begins an animated conversation. We are made privy to the identity of the call's recipient via the scene cutting to a disc jockey sitting before his turntables in a radio station. "Right," the DJ nods into the phone. "You got it, man." Meanwhile, the Dominators have reached the subway station but stand rooted in anxiety because of suspicious activity outside. Two figures shuffling along the sidewalk are carrying shopping bags that could contain weapons. Finally, the Domi-nators pelt desperately toward the subway entrance—and only realize as they pass the figures that they are bag ladies. With amused relief, they board a train, their relief intensified by the thought of being virtually home and dry.

The DJ, though, is broadcasting a coded message. "...we have been asked to relay a request... It's for the Dominators, and I do mean the Dom-inators." The mention of the name is coded confirmation to the listeners of who was the guilty party at the conclave. Another montage shows various gangs preparing for retributive action.

An act of God assists these revenge plans: the Dominators' train journey is halted by a fault on the line. When the Coney Islanders disembark and make their way to the street, it is to find they have missed the first tranche of the replacement bus service. They spot some menacing figures their age in wide-brimmed plantation hats, one of whom is clearly in the act of going off to fetch reinforcements. Unarmed and in enemy territory, the Dominators' only option is to be friendly. Hector walks across, all smiles and proffered cigarettes. However, things quickly get awkward when he insists that they are only in the area for the conclave. "How could there be a big meeting if the Barrio Blades wasn't there?" complains Jesus Mendez. The ice is at least broken a little when Mendez shows Hector his gang's mention in *La Prensa* and Hector responds with a Dominators *Daily News* clipping.

Just as things look like they might end amicably, onto the scene walks a mini-skirted, bare-midriffed, stiletto-shoed beauty whom her boyfriend Mendez addresses as "Merchy". Shaber's rationale for the name he has created for the girl is fairly ingenious. She approaches Hector, pointing at his hat pin. "Why you wearing my name? See, that's my name. Mercedes." Holding out a hand, she says, "Come on, gimme." When Hector declines, she angrily spins toward Mendez and says, "You let an army walk through here whenever they feel like it, how's that gonna look, man?" Flustered, Mendez says the Dominators can pass if they take off their pins. "That's just our mark, it don't mean we're at war," Hector protests. As the exchange becomes heated, Hector says, "We're not coolies, we're warriors"— the only time the titular word is used in the dialogue.

The Dominators stomp off toward the next subway station. They find themselves joined by Merchy ("I'm looking for some real men"). They are trailed by the Blades, who have somewhat less friendly intentions. The Dominators produce a bottle. Hector rips off a piece of Merchy's skirt. "You gonna jump me?" she says in semi-excited misunderstanding. Instead, he shoves the scrap of material down the bottle's neck, sets it alight, and tosses it at a nearby car. As the flames cause the vehicle's gas tank to go up, the Dominators make their escape. Merchy goes with them, although not so willingly this time. Hinton explains, "Sorry—you may not be much, but you're the only hostage we got..." This makes no apparent sense, as the Blades now have further reason to pursue them.

Waiting at 96th Street Station for the Times-Square connection, the Dominators have to scatter when a cop notices them. Hinton and Merchy wind up jumping off the platform into a dark tunnel. Caesar, Dewey and Grandpa have no option but to hop on a train going the wrong way. Hector, Tom-Tom, Crusher, and Frito end up out on the street, where they find themselves being followed by the All-Stars, a gang in baseball uniform. They flee to a park, where Frito is set upon by an All-Star whose knife flashes in the dark. He is never seen again.

In the tunnel, Merchy flirts with Hinton, excited by the idea that he wasted Ismael. It's the first time that any of the gang have become aware of the erroneous word on the street. Hinton is left cold by Merchy's advances, declining even to tell her his name. He also reveals that he has been left cold by Ismael's rhetoric about the gangs taking over New York ("No way. They'd call out the whole mothering army, they'd drop the atom bomb on Harlem first"). He also once more demonstrates ambiguity about being a gang member, sneering, "Be a Dominator and see the world!" Merchy has an opposing point of view: that one should live for the moment. "In two years I gonna be twenty, that's only two more years to live," she insists. "After that, what I got for a future, hah? You tell me. I see my sisters. A belly hanging between my knees and hair on my lip? I want something now, man—because this all the life I got left."

Their gutter philosophizing is brought to an abrupt halt by the appearance of Merchy's boyfriend, armed with a six-inch pig-sticker. The intended cause of Hinton's demise instead becomes that of Mendez's own expiry when Hinton knocks it out of his hand and, stooping to retrieve it, the Barrio Blade-man makes contact with the third rail. Merchy is so turned on by Mendez being fried alive that she insists Hinton take her right there. Hinton slaps her and walks off.

In the park, Crusher gets exhausted running away from the All-Stars and decides to stop and fight them. When he poleaxes one, the others turn and run. Almost by way of celebration, Crusher tries to seduce a middle-age, thick-set nurse sitting drunkenly on a park bench. Tom-Tom gets arrested because, just as a patrol car is going by, she takes loud exception to him trying to steal her purse.

Horniness is also distracting the other group, who have—by means not fully explained—found their way to a Manhattan gang clubhouse, where they are pleased to find a sprinkling of female company. Grandpa recognizes danger just at the moment that the door is bolted and guns produced. Although Grandpa and Dewey escape, Caesar is felled by a bullet in the back.

Hinton, meanwhile, has found his way to Times Square Station. Unfortunately, so have members of a gang called the Pool Sharks. Hinton coolly enters a penny arcade and plays a game that involves a shoot-out with a cowboy mannequin. Not knowing he is aware of the Sharks' presence, Merchy appears and makes to apprise him of the danger. When the cowboy's mechanical voice groans at him, "Yuh got me, Podnuh," Hinton blows imaginary smoke from the barrels of his pistols and enthuses, "Fucking-A." Aside from a few "shits," there are no other profanities in the script.

Tom-Tom, Dewey, and Grandpa arrive. When Hinton realizes that the Dominators are still not up to strength, he indicates that the group—including a reluctant Merchy—should make for the nearby men's room. When the Sharks enter, knives at the ready, they find the toilet apparently empty. The stall doors abruptly burst open and the Sharks are assailed by spray cans and mop handles. A Shark thrusts his knife into the retreating figure of Grandpa, but the only thing that has been stabbed is the toilet seat Grandpa has placed beneath his jacket. Sobbing for his fallen comrades, Grandpa manically swings the seat and the Sharks stumble out of the door.

The bedraggled remnants of the Dominators make their way to their Coney Island connection and collapse onto the train's seats. At the next stop, two young, smartly dressed college couples returning from a prom enter the carriage and sit opposite them. Shaber doesn't make them cartoonishly nasty and privileged, stating them to be "rather sweet." They are, though, representatives of a world to which the Dominators and Merchy feel they don't have access. When one of the prom boys protectively takes his date's hand, Hinton gets angry enough to pull down Merchy's arm as she tries to straighten her hair. The prom couples get off at the next stop, one of the girls dropping her corsage in her eagerness to depart. Hinton stoops and grabs it when the Warriors party disembarks at Coney Island.

In the harsh light of day, the place they had been so anxious to reach these last hours is not a prepossessing sight. Surveying the tenements, beach, and litter, Hinton shakes his head and says, "Funny. Spend all night fighting to get back to a place—and the rest of your life fighting to get out of it again..." It's a line that's unrealistic in its concision and poeticism, but powerful in its rhetoric.

The Dominators aren't the only attendees of the conclave who have made it to Coney Island. When the Dominators spot a Cadillac hearse crawling along behind them, Hinton explains that the Rogues won't ever leave them alone because "one of them pulled the plug on Ismael—*and I saw it*." Hinton hands Merchy the corsage and asks her to wait for him on the boardwalk as he and the gang prepare for a confrontation. They are cornered by the Rogues in a housing-project playground. There, Butcher-Boy responds to Hinton's improvised, non-lethal weapon—a chair—with a gun. Hinton calls out for help. "Hey, anybody. Anybody! We got the dudes who did it, we got the guys who wasted Ismael!" "Sure, we did it," Butcher-Boy laughs. "But by the time anybody wakes up to hear about it, you're gonna be wasted, too." It would have been more pertinent if Butcher-Boy had pointed out that there is no one in the vicinity who would understand Hinton's yell. Yet a miracle of implausibility causes the smile to freeze on his face as members of the Delancey Thrones rise from the nearby bushes. "This is ours, man," the Dominators are told by a character the script names as the New Ismael. "Go home."

Hinton makes for the boardwalk but Merchy is gone, the abandoned corsage the only clue that she was ever there. In Grandpa's two-room tenement apartment, his mother is remonstrating with him. When he had been trying to make it out the door for the journey to Van Cortlandt, she had asked him to buy groceries. He has only brought back potato chips and pretzels. "Better to eat shit in New York than steak in Haiti," responds her son. In Hinton's family apartment, he finds that Arnold has left him some dope he wants him to deal. Hinton tucks it under his brother's pillow and goes out onto the fire escape to hide his spray can. From his elevated position he suddenly notices the figure of Merchy walking toward the subway station. "It's Walter!" he shouts at her back. "My name is Walterrr!" She doesn't hear.

The script ends with a shot pulling back from the tenement, the street, Brooklyn…

Shaber's adaptation is impressive in the fact that he has turned a thin narrative featuring utterly unsympathetic characters into a properly structured plot featuring relatable people. Almost every scene in his script has its roots in the original novel, but Shaber significantly expands length and profoundly alters tone, sometimes even fleshing out into full scenes what had been mere thoughts and asides. Hinton's glum escapade in the Times Square women's lavatory becomes the men's-room showdown with the Sharks; Hinton's briefly seen drug-addict half-brother Alonso becomes a bigger character (as well as being given the name of the novel's gang leader); the nasty prom twosomes become a nice pair of couples yet also a vehicle for a statement about class pride; the live-for-today speech by Merchy and the take-what-you-can-get peroration by Arnold each seem informed by Alonso's advice to Hinton in the Yurick original.

The most significant changes Shaber makes are ones that render palatable source material that had cast the Dominators in a very bad light. With regard to the rape and murder that he wrote, Yurick admitted that the *Warriors* filmmakers "couldn't have sold the movie with those scenes." "We wanted to have heroes and villains and the Warriors were heroes basically, even though they were gang members," reasons Gordon. In lieu of being able to incorporate into a motion picture anything from Yurick that sullies the hero status deemed necessary for the Dominators, Shaber introduces Butcher-Boy, who has no equivalent in the Yurick book. This character not only gives the story a hinge on which to turn but makes the Dominators good guys by default. In the novel, the Dominators' peril is partly down to the cops looking for Big Meeting/conclave attendees, partly down to them being on other gangs' turf, and partly down to them being animalistic criminals. Shaber retains the element of the danger of them crossing enemy turf but jettisons the rapist-murderer component, making the Dominators' fear of the cops the same as that of any of the gangs who had attended the conclave. However, he adds a massive new peril by engineering the belief among the rival gangs that the Dominators are responsible for Ismael's killing. The only remnant of the book's rape is Merchy's "You gonna jump me?", a vastly toned-down version of a suggestion in the Yurick text that the girl to some degree enjoys her assault.

The invention of Butcher-Boy compels Shaber to provide a rationale—necessary in an age prior to the instant dissemination of information enabled by the internet and cellphones—for the fact that the gangs are able to stick to the Dominators' trail. In doing so, he comes up with an inspired piece of connective tissue in the shape of the scenes with the DJ character.

Another major change is the number of interactions with rival gangs. It's surprising to realize that in Yurick's novel, aside from an edgy passing encounter with the Colonial Lords on the way to the assembly, the Dominators only tussle with one other gang, the Borinquen Blazers, and even that face-off passes off fairly uneventfully. In order to engineer the sort of action set-pieces traditional in cinema, Shaber adds the All-Stars, the Pool Sharks, the unnamed gang in the Manhattan clubhouse, and the Rogues.

Aesthetically, Shaber's first draft is sometimes pat. One example is that mysterious and convenient materialization of the Delancey Thrones when the Warriors look doomed. Another is the equally mysterious appearance of Merchy's boyfriend in the tunnel, an arrival which is moreover described like something from a cheap horror movie (of a pillar that Hinton has just infuriatedly sprayed red, Shaber writes, "Part of the red is moving, inching like some slimy lizard, and we see it is a hand, a hand that was there when the paint was sprayed, followed by an arm—and then the face of Merchy's ex-boyfriend, the Blade"). Sometimes the action is limp. The final showdown in the housing project playground is a real damp squib, especially the way the Dominators call wimpily, randomly for help. (It's perhaps the only instance in which Shaber's rejigging of Yurick is not an improvement, being a remolding of the novel's hardly scintillating scene wherein a challenge is shouted to the Colonial Lords from such a venue.) More generally, Shaber's narrative never quite convinces that rival gangs would be upset by Ismael's demise.

The script's main fault, though, lies in how absurdly clean-cut the Dominators are. Shaber's notes find him exhorting himself, "The gang must be sympathetic, must be people we root for" but—almost contradictorily—"Watch tone: these guys are tough & mean, not wistful or soft." The latter impulse seems to have lost out to the former. The Dominators routinely—almost doggedly—respond to the deadly likes of switchblades and guns with non-lethal weapons such as spray cans, mop handles, and toilet seats. This unlikely sportsmanship leads to an overarching inauthenticity. This especially applies to Hinton. Shaber's notes show that his intention is to portray Hinton as in possession of an "apartness" and that he wants to create a "line" whereby it is seen that "through the evening—and especially as they get back to the home turf & he sees that this is what he fought for, getting back to this shithole is the prize—Hinton has been making a decision." This conceit is of course common in proletarian fiction, a way of exploiting a grungy milieu while asserting that the protagonist is better than what he is surrounded by. However, here it engenders ludicrous scenarios. For instance, when Merchy's boyfriend gets fatally electrocuted, a horrified Hinton turns to her and insists, "I didn't touch him, he did it himself, you saw I didn't touch him…" How did this delicate flower ever get into a street gang?

That is, if a street gang it can be called. The process of presenting the Dominators as victims/heroes results in an essential nonsensicality. We are never made privy to what precisely makes these people gangbangers. They are not shown mugging people, robbing stores, dealing drugs, engaging in violence, or any of the other means by which urban gangs are defined. Unless the graffitiing scene counts, we never even see them indulging in vandalism. To show such stuff, of course, would instantly reduce the sympathy of the viewer, especially those viewers who are residents of big cities and spend large portions of their lives in fear of being on the receiving end of such activity. In order to portray these people as heroes or at least nice guys, the very essence of being a gang member has to be discretely tucked out sight. Yet understandable though Shaber's policy is, the consequence of it is that the Dominators end up seeming like little more than a social club with a dress code. This is not completely because of shortcomings on Shaber's part. Although his vision would be subsequently toughened up by Walter Hill, this dichotomy would sit at the heart of all iterations of the Warriors film project.

Paramount, though, would seem to have been broadly pleased by Shaber's work. A log by Shaber of a January 31, 1978, phone call between him and Don Simpson, Paramount's production vice-president, does reveal the studio to have some misgivings. (Because Shaber did not date his scripts, it's not clear if the misgivings are about the first draft or a later one.) Simpson felt the viewer needed to "care more" about the gang, that there needed to be a "stronger sense of all the gangs looking for our gang," and that Merchy "needs work, needs to be more rounded; maybe somehow a spark of hope." Overall, though, Simpson felt it was an "excellent job" and something he would be "interested in making."

The movie would indeed be made, and in the theatres barely a year after this phone call. By then, though, Shaber had long since departed the scene.

THE HYPHENATE

THE CREDITS of *The Warriors* state that the film is written by "David Shaber and Walter Hill." The fact of an "and," rather than an ampersand, between the two men's names is significant.

In motion pictures, tradition and contract demand this distinction, as does a necessity for clarity about input. An ampersand would indicate that the two had actively collaborated on the script; the coordinating conjunction signifies that the second-named writer rewrote the work of the first named. Shaber had no input, either formal or informal, into Hill's rewrite. As Hill puts it, "Once I was started up, I was unleashed and on my own."

"He got an okay draft," says Lawrence Gordon of Shaber. "Nothing we were going to shoot. I don't think it was exciting enough for what I needed. I think he did a good job. It just wasn't a hit movie… He was disappointed we didn't go forward but he was very professional about it." Shaber's replacement would be a hyphenate. Gordon: "I worked with Walter, we were close, and I knew what he could do. I wanted to hire him to write and direct, just like we did on *Hard Times*."

Walter Hill was born in 1940 in Long Beach, California. From the age of fifteen or sixteen, he set his heart set on being a writer. He attended university in Mexico City, where he studied art and literature. Subsequently at Michigan State, history and literature were his subjects. After being excused the draft due to childhood asthma, he set his sights on being a writer-director.

"I always felt myself to be somebody who wanted to make films as well as write films," Hill reasons of his hyphenate ambitions. "But you have to kind of write your way into the job unless you have some other way in and I did not, and I think writing your way into directing is probably the best way to do it. I always felt whenever I was working in other jobs—assistant director for instance—that I was a writer and I was marking time in the other jobs, trying to make a living and buy a hot lunch while hoping to get a break." His director heroes tended to be non-Americans such as Japan's Akira Kurosawa and Italy's Mario Monicelli, although almost contradictory Hill had a desire to work in the mainstream, Americancentric realm of Hollywood, not least because of his love of genre films.

After working as an assistant director for a couple of years while knocking out screenplays in his spare time, Hill's writing breakthrough came with *Hickey and Boggs*, a 1972 nihilistic detective movie starring Bill Cosby. *The Getaway*, his next effort (also '72), featured Steve McQueen and Ali MacGraw as a sort of modern-day Bonnie and Clyde. Directed by Sam Peckinpah, it was a box-office success. That no less a superstar than Paul Newman starred in *The Mackintosh Man* (1973) and *The Drowning Pool* (1975) indicates that Hill was a writer making a name for himself. Hill also scripted 1973 comedy *The Thief Who Came to Dinner*.

Hill's dream of directing his own scripts finally came true in 1975 with Gordon's *Hard Times*. "Larry liked to take chances with writers," Hill told Robert Markowitz in a Directors Guild of America website interview. "He thought… if you give them a chance to direct, you could get the script at a reduced price and you'd get a better script if you hired the right person… And as far as he was concerned, the chances are you weren't going to be any worse director than most of those he had been working with over at AIP… He was quite a character. So I wrote the script for scale and I directed the picture for scale… Did it in 38 days." Although he adjudges the experience "harrowing," Hill also says, "It was the best deal I ever made. I got a career out of it."

In 1977, Hill and Gordon created for ABC *Dog and Cat*, a television drama about a male-female police-officer partnership. *The Driver*, the film with which Gordon and Hill followed *Hard Times*, was awaiting release when the pair began shooting *The Warriors*.

"Larry Gordon had optioned it and he had me read it a year or so before the movie got made," recalls Hill of his history with *The Warriors*. The director's reaction was similar to Gordon's. He says, "The truth is, I didn't like the book very much," but he also states that "it had a good narrative idea… trying to get from the Bronx to Coney Island through enemy territory." Hill was far more enthused, in fact, by Yurick's own inspirations. Of *The Anabasis*, he says, "I recommend it. It's a classic."

Despite his conviction that the book contained the potential for a good picture, Hill says he told Gordon, "Nobody will ever let us make this movie. There's no way you're going to have movie stars in it." He explains, "This was not a vehicle for your traditional kind of movie stars. They were generally older people and not right [for] that kind of environment either. There were a couple you might have gotten away with—Travolta or something. But he had just done other things." That, though, was just the start of the unfilmability issues he articulated to Gordon: "'It doesn't have the normal act breaks or the rise and fall of plot that's a Hollywood kind of thing. And you're also going to be skirting on the edges of reality. Most people aren't even going to get what it could be, especially readers in Hollywood.'" Hill adds, "I was quite confident in my opinion. Of course, I turned out to be wrong."

Although by the time that Hill formally joined the project the rise-and-fall-of-plot issue had largely been ironed out by Shaber, he was still determined to stick to his hyphenate role. "I came on board as a writer-director. There was a pretty solid understanding, at least from my view, that it would have to be rewritten." Hill says of Yurick's concept, "He was probably more interested in the social phenomena and problem with gangs than he was anything else. I think that there's a lot of politics in his approach, contemporary politics, and I have to say that wasn't of great interest to me." Of course, the political component discerned by Hill in Yurick's novel might have worked had the movie adaptation been approached as a mid-Sixties period piece, but neither Gordon nor Hill were attracted to that idea. "We thought of just doing it as a timeless piece," Gordon says. "You could do it today." Hill offers, "I thought it only worked as a kind of slightly futuristic fantasy. I didn't think it had much relevance to social realism or anything like that. He had written something I thought was quite interesting in its way, but it was very different than what I thought the film possibilities were." Ironically, though, there would be more than a smattering of social commentary in the finished movie, whether it be in the form of Cyrus' we-got-the-numbers rhetoric, Mercy's speech about living for today, or the subway scene with the prom kids. "I don't say the movie is without its politics," says Hill. "I just say they're a diversion from Yurick's."

Hill felt the Shaber screenplay was "faithful to Sol Yurick's book," which judging by his comments above would be something he considered a demerit. He also says of Shaber's script, "I just didn't think it was bold enough and special enough and didn't take enough chances.

It was too realistic, and I didn't think a realistic approach would ever work with this story... I thought you had to get kind of crazy to pull this thing off."

Hill says he didn't conduct formal research when preparing his rewrite but, "I certainly talked to a lot of people that had gang experience." Moreover, he found himself involuntarily acquiring knowledge. "I'd taken a little room [in] midtown Manhattan. While I was preparing the movie, there was a terrible incident of gang violence in Central Park. There was a gang—if I remember correctly, their name was the Budweisers—and they went on a rampage and beat up quite a few people."

Like Shaber and Gordon, Hill was of the opinion that the film's protagonists had to be far more likeable and noble than those in the book. "I wanted to make a film that was a little more approachable," he says. "It's a mass medium and what is perceived to be a success or a failure when you publish a novel is a very, very different thing than when you put out a movie. The numbers that you have to attract are vastly different. You're in a very different medium." He reflects, "I don't really remember using very many of the characters from the book. There were some loose archetypes that were used and then evolved in somewhat different directions, but it's not what I would call a character-driven movie."

In the usual movie-world swirl of rewrites and polishes, it's frequently impossible to know who did what and when. Confusion is added in the case of *The Warriors* not just by Shaber's habit of not dating his scripts but by the fact that he is now deceased and not available for query answering. What can be unequivocally stated is that a revised screenplay dated June 1978 is notably different to Shaber's solo first draft, if perhaps not deserving of the "total script revision" description placed on its first page, let alone its sole credit to Hill.

The June '78 iteration changes almost all the protagonist gang's names. It also blends and switches their previously established personalities and roles. The leader is now Cleon, a tough, wiry, and charismatic man of "great street intelligence" and "tightly controlled intensity." The Fox is the ensemble's "memory man," possessing enormous knowledge of the city's other gangs. Quick-witted, emotional, and verbose, his toughness is an attitude, although in terms of physical aptitude Fox is fast of foot, making him a perfect scout on military missions. War chief and second-in-command Swan is a combination of the first draft's Hinton and Hector, although is braver than the latter. He is tough, resourceful, and a natural military tactician, but is laconic by nature and dislikes the necessity of taking command. He's a dab hand at knife-throwing. Rembrandt is another mix of prototypes, inheriting Hinton's position of spray-can marker and Grandpa's status as youngest. Though shy, reserved, and small, he's also kinetic, an able climber, and a stealthy mover. (From a couple of accidental instances of its use in the script, it would seem that Rembrandt's name was originally envisaged as "Plato.") The rough-and-ready Cochise lives only to fight and fornicate but is nonetheless a good soldier. Cowboy is another good soldier, despite his amenable, smiling nature. The name derives from the Stetson he habitually sports. The raw-boned and complaining Vermin is undisciplined in a rumble but can at least be relied on to line up. He is the gang's bearer. The tall, lean Snowball is disciplined, if independently minded. He is described as having "the face and body of a Masai warrior." This reference to the residents of pastoral Tanzania and Kenya is the only allusion in this draft to the ethnicity of any member of the protagonist gang. The fact that, one line of dialogue excepted, Snowball never speaks makes him a vague equivalent of the first draft's Tom-Tom, although he has the additional role here of "music man," meaning he carries one of the then-fashionable oversize but portable radio-cassette tape players often referred to as ghetto blasters. Meanwhile, Ajax is similar to Crusher in his physical strength, but with added cantankerousness, cruelty, and sexual incontinence.

"I wanted to keep the Greek connection alive," explains Hill of the new appellations. "It wasn't really meant to be pure Xenophon. For instance, the name Ajax really doesn't have anything to do with Xenophon." One name that indubitably does is Cyrus, the new handle for the man who convenes the conclave. The knowledge this revealed of *The Anabasis* would impress Yurick about the film even if little else would. Hill meanwhile explains of Swan's oddly elegant handle, "I didn't want a tough-guy name. I wanted something that was in the opposite direction, even though he was a very tough guy." As well as a Cowboy, the gang now has an "Indian," Cochise being a name derived from a famous Native American. "The origin of that name was pop-culture's influence on the gang sensibility," says Hill. "I thought that they liked a certain kind of Western and that they would name themselves after attitudes that they liked when they saw movies."

There has also been a collective name change. The Coney Island Dominators are now the Coney Island Warriors. Hill: "I'm sure that was in conversation with Larry and Frank. Somehow it seemed to tie together better. We knew the title of the movie was going to be *The Warriors*."

Hill has publicly laid claim to the crawl that begins this script (although, as it transpired, not the movie). It makes explicit the story's connection to classical war chronicles:

> "In the Fourth Century before Christ, a mercenary army of Greek soldiers found themselves stranded in the middle of the Persian Empire.
> "One thousand miles from the sea.
> "One thousand miles from safety.
> "Enemy troops around them on every quarter.
> "This is a story of that army's forced march.
> "This is a story of courage.
> "This is a story of War."

The screenplay's action begins with a montage showing gangs of New York on the move, heading purposefully but peacefully toward the conclave. Our first view of the Warriors finds them killing time outside a graffiti-bedecked building on a Coney Island boardwalk. Swan is steamed that, because of the no-weapons rule, he can't bring his blade to the pow-wow. Nearby, Cleon is talking with his girl, Lincoln, who is worried about the conclave. "I don't want you getting messed up with something heavy way off in the Bronx," she says. "You never even been up there..."

A boardwalk scene later that afternoon finds Cleon reassuring the gang representatives, who are dubious about the big meeting. He tells them that their selection for the conclave is something that shows they are special. He then issues the instructions for their roles, after which they set off nervously into enemy turf, trading insults with rival gang the Mongols, to whom they "lost a cat" the previous year.

The conclave takes place in an open plaza accessed by a stairway. There, the Warriors are impressed to find numerous other gangs of multiple races and ethnicities. Not only does the script precisely specify the number of gangs (74), it provides their gang names, a strange wodge of data in the middle of the narrative. One of the gangs is the Rogues. Their leader is no longer "Butcher-Boy" but Luther. His second-in-command is Cropsey, which name seems to be a holdover from a reference in Shaber's first draft to Brooklyn's Cropsey Avenue. An exchange between the pair makes it clear that they are up to no good.

Attention is suddenly drawn to a voice demanding, "Can you count, suckers?" It is Cyrus. He is now the leader not of the Delancey Thrones but the Gramercy Riffs, a karate-expert ensemble. The script doesn't specify his ethnicity, but simply describes his aura: "Commanding presence, born to royalty..." Much of his speech is the same one that the first draft gave him, aside from his noting the "miracle" of the truce ("We've got the Saracens sitting next to the Jones Street Boys. We've got the Moonrunners right by the Vancourtland Rangers...") and his stressing the need to set aside petty differences for the pursuit of collective riches ("We have been unable to see the truth because we have been fighting for ten square feet of ground... Our turf. Our little piece of turf").

When the rhetoric is brought to an abrupt end by the report of a gun, this time it is Fox who spots the culprit. After the flashing lights, police bullhorns, chaotic fleeing for safety, Luther's fingering of an innocent (Cleon), Cleon's consequent disappearance under a swarm of Riffs, and the hero gang's reassembling in a graveyard, the Fox tells his compadres that he saw Luther kill Cyrus. This is a far more logical point at which to relay this information than the late stage that Hinton reported his sighting in the first draft. With the Warriors unaware that the whisper is going around that it is in fact they who are the guilty party, Cowboy comments, "I'd hate to be a Rogue tonight. Those Riffs are going to be on their ass." (This dialogue is an echo of a cop in the first draft noting of the Dominators, "I wouldn't want to be one of them tonight.") Another change is less explicable. Vermin says, "Fucking Coney Island must be fifty miles from here," a greater postulated distance than the twenty to thirty of the first draft, let alone the fifteen miles of Yurick's template. This time the presence of a memory man/scout means that there is someone able to proffer a correction. "It's 27 miles," says the Fox, an accurate estimate according to Google Maps. In the finished film, Vermin's estimate becomes "fifty to a hundred miles" and Fox's correction isn't included. The voiceover in the film's trailer, though, states the Warriors are "Twenty-seven miles behind enemy lines." (One can imagine the response of Xenophon's men to all this being, "Pah!")

"We're going back," announces Swan. "It's the only choice we got." Just as Crusher bristled at Hector assuming leadership responsibilities, so Ajax wants to know who nominated Swan for that role. "You're no leader without your blade and you ain't got one," Ajax sneers. Swan coolly challenges him, "Make your move." As previously, internecine violence is averted by an (as it were) "Subway station, ho!"

Meanwhile, the Gramercy Riffs have appointed a replacement leader, referred to in the script as "New Cyrus." Informed that Cleon is "Dead as a fucking doornail," New Cyrus responds that he wants the other Warriors alive if possible: "If not, wasted." We then cut to a radio station, where a DJ—female this time—puts the coded word out about the Warriors. In the next scene, gender is also changed from the first draft. It's now a female shop worker that the Rogues are terrorizing as Luther makes use of a candy-store phone. Luther then tells Cropsey, "They want them alive… But we don't."

The Warriors arrive at an elevated station but their path is blocked by the Turnbull ACs, a skinhead gang with a minimum height of 6'2" who are malevolently prowling in a graffiti covered bus. The Coney Island men have to make a dash for the train with the Turnbulls in hot pursuit. They just make it.

The ever-cautious Swan excepted, the out-of-breath Warriors are celebrating being home and dry. However, the train suddenly grinds to a halt, loudspeakers announcing that it can't proceed due to a fire. "We just better worry about who set the fire," notes the Fox. When they emerge from the station just in time to miss the replacement bus service, the gang the Warriors encounter is not the Barrio Blades but the Orphans. According to the memory man, they are as unimpressive as they sound. "So far down they ain't even on the map," notes the Fox. "Full strength…maybe thirty soldiers. Minor League." Vermin notes that thirty is a lot more than eight. The level-headed Swan approaches in ostentatious friendliness and runs into trouble when the gang leader's feathers are ruffled by the revelation that his crew wasn't invited to the conclave. As in previous versions, the intervention of a female gang associate destroys the chances of things passing off peaceably. There is no particular description of this woman except a designation by Cowboy of "trouble" and the Warriors' earthy verbal indications that they find her attractive. The Warriors' uniform is not described in this script except for the fact that they wear "vests." (Britons would describe what the Warriors wear as a "waistcoat." In British English, a vest refers to what Americans would call an "undershirt.") As such, there is no impetus for the girl to latch onto a component of their uniform—the Mercedes-Benz hat pin—as reminiscent of her name, therefore no reason for that name to be "Mercedes"/"Merchy." It is now "Mercy." What she does do is demand one of their vests, it later being revealed that she perceives their value as stemming from the fact that one of their wearers killed Cyrus. When the Warriors decline, Mercy wheels on her boyfriend and provokes him into demanding as the price for being allowed passage that the strangers remove their "colors." Although this isn't specified, the latter is logically their identifying brand traditionally to be found, in either letter or graphic form or both, on the backs of street gangs' vests.

Much as before, the girl and the Orphans separately follow the Warriors when they march defiantly in the direction of the next subway stop; the Coney Islanders send the pursuers' ranks scattering by use of a petrol bomb whose fuse is a piece of Mercy's ripped skirt. As the Warriors depart the fiery scene, Swan instructs, "Take her. We may need her for a trade."

The run for a train is another close call. At 96th Street, the Warriors have a tense wait for their Union Square connection. They scatter as transit cops spot them.

Swan, Cochise, Ajax, and Snowball are this time the ones stranded out on the streets. In a park they run into a baseball-themed gang, who are now not the All-Stars but the Baseball Furies. The name is hardly important—it will never be uttered—but what is is the fact that now they actually carry ball-bats. Ajax, like Crusher before him, gets too winded and bored to continue running. He deploys a commandeered bat, while Snowball utilizes his belt, which, when pulled off, transpires to be a bicycle chain. However, the Warriors permanently lose one of their number—Cochise—in the violence-torn darkness.

Down in the tunnel, Mercy and the Fox have much the same exchange as "enjoyed" by Merchy and Hinton in the previous script. This time, the scene does not climax in the melodramatic arrival of the girl's boyfriend but merely in the Fox rebuffing Mercy's advances on the grounds that "you're a jinx… You're just part of everything that's happening tonight and it's all bad."

Forced to take the wrong train, Vermin, Cowboy, and Rembrandt make their way to Union Square, where it was agreed everyone would congregate if they got separated. They are disappointed to find none of their Warrior comrades present. However, their spirits lift at the sight of three smiling "gang chicks."

Back in the park, Swan, Ajax, and Snowball come upon a nurse seated on a park bench listening to a transistor radio. To the disgust of his comrades, the perpetually horny Ajax decides to spend some time with her. That the nurse is no longer described as fat is explained by the fact that she's a honeytrap. She whips out some handcuffs and lashes Ajax to the bench and, flashing a badge, says, "Your fucking days are over for a while, honey."

Swan, walking alone after having dispensed with Mercy, finds himself accosted by the Dingos (as it's spelt in the script), a group of bodybuilder types in skin-tight t-shirts, each with a leashed Doberman. They address him as "dear" and describe him as "cute," and one says, "I wonder if you're the straight that shot Cyrus." They set about Swan and fling his bloodied form into a bare room, before going off—we infer—to contact the New Cyrus.

The enthusiastic Vermin and Cowboy and a slightly more dubious Rembrandt accompany the gang chicks to their clubhouse, where—unlike in the equivalent scene in the first draft—the company is entirely distaff. Later dialogue will reveal this gang (numbers unstated) to be called the Lizzies. However, this gang is no less malevolent than the co-ed prototype. Rembrandt's warning that they are packed comes too late: Vermin gets fatally shot. Cowboy doesn't make any concessions to chivalry as he coldcocks one woman and wipes out another with a chair before he and Rembrandt make their escape. Across town, Swan also makes an escape, in his case via a window to the accompaniment of a fusillade of gunshot and Doberman barking.

The Fox has made it to Union Square Station. So too have a gang referred to in the script as the Big Time Punks. This ensemble dresses in severe black and one of them glides around on roller skates. Aside from the name change from the Pool Sharks, much of the scene remains the same as before, including the materialization of both Mercy and a trio of other Warriors and a showdown with a penny arcade cowboy prefiguring a men's-room rumble. Gone is the reveal of the lavatory seat prior to the enemy's red-sprayed retreat, although the Warriors are better able to defend themselves in this script because of Snowball's confiscated Furies bat. Across town, meanwhile, the New Cyrus is being told by an informer, "We might be looking for the wrong family." Somebody has stepped forward who says he saw who shot Cyrus.

In the subway train headed for Coney Island, Fox is telling the exhausted, battle-scarred remnants of the Warriors delegation, "It's got to stop. This ain't the way people live." He also dismisses Cyrus' rhetoric. "Some crap that was. Those cats uptown aren't going to let anyone, much less us, take it away from them." Cowboy and Mercy disagree. Mercy says, "We do our part. They need us down on the bottom so that there's a top. We get even by ripping them off every time we get a chance." "That ain't much of a choice," says the Fox before turning to Rembrandt and saying, "I'll tell you something. Don't let go of your spray can. It's your passport in case you want to get out... You're great. You can make a living at it."

When after the disembarkation of the prom couples Fox hands Mercy the fallen corsage, she asks him his real name. Embarrassed, he says, "Francis. Francis Conroy. They call me the Fox because of Francis... you know... and because I'm smart." "I like that name," Mercy offers as a gauche way of expressing her growing affection for him. (Interesting that the name has been changed from the equivalent scenes in the first draft, where Hinton revealed his handle was, erm, Walter. Hill thinks the original name just a coincidence. Presumably, he changed it because it would look narcissistic if retained, although it all became moot in the end, as the exchange about names was excised.)

"We made it," says Rembrandt as they exit the station, but the gang are instantly underwhelmed by the sight of their scuzzy hometown. "Yeah, looks real great..." says Cowboy. It causes the Fox to reverse his previous sentiments. "Cowboy was right," he decides. "It's all there. All anybody's got to do is go steal it." Mercy, though, observes to him, " I don't think you're going to hang around here much longer."

Hill's bolstering of the Anabasis allusions are diluted somewhat by the fact that the gang's home turf does not transpire to be sanctuary, for their enemies have followed them back. However, there was probably no real way around this if the cinematic convention of a climax was to be adhered to. As the Warriors wearily clump down the station's stairs, the Rogues' hearse is waiting for them. Noticing it, the Fox explains to the gang, "We got one more bop to go... That's them... the ones what wasted Cyrus. Now they're here to waste us." For the first time, Snowball speaks: "Let's get even."

As the Warriors fashion makeshift weapons, a voice says, "You guys must be looking for trouble." It's Swan. He clearly hasn't only just got back: he's had time to fetch a huge Bowie knife.

On the beach, five Warriors square up to eleven Rogues. "Cyrus was a big man," says Swan to Luther. "He had a big idea. Why did you do it? Why did you shoot him?" "No reason," says Luther. "I just like doing things like that." Indicating Fox, he explains why the Rogues are on their tail: "If that prick over there hadn't seen me, you guys would be okay." Luther lifts his gun. The .357 falls to his feet as Swan's flung knife slices through his forearm. As Luther drops to his knees, clutching his arm and crying, the Rogues move threateningly toward the Warriors, but Fox apprises them of bigger problems than their fallen and humiliated comrade: a hundred Gramercy Riffs have appeared beyond the sand dunes. "You Warriors are good, real good," says the New Cyrus. "The rest is ours."

As the Warriors and Mercy leave the Rogues to their fate, a tearful Rembrandt says, "We made it. We made it. I don't believe it. We made it." "Why not?" says Cowboy. "We're the Warriors." Swan watches Fox and Mercy walk off together and turns and looks out to sea.

THERE WOULD SEEM to be a large demerit to this screenplay. By transposing the scenes involving the candy store and the first appearance of the DJ, a nonsense has been made of the sequencing: it is no longer clear—or even stated—that Luther's call is to the DJ and that this prompts the latter to put out the word to catch the Warriors. This has led to a decades-long debate about the identity of the mysterious figure to whom Luther is talking on the phone. David Patrick Kelly, the actor who played Luther, had to—in the absence of knowledge of the original script —come up with a complicated thesp's rationale. "Walter said, 'You're talking to the Big Boss,'" he recalls. "So I just made a combination of one of those guys who crosses the line from gangster into politician, somebody who's involved, somebody wants to make sure that the police are not overpowered and was tapped into their sources. They want to control the gangs and not have the gangs control them and so they hired Luther and farmed him out, 'cause Luther was working his way up, to take this guy down."

"I resist the idea it's a screw up," says Hill of the change. "I would suspect that I did not want to make it just one domino tips over the other. That the idea was that this was a universalized thing out there in the city, that they were networking with each other, they knew what was going on, there was communication from all gangs. When you had had the conclave, and what had happened at the conclave, this was now not exactly a newsflash. It was a newsflash to go out to maybe the city at large, the gang city. I suspect I just didn't want to make it, 'Oh, he was the one who was in touch.' [The DJ] was meant to be a more cosmic sensibility. So I would say that that was a willful change. But one might argue that it would have been clearer to the audience had what you described been in the movie."

The very-Sixties and already very dated Warriors uniform of paisley shirts and mod jackets had been transferred in the Shaber script wholesale from Yurick. This has been ditched. There is no replacement description: the clothes the titular gang actually wore in the film would be dictated not by script but by the combination of director and costumer designer. However, Hill, if by way of Shaber, still betrays his age by retaining another Sixties overhang in the shape of Ismael/Cyrus' cry of "Can you dig it?" (The first draft used it more frequently. Hinton's brother Arnold—not present in the new script—also said it.) As Yurick (who didn't use the phrase in his book) noted, "It had been out of fashion for ten years."

Other alterations made include the jettisoning of the first twenty pages of the first draft, which means a dispensing with preambles depicting spray painting, conclave emissaries, other gangs' clubhouses, and Warriors home lives. This may or may not be an improvement, but setting the denouement on the beach certainly is. It is not just a return to Yurick's deliberate analogy with Cyrus' trek back to the Black Sea but is more satisfying, both visually and conceptually, underlining the Warriors' geographical hinterland and the fact of their arduous journey back to it. It's just a mild pity its contrivance is called attention to by Swan's justification for the location to Luther (and hence the viewer), "When we see the ocean, we figure we're home. We're safe." The increase of the distaff element in the shape of the Lizzies and the new DJ also improves the narrative, making for a welcome variation of tone in an otherwise overwhelmingly masculine script.

The crucial change for the better in this draft, though, is the watering down of the mealy-mouthed approach. Although we are never shown what defines these young men as gang members and although more than one Warrior is revealed to be ambivalent about being in a gang, neither do we see a Warrior protest that he is only "considering the idea" of gang membership or prissily expressing disapproval of drug dealing. There is far less coyness about profanities. As opposed to the sole F-bomb in the first draft, it is present here more than fifty times. The Warriors are now pointedly cooler. The Dominators were barely less pathetic than the Barrio Blades, but when the Orphans produce a newspaper clipping it is a risible act, one not reciprocated by the Warriors, a gang who wouldn't be so crass as to be awed by press. The Warriors are also tougher than the Dominators. Where the Shaber first draft ostentatiously had them horrified at the idea that they might have killed anybody, here it is implied that, while they didn't do it to Cyrus, they could easily do it to other people, whether it be in the form of Swan's prowess with knives or Ajax's comment about the Orphans, "I said we should have wasted them." In the square-off for leadership in the graveyard, Swan—unlike Hector—is not shown as being relieved that he doesn't have to fight.

The action is still deliberately kept close to a bloodless comic-book level, but there is more grit and drama than in draft one, from the fact of the gang dashing into the first subway station not because they mistake two homeless females for gang members but because they're being chased by a busload of skinheads, to their first train stopping not because of a mundane act of God but a fire implicitly started by a rival gang, to the Baseball Furies being a far more menacing proposition than the unarmed All-Stars (something that itself gives rise to a lengthy fight sequence). The alteration of the park-bench scene to involve a honeytrap female cop rachets up the feeling of the Warriors being persecuted. The final Coney Island confrontation is far superior: Hinton meekly, vaguely shouting for help when surrounded by the Rogues hardly compares to Swan hurling a knife into Luther's gun arm. Hill notes of his vision of the gang, "They accept their world and they don't apologize for it." For Hill, this was crucial to the picture's ultimate commercial fortunes. "I think the reason the film got a very large audience among young people is that it was the first film that saw gangs and this kind of youth involvement from their point of view. That did not examine it as a social problem. It examined it as a defensive measure for attitudes and survival in a hostile environment. That sounds a little high falutin'. The movie comes off almost simplistically within that framework, but that framework was radically different for its time. Now it seems to be common as tap water but, before, gangs were always approached as social problems: 'Why are these kids not in school and going to college and becoming lawyers and dentists?'"

HILL AND GORDON now had what they felt to be a viable product. However, that *The Warriors* was put into production was to a large part because of the misfortune that befell another of their joint projects.

Despite acquiescing to a production deal, Paramount blew sufficiently hot and cold about *The Warriors* that it lay dormant as a project. In lieu of its immediate production, Gordon and Hill had intended following up their collaborations on *The Driver* with a Western story called *Last Gun*, an original screenplay Hill had written with Roger Spotisswoode. "The finance pulled out at the last second," reflects Hill of *Last Gun*. At that juncture, Paramount Pictures announced that they had a short, eight-week window that Gordon and Hill might want to exploit to turn around *The Warriors*.

Some have detected wild-west themes in *The Warriors*, whether it be the costumes of some of the central gang or the *High Noon*-like climactic showdown. Could these have been in part a manifestation of Hill's frustrated *Last Gun* ambitions? "You're attributing front-of-brain attitudes to a lot of this," he responds. "You just do these things. You don't even know why you do them. You just stage 'em and make choices and I always think the more you're operating almost instinctively with storytelling… What's the Keats idea? You don't invent things—you discover them and they're already there."

The suddenly renewed interest in *The Warriors* on the part of the studio appears to have been opportunistic. "Paramount suggested this movie because gang movies were all about to come out at the same time," says David Patrick Kelly. "There was just a whole gamut of gang movies going on at that time," backs up Deborah Van Valkenburgh. At that juncture Hollywood had green-lit or was just about to the similarly themed *The Wanderers, Boulevard Nights, Over the Edge, Sunnyside,* and *Walk Proud.* Thomas Waites, who would nab the role of Fox, was surprised at this explosion in street-gang chic. He says, "This was a culture that was coming off the Sixties. It wasn't even ten years after '68. We still had the vibe in the air of non-violence, of peace, of love. Everybody was smoking pot."

Although the idea of *The Warriors* and the other gang movies might be antithetical to the zeitgeist, Hill was hardly about to inspect his gift horse's maw. "Larry told me that he thought he could get it on at Paramount if we would go right away," he recalls. "I believe a week after the Western went down—a week or two—I was in New York and we were setting things up and I was writing in the hotel at night." It wasn't just writing that was being done in an extraordinarily short timeframe. but also casting, crewing up, location scouting, film-permit acquiring, and everything else associated with motion -picture production. It's Hill's recollection that *The Warriors* was given the studio go-ahead in April or May of 1978. "We were shooting by the end of June," he says. "So it all went like a whirlwind."

THE ASSEMBLY

THE PRODUCTION BUDGET of *The Warriors* was reported at the time as being between $4m and $4.7m. "I'm under the impression that the movie cost slightly less than three in the end, but I don't know," says Walter Hill. "I think we can agree that *The Warriors* was made threadbare."

Certainly, the upper end of that range would be low even for the time. Estimated budgets for other films released in 1979 include *Escape from Alcatraz* ($8m), *Kramer vs. Kramer* ($8m), *Hair* ($11m), and *Apocalypse Now* ($31.5m). Even *Manhattan*, another New York movie but in Woody Allen's established low-key mold, came in at $9m. It then has to be taken into account that the *Warriors* production team had little to spend above the line because the film's below-the-line costs were inordinately high. It was shot almost entirely on location (i.e., not in the more controllable and relatively inexpensive environs of a studio set or backlot) and involved predominantly night shoots, which meant considerable crew overtime pay.

Hill, though, didn't let his scant resources dampen his ambitions. "You have to present yourself to best advantage whatever limitations you have when you make a film," he shrugs. "We were all younger and a lot crazier then. I decided I wanted to make the movie around the kind of editorial principles of Eisenstein and, if you look at the way the movie's edited, I think you'll see that. Nobody's ever pointed this out, and I've never really talked about it much and I realize it sounds a bit ludicrous, but that's one of the guiding principles that I had in making the movie." Legendary Soviet Union director Sergei Eisenstein (1898-1948) was responsible for *Battleship Potemkin*, which—although made in 1925 and without sound—still regularly features in critics' polls to determine history's greatest motion pictures. However, he is not just remembered as a maker of great films but as a pioneer who helped devise some of the vocabulary of the medium, particularly montage and cumulative effect. "His directorial style is inseparable from his editorial style," opines Hill. "And he was most fascinated by the potentials of editing within film and how the assembly of images in a certain order could produce a greater effect."

While the paucity of funds affected the film's tone, it was not necessarily in a bad way. Hill attributes to his lack of resources the picture's non-naturalism. This quality conferred on *The Warriors* a surrealism that is pleasing to its fans and has prevented it from dating. "I don't know how to say this gracefully, but the only chance it had was to make it as kind of wild and crazy as you could within the budget," he says. "When I say wild, I mean stretch the limits of realism... You didn't have a normal story and how do you just tell it?... I thought that there was a hint within the book. He's got one of the guys reading a comic book on the subway about the Xenophon march and I thought that was a window into an interesting way to make the film... I wanted to make a kind of comic book... The principle that the gangs are going to take over the city of New York is fairly ludicrous. That immediately puts you into the areas of fantasy and science fiction." Ergo, the film he made would necessarily be "dystopian, and set in a kind of immediate future, if that's not a contradiction in terms—a future about to happen."

Another impetus for the comic-book approach arose from the casting process. Sol Yurick said of the characters in his book, "I was essentially looking at Hispanics and blacks." Perhaps surprisingly for such a proven populist, Hill was initially keen to be faithful to that all-ethnic vision, feeling it was the only way to do the film properly. Paramount, however, were not so enamored of the idea, feeling it would narrow the picture's appeal and commercial prospects. The studio gravitated more toward the racial variety seen in Shaber's script. The Warriors delegation to be found in the finished film was comprised of five whites, three blacks, and one Latino (two, if one counts the implicitly Puerto Rican Mercy as an honorary Warrior). In today's climate wherein "diversity" is a mantra, such a line-up wouldn't seem at all unusual. In the late Seventies, an era of largely white casts with the occasional ethnic (classically, the "token black"), it was highly progressive—or at least it would have been to a public unaware of the hard-nosed business exigencies that lay behind it.

Which, of course, is not the same thing as believable. "Almost impossible," Yurick said of the notion of such a blend. In any era? "Very much so." As to the reasons that gang loyalties can't in real life cross racial lines, Yurick said, "You have a combination of localism and an overall, overriding global economic structure. Racism is very strong and alive and well in the United States, Obama notwithstanding. For instance, motorcycle gangs almost always tend to be white, of Germanic-Irish-English descent, and violently racist."

Dorsey Wright—an African American and New York City native who would be cast as the leader of the Warriors—agrees about the impossibility of an interracial gang. "I graduated in '74 and there were tons of gangs in New York, but there was no such thing as an interracial gang," he says. "You might find a gang that has maybe blacks and Puerto Ricans, but you would never find a gang that had whites, blacks, and Puerto Ricans. So when they did that in the film, it kind of threw me." Like Yurick, he asserts that this lack of real-life blending hasn't changed since.

Fellow black New Yorker Brian Tyler (the film's Snow) was also surprised at the rainbow coalition but feels the filmmakers should be cut some slack. "I'm not gonna say it's unrealistic," he says. "I'm sure somewhere in the world, there is probably a mixed gang of some type or another. It's a theatrical production. It's art, and art is in the eyes of the creators and the beholders."

For Hill, though, the project's unrealisticness gave further cause for him to create a different kind of reality, one in which nobody could cite lack of verisimilitude because in a universe of his own creation he was the one making the rules. Whatever grittiness there was in the script—and there had never been much—would now give way to something approaching a dreamscape.

THE WARRIORS PRODUCTION team that proceeded to set up in New York included the "Frank" previously mentioned by Hill. Frank Marshall would be the film's executive producer. As well as collaborating with Hill and Gordon on *The Driver*, his so far miscellaneous career had encompassed some acting jobs, working on several Peter Bogdanovich pictures in roles ranging from location manager to producer's assistant to associate producer, assisting on the Band's in-concert movie *The Last Waltz*, and trying in vain to get off the ground the Orson Welles project *The Other Side of the Wind*.

Today, Marshall's name is attached as producer to some of the most successful motion pictures of all time, including *Raiders of the Lost Ark* and the Bourne films, but in the late Seventies he was a humbler figure in that area, with just two (co-)production credits to his name, on *Paper Moon* (1973) and *Nickelodeon* (1976). As such, he handled many of *The Warriors* day-to-day chores. "I was really the line producer and Larry was the producer," he notes. "I was on the set every day... But in those days, 'executive producer' was the title that you got."

One of Marshall's relatively mundane tasks was to scout locations that matched the backdrops in the developing script. "I would go and try and find something that was interesting that we could shoot at. I literally drove around all of New York. There were a lot of places that were pretty dangerous. I had a production manager and we had a liaison with the police department with us as well, so that was a big help." Although Marshall says, "I wasn't really involved in the writing," he also states, "I was a researcher [on] the original story." This sometimes fed into significant alterations as, for instance, when Hill desired a plausible reason for the gang's train to be stopped that was more dramatic than Yurick's/Shaber's happenstance rationale of a fault on the tracks. "I had a very strong connection with the Transit Authority, so I asked," says Marshall. When the answer came back that a fire was a likely cause of a subway line grinding to a halt, it duly made its way into Hill's script. Marshall also assisted in the task of populating the picture, attending auditions with Hill and Gordon, although says, "I was more the person who got things done and made the deals. Walter always respected my opinion, but it was really Walter and Larry that made the final decisions."

The film's press book would reason, "Newcomers were cast in the film in order to maintain the look and feel of real people caught in dangerous situations." "It just didn't lend itself to star casting," says Hill. "Even the studio felt that. I didn't get along very well with the studio, but Eisner and Diller had come out of television and they were not as star oriented as most of the movie studios were. They very much had the notion that lead players could be developed... Their dream was to find I don't know how many people and then make option deals and keep them for a long time." It should be pointed out that the Paramount men's hankering for a return to the "studio system" was to some extent motivated by financial interest: unknowns were handy for *The Warriors*' tight budget. Hill: "That was part of the charm of the idea." David Harris, another of the young men cast as a Warrior, observes, "What we got paid when we did that movie was the least that SAG [the Screen Actors' Guild] said that we could get paid. It was the bottom of the bottom." On a similar note, it has been claimed that the production didn't look outside the Big Apple for actors so as to maintain a Gotham verisimilitude. However, this is hardly consistent with the fact that roles were awarded to people who hailed from places as far away as Memphis and Philadelphia. The reality was slightly more complicated. As Marshall explains, "As long as they lived there, it was fine, 'cause we didn't have enough money to pay anybody to come in."

The acting profession, of course, is never short of people hungry for their big break. When *The Warriors* shoot was announced, therefore, Howard Feuer and Jeremy Ritzer—the directors of the casting company with which the producers were working—were inundated with applications from young unknowns. Those fledglings would find that it was not enough that they had talent and fit the character profile. Not for nothing did the recruiting process include a group reading. Hill wanted to hire people who collectively felt like the gang they were supposed to be. "Walter was very astute in the way that he put us together," says Michael Beck, the man who would be Swan, "and the way that he—I don't know if 'manipulated' is the right word—but certainly created an atmosphere for the cast members, the gang, the Warriors, to bond as that. To become close to each other and to watch each other's back... I'm sure from Walter's point of view he was thinking, 'The lens is going to pick that up.'" It could be suggested that part of the reason that this strategy worked is an element of human nature that wasn't part of Hill's reasoning: the cast of beginners were coming into the project as equals. Whatever the reason, its success did not evaporate once shooting wrapped. Decades later when the cast reassembled for commercial events, Beck noticed that the camaraderie was still very much intact. "We still feel a strong connection with each other."

There was another unusual consideration in the audition process. Interested thespians needed to be blessed with above-average levels of fitness. "When you read the script you go, 'This is going to be pretty physical,'" says Beck. "We did have some week-long stretches where all we did every night was run, from dark to sun-up."

It's not only morals and skin shades that differentiates the central gang of the film from the one in the book. "That really had to do with the labor laws more than anything else," says Hill. "I would have probably liked them to have been a bit younger but, to work nights and things like that, they had to be of adult age." Marshall explains, "We needed people that could work at night, all night, so they had to be at least eighteen."

Once again, tight finances were also part of the equation. Hill: "We'd have never been able to make the movie under any economics that Paramount was prepared to put up with if we'd have shot [within] the kid laws that prevailed, because they worked such a short working night."

However, while this might make sense on a practical level, rendering the Warriors grown adults—they all look in their late teens to mid-twenties, although in reality some of the cast were at the upper end of their twenties and one had even entered his thirties—introduces a large, and for some fatal, flaw into the whole project. It's one that can best be summed up with the question, "Why didn't they just catch a ride?" An adult gang stranded miles from home in enemy territory would surely have hailed cabs, stolen cars, or any number of things involving the safety and speed provided by a vehicle that is not offered by trying to catch subway trains and trudging between stations on foot. Of course, such recourses didn't exist in the ancient world inhabited by Xenophon's men. Nor was it an issue when Yurick transposed the Ten Thousand's adventures to the modern day. Although he doesn't particularly explore it in his novel aside from the Dominators' abortive attempt to procure a ride from their social worker Wallie, Yurick later explained of gangs of the period, "Automobiles were not available to them." The writer seemed to be referring to the lack of money around in the mid Sixties, but could equally have cited the tender age of his protagonists. Moreover, as mid-teens, it was plausible that they would not know how to hotwire a car. Meanwhile, their ethnicity made it unlikely that a cab would stop for them. The Warriors of the film, though, were a different proposition.

"Yeah, but it's metaphorical," shrugs Marshall. The metaphorical/futuristic/heightened realism tone of the *Warriors* movie is undeniable but is also frequently used by its principals as a get-out-of-jail card for all sorts of illogic. However, Marshall does also offer, "It's about getting back home on the transportation that they use. They don't have any money. They jump the turnstiles—that's how they roll. And back in those days nobody drove in New York. That was a California thing. Nobody had a license. A lot of people don't have their licenses today in New York, 'cause the public transportation is so good." "I guess they wanted to get home the way they got there," says Hill of the car/hotwire issue. However, the fact that he knows he's on shaky ground seems to be indicated by another comment, which he makes while laughing: "The temptation is to say, 'Well, that would have ended the movie, and it wouldn't have been a very good one.'"

Dorsey Wright bats away all the torturous rationales. "A gang would have hotwired a car," he cheerfully admits. "There's no way in the world I'm gonna try and, as they say in the movie, 'bop' from one territory to the next. That's insane. You would hotwire a damn car and get the fuck out of there. There's only nine of you. When you go into somebody else's neighborhood, you're not looking at nine gang members in that fucking territory. You're looking at two to three hundred or better."

If Shaber, Hill, Gordon, Marshall, etc. ever thought at the time that this matter was a gaping lapse in logic—and it's possible that in the hurly burly of bringing the project to the screen in such a short timescale they didn't—they had, as Hill merrily indicates, every incentive to ignore it. However, it has to be said that curiously few reviewers—whatever any other misgivings they may have had about the picture—have ever taken issue with it.

THE MOST IMPORTANT ROLE in *The Warriors*—at least initially—was that of the Fox, the man who the script dictated become the de facto leader of the decapitated Coney Island unit. In a way, it's surprising that Thomas Waites (later professionally known as Thomas G. Waites) should have bagged the part. "I'm a classically trained actor from Julliard and I'd done a lot of Shakespeare and I was kind of a theatre guy," he notes. "I guess I'm more literature oriented than action oriented." Nonetheless, in '78, the career of the Pennsylvania-raised 23-year-old was showing great promise. Waites had obtained stage work at the O'Neill Foundation in Waterford, Connecticut, the Spoletto Festival in Charleston, and Center Stage in Baltimore. Moreover, "I had done two pictures before. One was an independent movie (before the term independent was in vogue) called *On The Yard* directed by Ray Silver, based on a novel by Malcolm Braly. I had the lead in that. I did another small picture for PBS, a movie for television." "He was kind of the hot actor at that time," says Marshall.

Waites recalls being in a theatre one night when casting director Scott Rudin said to him, "The most amazing thing just happened—two movies have come into town: *The Warriors* and *The Wanderers*, and they're both about gangs. They're going to be shooting in the city this summer and I'm sure you'll be auditioning for them." Observes Waites, "It was a coup at the time to get one of those pictures." Waites, in fact, could have had either.

Despite all the other gang movies in production, it was Philip Kaufman's *The Wanderers* with which *The Warriors* would most be compared and bracketed, partly because they were both set in New York, partly even because of the assonance of their titles. Quite deliberately, though, there was no overlap between the two films personnel-wise. "I had no idea what their project was," says Lawrence Gordon of *The Wanderers*. "I just knew they were casting around the same time we were. I think our movie speaks for itself. I don't think they're similar movies. I think they're similar genres." Says Walter Hill, "I remember people talking about it, but Phil's movie as I recall was shot a number of months after ours... We were casting at the same time and quite often everybody wanted to be in the other movie. I never felt I was in a race... When you make pictures for a living, the only race you're in is with yourself and how good a job can you do with the conditions that you're given. I had plenty to worry about without having to worry about somebody else's movie." However, the director does concede, "It worried the studio and it worried the business producer elements."

"There was a lot of competition between *The Wanderers* and *The Warriors*," Terry ("Vermin") Michos recalls. "I was called in to go in and read for *The Wanderers*. I thought they were very interested in me, and then the guy said, 'Anyone that's in *The Warriors* we're not casting in *The Wanderers.*' They had some little parts like Konrad Sheehan, who was the head of the Punks on the roller skates. He did do a part in *The Wanderers*. But no big roles were double cast."

Waites, therefore, had to make a choice. Kaufman was at the time arguably a bigger name than Hill: his last two pictures had been the 1976 Clint Eastwood Western *The Outlaw Josey Wales* (writer) and the 1978 remake of *Invasion of the Body Snatchers* (director). As such, it took some courage on the part of Waites to reject his overtures. "He asked me to turn *The Warriors* down," says Waites. "He said, 'Just give me a little more time, don't say yes to the other picture because I'm interested in working with you.'" Waites' deal from Paramount was reported to constitute $1,500 a week and a $50,000 option deal. Even adjusted for inflation—approximately $6,000 and $200,000 respectively—it doesn't sound like much, but he has said it was more money than he had ever seen in his life. However, when asked why he chose to go with *The Warriors*, Waites says, "I liked Walter better as an artist. He had a sensitivity beneath his tough/quiet exterior."

The prominence of Fox in *The Warriors* may also have been a factor. "The Fox was the guy that was supposed to get the girl in the end," Waites points out. "He was the main character." Waites recollects, "I think they started seeing people April of '78. I auditioned and then I was called back, then I was called back again. This was way before cellphones or beepers or any of that stuff. I was walking around the city, it was *really* hot, and for some strange reason I just happened to call my agent. 'Oh my God! I'm so glad you called. Hurry up. You have to get ever to Paramount. You and Deborah Van Valkenburgh have to do [an] interview with Larry Gordon and Walter Hill and they need you there right away.' So I went up for the final interview and sat and talked to Walter and Larry, then I think it was the next day that they offered me the part."

Although Waites did some preparation for his role, he doesn't sound too sure about how much. "I think I did go down to Brooklyn and Coney Island and tried hanging out. Not an extensive amount that I recall. I remember hanging out on the streets as it became summer before we started shooting in June. And I remember screening a bunch of movies with Walter to try to get an idea of his vision of it. *Rebel Without a Cause*, which has also the gang thing going on in it. *East of Eden*, which has more of the tortured romantic. *West Side Story*."

Waites saw his character as a cut above the other Warriors. "One of the things that Walter used to stress to me is that there's a difference between a verbal actor and a non-verbal actor. For example, he had directed *The Driver* with Ryan O'Neal and Bruce Dern and he said Bruce Dern is an example of a verbal actor whereas Ryan O'Neal was an example of an actor—not that he can't do lines—but that his power lay in his ability to convey silence. What he wanted from me was to be his verbal actor. That I was the guy he wanted to carry the intelligence of the story. [Fox] was on a level above in the sense that he was the most knowledgeable and I tried to garner respect from the other guys in my physical prowess, my ability to use my own physicality, to be able to move more quickly, run faster, use my body in a more agile fashion than just the muscle."

Despite the studio resisting Hill's desire for an all-ethnic cast, the director was able to recruit 21-year-old black actor Dorsey Wright as the Warriors' leader, Cleon. The importance of the role is not diminished too much by the fact that the character disappears from the proceedings at the quarter-hour mark because of his capture or killing (the finished film doesn't make it clear) at the conclave.

Born in Philadelphia in 1957, Wright was raised in New York City. He enrolled at Pratt Institute to study scenic design but stumbled into acting when asked to fill in for a player who was ill. *The Warriors* would be his first released film, but he shot his role in Miloš Forman's movie adaptation of hippie musical *Hair* shortly beforehand. He was also working as a disc jockey in several New York clubs. "I went for a quick reading right behind finishing up *Hair*," Wright recalls. "I knew nothing about the film… My agent would point me in the direction and was like, 'Yo, go audition. Get that job'… I went up there and read for a couple of parts. I was called back not too long afterwards and basically was told about the part for Cleon. Also I was told that his girlfriend would be Pamela Poitier, which I felt was exciting. You know: Sidney Poitier's daughter."

"I didn't have to do any research," Wright states. Not only did he grow up in gang territory but, he notes, "I was in a gang for a short period of time because it was convenient in order to go to high school. I went to high school up in Missoula Parkway. Where I lived was 174th street. From 174th Street to Missoula Parkway, you went through maybe three or four gangs' territory." Accordingly, he became a member of the tautologously titled Black Spades. "If you weren't part of a gang, you were liable to get your bus pass taken, your lunch money taken, so it just became a convenient way to go to school without getting your ass kicked."

Wright says he based Cleon on "a million people I knew." His character's leader status necessitated him projecting an authority but, Wright states, "Not the whole gorilla authority." He explains, "The people that I was scared of in real life are the quiet ones. Those who talk and tell you, 'I'm gonna kick your ass,' they're just talking. I learnt that a long time ago… Most of the people that were in gangs were quiet. They were just the opposite of what people thought they were."

Interestingly, he echoes the nomenclature in Sol Yurick's book as he elucidates, "They needed a family. And they were ready to do anything that the family needed to be done. But they weren't talkers, they were do-ers. It was like, 'Yo, what are we gonna do today?' 'Well, we need money for beer.' 'All right then, we're gonna go into the store, we're gonna go steal somebody's beer, or we're gonna rob somebody.' And that was the end of the talking. You'd go do it. If you don't do it, you can't be part of the gang.

"That's all a gang was. It was an extension of family. Most of the guys I knew, they had family. It might have been a single mother at home. It may not have been the complete American happy-family routine. But they needed more in the streets because there were people out there who would take advantage of you. It was dangerous. There were people out there that really weren't like gang members, they were just solo and they would do dumb shit. So gangs popped up so that, 'Hey, we all together become a family, we all protect each other.'"

The scenario he posits of gang-as-defensive-maneuver might well cause raised eyebrows among those who have had the misfortune to live in the same vicinity as gangs and who perceive them as aggressors. Wright: "Yeah, but those were rogues. Because if you belonged in a gang, it was specified that, 'Hey, you do not rob civilians, you do not beat up civilians.' Unless you are told to. If you did, then you're kicked out. 'You don't shit where you eat'—that was a gang expression. Don't do dumb shit where your gang live, because now the people in the neighborhood don't like you, and on top of that, the people in the neighborhood is my fucking family, that's my mother."

Wright had an NYC-dweller's disdainful view of the Warriors' home turf, which he describes as "suburbs." "Coney Island is like a cheap Vegas. Most people in New York, we basically just go there for entertainment and we leave… Most of Coney Island was this huge complex of projects. They live near the ocean and their rides, so it's like fantasy land." This "'burb" ambience extended to the area's paucity of street gangs. "Most of the gangs were Brooklyn, Bronx, and Upper Manhattan, Harlem."

Michael Beck, the film's Swan, says, "I was born in Memphis, raised on a farm across the river in Arkansas, went to college in Jackson, Mississippi. I went to college on an athletic scholarship so acting was not something that was even on the radar for me, but halfway through my junior year a friend of mine dared me to try out for a play. I auditioned for *Romeo and Juliet*, got the part of Tybalt, and never looked back." Like many American actors, he relocated in order to finish his training, although not to the more common New York or California. "The professor who was the director of the players of the drama department, I think he saw some gifting there as an actor and he was a real Anglophile. He wasn't English but he loved the British drama-school mold. His advice to me was, 'You can either go to New York and go to the Actors Studio or Neighborhood Playhouse or one of those, or what I would recommend is that you go to London and audition for RADA and Central and LAMDA and all these drama schools and see what happens.' Having only had a year-and-a-half of acting under my belt and having been graciously given lead roles and everything, I thought it all came easy. So I went, 'Sure, I'll go to London and get in drama school.'" Beck failed his audition for the top-tier Royal Academy of Dramatic Arts. However, a friend he made early on in his time in the UK was a graduate of and sometime teacher at the Central School of Speech and Drama and obtained him an audition there. "I fortunately got picked as one of the thirty for that year. Spent three years in drama school there and then loved it so much that I didn't want to leave and so finagled getting a work permit and stayed another two years working in rep."

Beck fell in love with London at first sight. "The only time I had been out of the rural south of the United States was on the eighth-grade trip to Washington, D.C. I remember vividly coming in on the final approach on British Airways into Heathrow and just looking out: the architecture was different, the cars on the road were different, riding into London on a bus—everything was different. I was there from late '71 to '76. It was a great time. Everybody went, 'Well, you missed the Sixties,' but it still had some of that flavor to it." His assimilation of the local argot is revealed when he adds, "Still got great mates from those days."

Some might find it curious that Beck should have been so enamored of Britain in an era when crises beset the nation. The indigenous British often remember life in the Seventies made perennially grim through balance-of-trade deficits and wildcat trade-union strikes. The perception of decline in the U.K., in fact, was rather similar to that in contemporaneous New York. The latter's sense of decay would be an underpinning of *The Warriors*. Beck acknowledges the parallels. "I remember the early days of punk rock. It was a whole different kind of rage going on then."

While none of this could spoil his enchantment at this exhilaratingly unfamiliar society, one thing that rather brought him up short was how early Britons tended to decide that acting was their vocation. Although only born in 1949, Beck was a veritable old man compared to his classmates. "In that year of thirty students, I was the second oldest. An Aussie mate of mine was a few months older. We'd both gone to university. There was one kid that was sixteen years old. I was 22 when I started. At drama school, probably the average age of my year was eighteen or nineteen. Little kids just right out of school going to drama school. So I was thinking, 'Man, I'm getting into this game later than most people.'"

Any fear that fact instilled in Beck was faint—he says he never at any point felt that he'd missed the boat—and was in any case dispelled by the progress he made on his return to his native country after working in British repertory in various companies and appearing in several BBC productions. "Things happened pretty quickly," he recalls. "Summer of '76, I came back to the States. In early November I moved to New York and by January I had gotten an agent. I had the lead in an independent movie that was being shot in Israel. So I felt, 'I'm on the road here, it's all happening.'" He racked up some significant TV roles, including NBC's *Holocaust*.

None of his success was under his given name. After finishing at the Central School, he had signed up with Equity, the British equivalent of the Screen Actors Guild and, as often happens when people join thespian unions, found that the presence in its ranks of a namesake prohibited professional use of the name with which he was born. "My legal name is John Michael Beck Taylor," he explains. "I have never been called John except on the first day of school each year and on government forms. There was already a Michael Taylor, so I took my middle name instead of making up a stage name. It seemed to fit. Glad I did."

Feuer and Ritzer were initially somewhat skeptical of the idea of casting Beck in *The Warriors*. "The way I got that part is kind of interesting," Beck recalls. "Feuer and Ritzer knew me as this Anglophiled theatre actor. My agents kept submitting me for *The Warriors* and they didn't see me as this street-gang kind of [actor]. They wouldn't even put me up for the part." By coincidence, however, Walter Hill had had occasion to watch Beck's screen debut, *Madman*, the aforesaid Israel-shot independent. "He screened that picture to look at Sigourney Weaver, 'cause Walter was one of the producers on the picture *Alien* and that was Sigourney's only film work at the time. So he got in touch with Feuer and Ritzer and said, 'I want to see this guy Michael Beck.'"

Once Hill met Beck, the latter's acting chops got him over the hurdle of being perceived by some as too effete for the role of a street-gang member. However, with the part secured, Beck's euphoria died down a little and his own doubts began to set in. "I thought, 'Well, I'm a little long in the tooth for this deal,'" he reflects. Although he possessed gaunt good looks and a fairly youthful appearance, he points out, "I was actually 29." With a little rationalization, he got over it. "Some of those hardened kids, they look a little bit older than what they are. Also, having grown up seeing movies all my life, high schoolers are always played by people in their twenties and thirties. Which is kind of crazy, but that's just how it is."

In preparation for his role, Beck read Yurick's book. The other research he did involved associating with a New York gang. "I was living up on 79th Street between Columbus and Amsterdam and there was actually a street gang headquartered up on 82nd or 83rd Street just a couple of blocks away, so I went up there and observed and chatted with some of those kids. Not letting them know that I was going to be in a movie." Who did they think this inquisitive stranger was? "Just a guy. I didn't ask them so much about what they did. It wasn't an interview process. It was more just taking up conversation as I went down the street." When pressed,

Beck has a memory of Hill screening some teenage angst movies, but his recollection on this score is even vaguer than Waites' ("I think he did—but that was years ago").

Beck feels that there was little instruction in the script about his character. He says, "I viewed Swan very much as a loner, as someone who wanted more out of life than life was giving him. That line at the end when they get back to Coney and he goes, 'Is this what we fought all night to get back to?' kind of describes [him]. I think he had some sense of a larger world outside of the place where he lived and a longing for that. I also saw him—this may be looking back on it; I don't really know that I was that in my head about it, I was just playing the part—in a same kind of mold as some of those roles that Gary Cooper played back in the Thirties and Forties. That loner person who had a tough exterior but underneath there was a softness that he didn't want anyone to see."

Emphatically not harboring a hidden softness was the character Ajax, played by James Remar. Born in 1953, Remar is a Bostonian. "I stopped going to high school when I was fifteen, but I went to kind of an alternative school until I was like sixteen," he says. "Then I stopped going to class and I just thumbed around the United States. It was pretty much the height of the Vietnam War and seeing kids on the street was not a unusual occurrence." At the age of seventeen he worked with a low-level rock band for almost a year. Although "a hobbyist guitar player," Remar wasn't operating as a musician. "I travelled as a roadie… And then I went back to high school and graduated."

His decision to become an actor came when he was "about twenty." He recalls, "It was just a culmination of events. I had done some acting with a summer community, a summer camp, and then I had been a roofer after I got out of high school—I didn't go directly to college—and I got laid off of my roofing job." Remar travelled down to St. Augustine, Florida, where he obtained a part in the long-running outdoor performance of the state's official play, the historical drama *Cross and Sword*. "They paid me fifty dollars a week to play a Spanish colonist. Richard Boone, who was a very famous actor back then, lived in that community. He came and visited the show on our final night. We all had a few drinks afterwards and we got to pick his brain and I said, 'Where do you go from here?' He said, 'Neighborhood Playhouse School or the theatre.' So I let that stew for a while. I went back to work painting houses and roofing and had an epiphany when I was on a ladder. I thought, 'I want to be a doctor or a jet pilot.' Military was very unpopular. I didn't even think I could get in back then. Doctor was a lot of school and I didn't like school, even though I had *some* brains. And I thought, 'You know, an actor can experience a lot of things in life and do a little bit of everything.' I decided right then and there that I would enlist as an actor. Give myself to it for three years and if nothing happened I'd be young enough to do something else. In that moment, I decided to go to the Neighborhood Playhouse.

"The Neighborhood Playhouse is an acting Academy. You're not even permitted to audition. [It's a] two-year academy. You have to be asked back for the second year. I went to the first year. They did not invite me back to the second year, which was a devastating experience. But I took comfort 'cause Steve McQueen went there and they didn't ask him back either. Then I started auditioning, and I got *Grease*, the Broadway road company." His role in said Fifties musical as Kernickie involved some trilling, but he says, "They didn't hire me for my singing. They hired me for my energy."

By the time of *The Warriors*, Remar had also appeared in productions at the Ensemble Studio Theatre and the WPA Theatre, but reflects, "I was pretty raw." However, unlike most of his new colleagues he could boast that he had appeared in one previous motion picture. It so happens, it was *On The Yard*, in which Waites had also appeared. "It was a prison flick made by the same people that made *Hester Street* and *Crossing Delancey*," Remar says. "It was a small independent company back when you could do that sort of thing. It was not a big hit, but it didn't need to be."

Those assuming that the two ex-colleagues coalesced again in *The Warriors* because they were comparing notes would be mistaken. "We were completely parallel. My agent submitted me for *The Warriors* and Tom Waites just happened to be another one of those thousands of New York actors that was in the audition circuit." He continues, "The first character that they sent me the script for was Swan. Swan was a very different character in that version. Then they said, 'No, it's gone to another actor,' and they asked me to audition for Ajax."

As Ajax was probably the roughest character within the Warriors' ranks, it's appropriate that Remar's audition was possibly the wildest the film's production staff witnessed. Remar says, "Ajax was a counterpoint to Swan. He was the rowdy guy, he was the loose cannon." The 5'10" actor also says, "He was written initially as a much bigger person, like 6'9", 300 pounds. A guy that could really move things around. So I brought to it a side in terms of my vocal energy and just swagger that was to compensate for what I didn't have in actual physical size." Even so, at this audition

Remar did exhibit some physicality. Acting out his character's key scene wherein he is ensnared by the undercover female cop and finding his only available prop a "huge conference table," he had to improvise. "I held on to the corner of the conference table as if I were handcuffed to the park bench. I picked up the corner of the table… It was just in the heat of the moment. I just moved it a little bit. It was heavy enough and I was into it enough and I was holding onto the thing just tight enough to make that impression." Gordon, Hill, and Marshall, seated around the heaving conference table, were duly impressed. Remar: "It was a little bit startling and at the same time it was just under the wire being over-the-top, so it became impressive, rather than off-putting… That sealed it for me—in a good way." Possibly, but as ever with the casting process there may have been another factor: aspects of physiognomy over which an actor has no control. Remar's handsomeness was undercut by a faint suspicion of brutishness and by a gap in his front teeth that was exposed whenever he smiled. In other words, he innately resembled the low-rent Lothario that Ajax is.

Remar says he didn't "to any great extent" have experience of gang members or their strata of society but that "I did my own little share of teenage nefarious activities and we'd run around in packs. Not real solid street gangs with colors and everything. That was much more a New York thing at that time." For research, he "went down to talk to people who lived in Coney Island and read about gangs." He also prepared physically: "Got myself beefed up, lifted weights, and swung the bat around, and more or less tried to get in tune with life as a young person on the streets of New York." However, he points out, "You didn't get six months to, like, pack on muscle. We were jobbing actors that had to be ready to do any role at any time. You get the job and then two weeks later you're shooting. It's not like it is now. And that's all a lot of hype—how actors prepare for their role and that makes them a method actor. None of us had the time to do that. You get the job on Thursday and shoot on Monday—that's method acting."

Although those Big-Apple streets to which Remar refers were much more dangerous than they are today, his character was well-equipped to take care of himself on them, perhaps too much so. Did he view Ajax as slightly unhinged? "Sure. Yeah. I don't behave like that. I hope." He adds of Ajax's gang milieu, "It's a funny kind of life. From what I've learned now, they don't really view life as having any kind of future. It's just grab what you can and don't take any shit. A hundred bucks in your pocket is worth far more than going to school and learning a trade that's gonna make you a thousand down the line. It wasn't in his frame of reference." The argument could even be made that there is not much moral difference between Ajax and the movie's villain, Luther. However, here Remar defends his character. "I'd say there's a pretty substantial difference. Ajax, you could reason with him. (Except when it came to the girl. He wanted to get some of the girl.) He was not as manic as Luther. Luther refused to play by the rules at all and he was devious. Ajax would stand up and have a fair fight with you. He'd look you in the eye and go man to man with you, toe to toe, whereas Luther was more of a sneak. He brought a gun to a knife fight. Ajax wouldn't do that."

Considering the audacious diversity of the casting, it seems odd that Hill didn't employ a Native American as Cochise. The role did however go to another African American, David Harris. Born in 1959, Harris was a graduate of the American Academy of Dramatic Arts. "I'm a native New Yorker," Harris says. "I'm what you call one of the original Bowery Boys [from] the Lower East Side, Avenue D… I grew up around gangs. I wasn't in one when I was much younger. My mother kept a tight range on me and my brother. She sent us to Catholic schools so we'd avoid all of that, and we were not allowed to hang out at night and all that stuff. But I grew up at the heart of it." Although he says, "*The Warriors* was my first major feature film," he also notes, "I was quite seasoned. I did some guest shots in New York City when they were shooting some TV series and I was doing a lot of stage." Harris had appeared on television in *Madigan*, *Kojak*, and the Emmy Award-winning *Judge Horton and the Scottsboro Boys*. Stage-wise, he had been seen in the New York Shakespeare Festival production of *Wedding Band*, Ron Milner's *What the Wine Sellers Buy* on Broadway, and the Phoenix Repertory Company production *Secret Service*. In the latter he was on stage with John Lithgow and Meryl Streep. A presentation of the play was broadcast on PBS' *Great Performances*. "When Walter Hill came to New York to cast *The Warriors*, I wasn't even in New York. Walter was still looking for Cochise and my agent sent me up. I had two scenes prepared. 'Whole lot of magic' was one of my lines at the audition… I read one little scene and then he said basically, 'Thank you and I'll see you.' My agent called me back and said, 'You got the role.' I went down I think the next day and I met the entire cast."

That cast was, with the exception of the diminutive, slightly built Marcelino Sánchez, notably bigger than the matchstick-thin Harris. He says this didn't make him self-conscious about playing a tough guy. "In my mind, I was a tough guy, came up from a tough neighborhood, and I always had a tough attitude. If I got into a fight you better really hit me hard to keep me down, because I'd get back up and come right back at you."

Acting school had taught Harris to think deeply about things like a character's voice, mannerisms, and motion. This came in handy for what was one of the subsidiary Warriors roles: outside of Fox, Swan, Ajax, and possibly Cleon, it has to be said that the personalities of the gang members are not well differentiated. The defining characteristic of Cowboy, for instance, is surely his hat, a device more usual in comic books, and in pre-Sixties ones at that. "I tried to make Cochise a little bit different," says Harris. "His gestures, his voice. I tried to make him funny. I tried to make him serious. I tried to make him street. I tried to make him a guy that you would like. The way he walked—he had this kind of little shuffle."

The other black face in the Warriors' ranks belonged to Brian Tyler, who played the character originally called Snowball. "I'm from New York," Tyler says. "When the movie was shot, I actually lived in the Bronx." Born in 1960, Tyler was making his screen debut. His acting ambitions had begun in his high school drama club, from which he graduated to New York's American Community Theatre. He felt that his new colleagues were "all much more experienced actors than I was," saying, "I was doing a couple of way, way off-Broadway productions." Of his initial *Warriors* audition, Tyler recalls, "I remember having to go down to Manhattan and I was given some sides—a little bit of script—and a couple of pictures were taken. The second audition, I was given a little bit of script to go out and study and then come back. So I walked across the street to Central Park."

He recalls that when he first auditioned, the producers weren't exactly sure what they wanted to do with him. "But I do believe by the second or third audition they were looking to me as Snow… Originally, the name was going to be Snowball, but that was never said in the movie. I think it just flowed better." Asked if, had the opportunity arisen, he would have liked to have played a central character like Swan or Fox, he says, "No. I think I played exactly who I was supposed to play." This, though, is not because Snow is the only character identifiable from the script as black, which is something Tyler appears not to have noticed. However, this equanimity ties in perfectly with his aura and appearance, him possessed of oval, cat-like eyes and a serene expression. Of his preparation, he says, "I read the book, I had the script and just practice, practice, practice. I pretty much went with the book and the script, but mostly Walter's direction."

Before being bitten by the acting bug, Marcelino Sánchez studied painting at New York's High School of Art and Design. (Although it wouldn't be evident from *The Warriors'* credits, his surname was spelt with an accent over the "a.") It was perhaps apposite then that Sánchez was picked to play the Warriors' resident artist. The bushy-haired, voluptuous-lipped, soft-voiced Sánchez was born in 1957. "He and my brothers and my parents were all born in Puerto Rico," explains his sister Mayra, thirteen years his junior. "I was the only one born here." Sánchez was six years old when he, his younger siblings, and his mother made the passage over in December 1964 to be reunited with his father. "He had to learn how to speak English and all that here in school," says Mayra, who adds that, despite this initial disadvantage, Sánchez was "very gifted academically." He was also "very good at painting. He just was incredibly artistic." Mayra notes, "According to my mom, he discovered his talents in Art and Design and decided at that time to pursue an acting career." Sánchez joined the 13th Street Theatre and studied at the HB Studio. Prior to being awarded the role of Rembrandt, he had appeared in the shorts *The Stowaway* and *Big Apple Birthday* and had toured Spain in *Hair*.

It wasn't just Rembrandt's race that tied in with Hill's designed diversity. "I always thought the character he played in the movie was gay," says Hill. If this seems like a retroactive rationale linked to the fact that Sánchez himself was homosexual, the Dingos gang—patently gay—support the director's claim. "I wanted to present a gay gang in a rather positive light," Hill explains. "I thought that would have been really terrific."

"It was not exactly a secret that he was gay, but I didn't have any conversations with him about it," adds Hill. "Everything about Marcelino was gay," says Beck. "It was part of who he was and part of the reason you loved his kind of flamboyance... At the time we were doing that movie, Donna Summer and disco was in the air and he was just such a lover of her and that kind of music." Sánchez's sister seems to have had a different experience, possibly partly because she was a child at the time, possibly partly because of a Puerto Rican culture that she admits was conservative about homosexuality. "That wasn't something that was overt," says Mayra. "He and my mother were close and my mother was aware, but he wasn't necessarily flaunting his lifestyle in terms of the family. He was very conservative… I don't believe that he made it a secret, but it wasn't something that was discussed in the family often or openly."

As for the question of a man with his artistic hinterland playing the gang's resident artist, Mayra says, "I think it was a coincidence. I don't think that any of the other roles would have been right for him." She adds, "He wasn't a graffiti artist. He definitely was not into that."

"My brother did not have to do research," Mayra notes. "By the time I came around, we were moved into a calmer area, but before then he lived in Bushwick." The latter area of Brooklyn is presumably what Sánchez was referring to when he told the *Village Voice* that he grew up in a "rough ghetto" only a few doors away from the hangout of the Devil Rebels street gang. "My brothers definitely lived in a different kind of neighborhood," says Mayra. "So they saw plenty." Sánchez could also plug into the psyches of intimates less gentle than he. "I think that he drew from his brothers. My other brothers were much more rough around the edges and much more boisterous. Not that my brothers were gang members, but he had plenty to see in the environment for him to choose."

Although Mayra notes that Sánchez was "very excited to be film-ing in New York," from what she says obtaining a role in a Hollywood production may have been a bigger deal for his parents than it was for him. "It was something that he could present to my parents to let them know that he had not made a mistake. There was a little bit of a challenge between him and my parents, because they wanted him—my mother es-pecially—to pursue academics. He told her that he was willing to finish high school but after that he wanted to pursue his acting career. That was their arrangement. So he never tried anything in acting officially until he finished this agreement to our mom."

The other Warriors were Caucasian. "I was born in Cleveland, Ohio," says Tom McKitterick, a slightly built man whose jutting bottom lip gives him a look of permanent skepticism. "I came to New York in 1970 after college." His relocation was not to fulfil acting ambitions, of which he had none. "I drove cabs and I smoked pot and I was a hippie. You could get by working three nights a week driving." Becoming a stagehand at the New York Shakespeare Festival Public Theater opened his eyes to the possibil-ity of a new career. "I thought, 'Boy, I love the theatre.'" He was particu-larly inspired by a production of a play called *The Black Terror* by Richard Wesley. "There was this actor named Gylan Kain who was a poet and he and Susan Batson, an actress who later became an acting coach, had this… red hot scene and they just went at each other. I saw it night after night after night, and just the energy and the precision and their ability to repeat this intense altercation so completely without it ever being stale… I thought, 'Wow, maybe I want to give this a go.'"

Looking back, McKitterick realizes he was up against it from the beginning. Michael Beck may have wondered whether he was a bit long in the tooth for his part, but McKitterick—born in 1948—has the questionable honor of being the oldest Warrior. "I started late. I was thirty." The matter has been confused by the—possibly disingenuous—claim made in the *Warriors* press book that he was a 1956 baby. "And they said I was born in Camden, New Jersey or something. I don't know where that stuff comes from." He explains of the drawbacks to a late start, "I felt, 'Shoot, I should have gone to England and had some classical training. I should have done this… I wanted to play Hotspur in *Henry IV Part I*. I wanted to play Edward in *Long Day's Journey into Night*. I wanted to play Chance Wayne in *Sweet Bird of Youth*. I could see these parts were going to be out of my grasp very rapidly." His build meant he did at least look younger than his years. "I ended up playing a lot of teenagers," he notes.

McKitterick's early acting career was a mixture of highbrow ("I had appeared in off off-Broadway productions") and low culture. "I had been on an NBC soap opera called *For Richer, For Poorer*. I was a non-contracted player. I worked about four months on that. That was my first paying job and that gave me confidence." Interestingly, he notes of the part, "I played a juvenile delinquent." Presumably, the latter fact is what prompted his agent to submit him for *The Warriors*. McKitterick offers, "My first three [major] jobs—a soap opera, this, and then Jack McCall in Thomas Babe's play *Fathers and Sons*—I was playing outlaws. I think there's something about my personality or my demeanor or something that was appropriate to the movie."

"I went in and did a reading as Vermin," McKitterick recalls. "I think Frank Marshall read the sides with me. It was the scene with the Lizzies. The sides were five pages or four pages of dialogue. I knew nothing of the whole script. I vaguely understood that it was a gang warfare picture. Two days before, I went over them and I decided how I was going to say the lines and what I was going to do with this material. I felt I nailed it." So, clearly, did the producer and director. McKitterick: "And then, I don't remember how, I learned that I was going to be Cowboy and someone else was to play Vermin."

That turn of events itself involved a tangled tale. With every aspiring young—and young-looking—actor in New York seeming to want a part in *The Warriors*, the film's production team naturally spent a large part of their time saying "no" to people. There was one actor, though, who turned *them* down. McKitterick: "Tony Danza was cast as Cowboy in the first assemblage of actors. I met Tony." "He was quite something," recalls Marshall of Danza. Part of this impression seems to have derived from more than merely his acting talents, Marshall noting, "We actually went to see him box in an amateur fight." Either way, "We offered him the role." However, at around the same time Danza received a verdict from the makers of a putative television series for which he had previously auditioned. "To his credit, he was very loyal to the people at *Taxi* and he turned us down," says Marshall.

Enter Terry Michos. Also a screen rookie, Michos was born in 1953. "I came from upstate New York, a place called Poughkeepsie," he says. "In *French Connection*, Gene Hackman says to some heroin addict, 'What are you doing? Pick your toes in Poughkeepsie?' I went to New York in 1975 and I studied acting at the American Academy of Dramatic Arts." At the time of *The Warriors* auditions, Michos was in the national touring company of *Grease*.

He was an interesting choice by the *Warriors* production team, his physical appearance—slightly puffy face, slightly spoiled and even dopey demeanor—a marked contrast to the mean and lean types by which he was mostly surrounded. This may be why his road to being cast was a rocky one. He recalls, "Frank Marshall said, 'Well, we're looking at a lot of guys.' He wasn't really interested and I knew they were kind of cutting me off. So then I said to Walter, 'Well Walter, why don't you look at some of my pictures?' and luckily I'd brought in a bunch of different pictures. And he said, 'Hmm.' Walter's very measured. He said, 'Huh. I like that look. Try to come in with that look and I'll let you read.' And then I read and I did a good job. So then they had me come back and I think I read again." Michos did a generalized audition related to the Lizzies scenes. "I did the scene where we come in with the girls and say, 'Hey, you must have a lot of guys around here, where are your guys, and how did you hear about us?' I did all Cochise's and [Vermin's] lines. The person reading with me read all the Lizzies' lines." Michos fell at the next hurdle. "There were nine Warriors and they had brought ten or eleven of us up to the Gulf + Western building as the final guide cast," he explains. "They were going to look and put us in costumes and they did that and I was so ecstatic. Two weeks later I got bumped. I was devastated. Broken-hearted. I remember going with my girlfriend out to dinner and I just cried."

Taxi was an American TV comedy that was both fairly long-running—it went to five seasons—and uncommonly witty for the period. It's a matter of opinion whether Tony Danza made the right choice in opting for the role of Tony Banta—a pugilist slumming it driving a cab—over Cowboy. It was certainly the right decision from Michos' point of view. "If he didn't get *Taxi*, I would have never been Vermin," says the latter. "All of a sudden I got a call months later to come back and read. I had to reread against a bunch of guys that I knew from *Grease*." With Michos having passed the new audition, a specific role had to be decided on. "I think I could have been cast as Cowboy or Vermin," he says. "I don't think I had the demeanor they were looking for for an Ajax or a Cochise. Walter said, 'Hey, you look slimmer, and more in shape.' I was always working out. Frank or Larry said, 'What do you want to do: Vermin or Cowboy?' I said, 'I don't know.' Then Walter said, 'Alright, why don't you do Vermin?' That's how simple it was. They were obviously trying to get different types and different looks. The guy who ultimately got Cowboy was the little, slim Irish guy."

The little, slim Irish guy thinks he was a bit wasted in his reassigned role. "Cowboy didn't seem to have verbally any place where I could assert myself," McKitterick reflects. "It did seem that the part was underwritten… Vermin had a really good scene with the Lizzies. I studied that scene and I felt, 'I can make a mark with this.' I didn't quite see Cowboy having that type of special sort of sidebar scene, so I was slightly disappointed. But what the hell. I felt incredibly lucky to get in a Paramount movie. I was astonished."

Michos made a research trip with Beck to Coney Island. "We stayed there the whole day. Just walking through Coney. We would sit down in little alleyways and we'd talk and try to get a feel for our home turf." However, he says, "My acting was never Stanislavski, never Method. It was, 'I'm gonna go raw, I'm gonna read what this character is giving me and I have enough experiences in my life that I know I'm going to make this work.'… I was always an actor that believed in, 'Acting is reacting.' Even when I directed plays years later, when I would get non-professional actors, for me an action always released the emotion. In other words, I was never great at having emotions come out by just having an inner self of deep contemplation for a long time on who this character was. I created a character."

McKitterick had a similar attitude but took it even further: he did no research whatsoever. "That goes back to my training," he says. "I'd studied with Mira Lostova. She was Montgomery Clift's mentor and her whole technique was based on line readings. Her idea was the actor's responsibility is to do the expressions of the line that the author intended and it's not to embellish and add other stuff... My technique was basically an interactive thing where I'm just there and I'm doing what I'd do if I were in that situation."

Another film rookie was Deborah Van Valkenburgh. Born in 1952 in Schenectady, New York, *The Warriors'* female lead was a Pratt Institute alumnus with a BFA in Painting & Drawing. She studied puppet production under Jim Henson. However, performance was in her blood, whether it be as a singer (she played in coffee houses) or acting. She appeared in the Broadway revival of *Hair* before moving on to another youth-oriented drama from a different generation. "My agent submitted me," she says of *The Warriors* auditions. "The casting directors thought that perhaps I wasn't visually the type they were looking for, but he pressed them to bring me in and I met the director." Also dubious about her potential for the film was her current boyfriend, who suggested she wasn't sufficiently "well endowed" for what the producers were looking for. Her agent reassured her in that respect. Whoever was right with regards that, Van Valkenburgh was unquestionably striking in appearance: her oversize lips were sculpted into a permanent pout, part sensual, part defiant. "I'm pretty sure I had one or two call-backs and I was competing with everybody else who was working pretty steadily at that time, so it was very extraordinary when I finally was cast," she reflects. "I think Walter said I was the 'unobvious choice,' so in the end what everyone thought was the appropriate visuals turned out to be not necessarily what he was in the mood for that day. He was in the mood for me. Thank God." She also points out, "All of my romantic scenes were going to be with Thomas G. Waites, so actually they were casting me to be a complement for another character. I have a still photograph of the two of us standing up against the wall in our civilian attire just to see how we looked together."

Van Valkenburgh didn't feel there was much of a description of Mercy in the screenplay she read. "What I really loved about this script was how incredibly lean and spare it was," she says. "You could imagine what everybody looked like, you could imagine where they were, and what the mood was. Your imagination could take over. You could infuse the character with any of the qualities that just popped into your mind while you were reading it. For some reason, it reminded me of old-time matinee movies where you get lost. You go on a really bright sunny day into a theatre and you get completely lost in this adventure and you walk out and you feel like you've gone to another planet and you're smiling."

With regards to preparation or research for the role, Van Valkenburgh says, "A lot of it was pretty organic." While raised upstate, she by now felt part of New York City. She explains, "I was going to school in Brooklyn prior to that and it's just an environment that you're in every day. One of the things I really love about New York is how diverse it is and how you're just always with such a variety of people. You just can't take the stance of, 'I live here, this is my world.' It's everybody's world and you get to integrate yourself with so many different kinds of people that you just absorb energy every single day.

"So there was that sort of more organic research of the environment that I'd already been in. Then I had been reading really evocative books, so I continued with that to just keep filling myself up with textures and moods and attitudes. I also read Sol Yurick's novel, which was just so much more brutal than the film. It continues to give you flavors that are very useful. And I just have a really crazy imagination, so she just became some sort of composite of all my thoughts and feelings and whatever I absorbed visually. I wasn't trying to play a Puerto Rican chick or anything. I just had an invention going on in my head and that's what came out… I was not actually cast to play a Latina. For me, Mercy is an amalgam of urban female energy circa 1979 and that is how I inhabited her. I don't think I have any Hispanic ancestors… My heritage is generally Dutch and English, but I recently learned there's a little Scottish in our history as well." Some might suggest that her surname sounds wonderfully like that of a princess from an olde-worlde Eastern European principality. This might not, in fact, be too fanciful. "There is a small community in the Netherlands called Valkenburg aan de Geul with caves and an ancient castle in the hillside. I believe my name means 'Castle of the Falcons.'"

Van Valkenburgh was certainly one of the film's more impressive performers, and not just because the Warriors themselves weren't often required to be anything more than strong, silent types. "There's something about what she brought to her scenes," enthuses Hill. "A humor and irony and a bit of vulnerability that the movie needed."

While Remar considered Ajax a little unhinged, David Patrick Kelly says he considered his Luther character to be flat-out insane. "For a lot of different reasons. And I think he was being mentored by corrupt, political gangster people and was just a tool of them." Kelly says he saw a fair amount of such people in the back room of famous NY music venue Max's Kansas City when employed there shortly beforehand. "I didn't think of him as a druggie or a junkie or anything like that. I saw him more as a kind of assassin that were around at the time, Arthur Bremer and Berkowitz, those kind of people, except he had a power position too. " He admits that coming to his opinion that Luther was "deranged" was an unseemly defiance of a method-acting commandment: "I judged the character beforehand."

Born in 1951, Kelly was raised in Detroit. He was for most of his adult life pre-*The Warriors* as much musician as thespian. "I've always been an actor but music defined it," he says. "My thing was always plays with songs in them, imitating Shakespeare and Brecht. Those were my twin poles. I didn't like musicals. I like rock. I'd written about four plays with songs in college in '69 to '73."

The first half of Kelly's twenties saw him soak up inspiration and experience in a journey that ends up sounding not unadjacent to the narratives of *Zelig* or *Forrest Gump*. "I had a college deferment. [In] my freshman year, I got the lead in the national touring company of *Hair*... I had to go back to college, but I got credit to go to Paris and study in 1970 with Marcel Marceau, so that brought me to a whole other thing in the theatre world: all this *avant garde* stuff, the mime mafia." During the Christmas vacation period of that year, Kelly hopped across the English Channel and took the opportunity to take a demo to the Beatles' Apple Records. "Tony King was their A&R guy and listened to the record... He liked the record, said 'Sounds like Dr. John'... but the headlines at the time in London were, 'Beatles suing each other and breaking up.'" In 1973, Kelly made his way to New York. "I was thinking about going to Juilliard and Yale, but I ended up—because I had to work, I was broke—at Max's Kansas City... I worked in the music room upstairs." It wasn't long before Kelly secured himself a berth in *Sgt. Pepper's Lonely Hearts Club Band on the Road*, a 1974 Robert Stigwood production that played off-Broadway at the Beacon Theatre. "It was just like a operetta—sung through," Kelly explains. "They made up a little story about Billy Shears. Teddy Neely, who was Jesus in *Jesus Christ Superstar*, was Billy Shears... It had *Sergeant Pepper*, *Abbey Road*, and some select songs like 'Nowhere Man.'" At a point where the ex-Beatles were inclined to look on such projects as a tribute rather than a cheapening of their corpus, Kelly and his colleagues were paid the honor of (separate) visits by the Fab Four's songwriting axis. "John came to rehearsal and he came to the opening-night party. McCartney came—and the kids—after it opened... I don't remember being daunted but imagine having to sing 'Get Back' for Paul McCartney, which was my song in the show. But they were complimentary and really nice."

From this retro scenario, Kelly moved on to the musical cutting edge, and from the Max's Kansas City staff rota to its performance bill, serving as frontman, guitarist, and songwriter for a band called Toivo. (Significantly, the name is an obscure literary reference, alluding to the lesser-known Tennessee Williams play *The Gnädiges Fraulein*.) He found himself part of a scene that would retroactively acquire the term "punk." "That was where Patti Smith first started doing stuff with Lenny Kaye, the New York Dolls performed there a lot, and Television played there. Then it moved over to CBGBs. Television essentially discovered CBGBs, and everybody went there… I had a very good band, 1975." He adds, "But was always acting at the same time: I was in Chekhov and experimental theatre downtown at the MoMA." This helps explain why Kelly, unlike so many other fixtures of the CBGBs scene, didn't end up signing to a record label. "People were interested. I had Patti Smith's manager, Jane Freedman, very interested and we were doing good, lot of gigs." However, "Acting took precedence… I said, 'Films are starting to happen, things are calling. I gotta just do acting now.' It was hard, because the band was so gifted, but we were getting into that kind of gamey situation: whose arrangement are we going to use?' I wrote all the songs, but it's that band environment where we start tussling and people are showing up late for rehearsal and stuff like that."

As to how he came to be cast in *The Warriors*, Kelly says, "I owe it all to rock 'n' roll and Studs Terkel. I was cast, because I could play guitar, in a musical version of Studs Terkel's book *Working*." A 1978 Broadway production directed by its co-librettist Stephen Schwartz, *Working* featured songs written by different people so as to reflect the show's panoply of characters. "He had five different composers that worked on that score." As well as Kelly and others, songs were provided by a celebrity. "James Taylor wrote two or three songs for it and he came in and worked with us. It was great." However, it wasn't actually his composing, guitar work or trilling that got Kelly the Warriors gig. "In that book there is a monologue by a character named Charlie Blossom, who was a—on the surface—peace-and-love holdover but who was quite murderous inside." Kelly auditioned for Walter Hill's movie "several times," and says its producers "thought I would be good for one of the Warriors" up to the point that they saw him as Blossom. "It was just a five-minute monologue and Walter Hill and Larry Gordon, at the behest of the casting director, came to see that. They decided to cast me as Luther." It may have been at this same performance that Hill and Gordon spotted Kelly's fellow *Working* cast member Lynne Thigpen. She would play the disc jockey in *The Warriors*.

Kelly also recollects, "Another person who came to see *Working* was the late David Shaber, who came with Ellen Burstyn. I'd been in a Chekhov play with Ellen Burstyn. I didn't know but they knew that I was going to be in the movie." While Shaber may have contributed nothing to *The Warriors* script after Hill came on board, this anecdote does suggest that he remained to an extent in the production's loop.

There is certainly a logic to the producer and director of *The Warriors* perceiving Kelly as more villain than hero. While we can probably attribute to his acting skills the maniacal gleam in Luther's eyes throughout the film, Kelly—in real life as well as in performance—has a speaking intonation that is nasally meticulous verging on menacing. Adding to the aura of danger is a pointed chin that creates a lupine appearance. One could instantly see what Hill meant when he once proclaimed that Kelly has a "Richard III kind of quality."

Kelly was 27 but doesn't feel that he was too elderly for a street-gang movie. "We knew it was a genre thing. I did, at least. So a kind of exactness, I don't think it was required. In our youthful vanity, we thought we were quite young-looking anyway... The attenuation of the youth culture wasn't as pre-eminent as it is today. Today, if you're seventeen you have a better chance of getting a part than someone's who 21, even though they have Broadway credentials, because we're so youth-obsessed as a culture. If they made that today, they'd make it with fifteen-year-olds, seventeen-year olds. Which I find appalling, frankly."

Kelly's practical research was "just to go to a halfway house and talk to some prisoners." He didn't read Yurick's original novel. "I read Xenophon while making it... I wanted to stick to Walter's script and the source material—*Anabasis* and stuff—and not be distracted by the things that weren't in it... I was more interested in trying to do anthropological research. Reading sociology tracts. *Street Corner Society* about gangs. Piri Thomas had a book, *Down These Mean Streets*. I had read a critique of *Saturday Night Fever* in a little journal and the guy mentioned Hubert Selby, Jr's *Last Exit to Brooklyn*, and that was a big influence on Luther's character."

However, as a resident of downtown New York ("mafia territory at the time"), the raw material Kelly needed was to some extent in the ether. In the second half of the 1970s, such an air of deterioration enveloped the city that it resembled something from a dystopian novel. Crime was rampant and murder everyday. An inordinate number of disturbed and/or disturbing people were to be seen wandering the streets. Times

Square was packed with porn merchants, prostitutes, pimps, drug dealers, and lowlifes. There was little money to address these problems. Profligate city spending had led in 1975 to a situation adjacent to bankruptcy when NYC indicated it might default on its debts. Things only worsened when spending was subsequently slashed: police were laid off, which led to crime figures climbing even higher, while sanitation workers were fired, resulting in overflowing garbage cans and rubbish-strewn streets. NYPD and fire department unions issued a mock tourist survival guide handbook entitled *Welcome to Fear City*. It advised people to only travel by public transportation, stay off the streets after 6 p.m., and to remain in Manhattan. Although an alarmist text written by people in dispute with Mayor Beame over his labor policies, many of the city's residents would have considered its advice honest and reasonable. This state of corrosion applied particularly to the subway system that formed such a key element of the *Warriors* narrative: in 1979 it played host every week to more than 250 felonies (crimes punishable by over a year's imprisonment or death).

Kelly recalls an incident from his Max's Kansas City employment tenure. "I remember a guy there sending me—naïve Detroit kid—out about three o'clock in the morning with a lot of cash. He said, 'The bar needs ice.' I was sat in a taxicab with a very nervous taxi driver and we went to some truck where a fat guy in shorts gave us a single bag of ice for a huge wad of cash. I have no idea what was in that ice. It may have very well been expensive ice, but I don't think so. I could have gone up the river. Light bulbs went off afterwards. That's how naïve I was at the time." Fellow NYC resident Terry Michos remembers a traumatic New Year's Eve incident from the turn of the Eighties that also gives a flavor of the place and times: "I was on the subway with my girlfriend and a few people going to a party and all of a sudden there was screaming in other cars. Guys were coming through and stealing things from people and pushing them up against [walls]. They were coming car to car to car... These guys are coming into our car next. Everybody pushed back to the end of the car in a bunch, in some sort of [hope] they would be intimidated by the group." "The atmosphere in the Seventies in New York was quite intense and you could feel it everywhere," says Kelly. "There were places you didn't go and questions you didn't ask, and you just tried to be as streetwise as you could."

Playing Luther's right-hand man Cropsey was Joel Weiss, who bluffed his way into a *Warriors* audition after having been turned down for *The*

Wanderers. Interestingly, he has recalled that his character's name was originally "Butcher-Boy." Born in 1953, Weiss had previously appeared in the short *Housing Project USA*.

Across such a large main cast, it was perhaps inevitable that resident among it was the whole gamut of acting approaches: classical, method, re-action, extemporization, line reading… This begs the question of wheth-er, at the end of the day, specific schools really make any difference to quality of performance. "Absolutely none," McKitterick says. "Everybody has their own way and, when you get on stage or on the set, you're not there to dictate what others give you in their line readings. You just have to go with the flow and do what you feel is appropriate." Waites may have studied at classical-leaning Juilliard but became a member of the method oriented Actor's Studio in 1985. "I'm a hybrid of both classical training and the method," he says. "Instinctually, I use the method anyway. They're all just terms, really. You have to just make it work, man. It's got to be true." "Method acting has a bad rap," says Remar. Method is the acting approach in which a performer attempts to portray a character by effec-tively becoming him for the duration of the run or shoot, a technique that involves inhabiting that persona even in downtime. For some of the pub-lic, and even some of the acting profession, it is not just pretentious but a license to be a jerk (obnoxious behavior can be passed off as a function of staying in character). "Method acting is applicable to classical acting," insists method-man Remar. "Most people don't even know what method acting is when they say it. The Stanislavski system was developed by Kon-stantin Stanislavski at the Group Theatre and it evolved into what became the Method with the Group Theatre in New York with Stella Adler and Lee Strasberg and Sanford Meisner. Essentially all it is is that you're play-ing characters from an honest emotional place. You're not faking it. You're portraying genuine emotion. But that can always be applied to good clas-sical acting as well, as opposed to what they call the declamatory style of acting, where you just say the words and don't feel a thing."

Did the assembled cast of various techniques consider themselves to be about to make a naturalistic film? "Semi," says Remar. "We knew it wasn't *Rebel Without a Cause*. We knew it wasn't an insightful probe into the emotional lives of troubled teenagers, but we tried to bring that to the screen anyway as authentic actors." "We knew it wasn't cool," says Kelly. "You try to do the best you can. It was my first movie, and so that was very exciting. My big influences were Kurosawa and Bergman and the French New Wave. You had an opportunity and you wanted to bring it. But then

I had to research Walter and found out he was from Peckinpah and I really felt fortunate." Not that he thought this project was as elevated as the art of the people to whom he refers. "I said, 'This is a Roger Corman motorcycle movie.' It's not [a] Martin Scorsese movie. It was a stylized entertainment movie."

An observation by Beck, though, is echoed by several of the cast. "We were approaching it initially as 'Oh God, this is going to be this realistic, gritty street-gang movie,'" he says. "Once we got into it, we went, 'No, that's not what this is at all.'"

CLOTHING AND COMBAT

WHEN THE *WARRIORS* PRODUCERS turned their minds to the issue of the clothes in which they might swathe their young cast, it's doubt-
ful that they appreciated just how important that part of the pre-produc-
tion process would be to the stature that the finished film would come to
enjoy. *The Warriors* is a thoroughly stylish movie.

While costume is a very important part of any motion picture, dressing screen characters appropriately is often an "invisible" virtue. By its
nature, it's usually only noticeable if it goes wrong. In the case of *The Warriors*, however, the wardrobe choices were what people ended up remembering about the picture as much as any of its other qualities, and very
much in a good way.

That a movie taking place both in insalubrious parts of New York
City and largely at night was unexpectedly rendered a feast for the eyes
seems to be in large part down to serendipity. "I realized when I read the
script, there was this huge meeting, conclave, and there was 120 gangs,
ten members deep," explains the film's costume designer Bobbie Mannix. "In my mind I said, 'How am I going to separate one gang from the
other?' Because in reality everyone would wind up in denim or leather in
those days, or t-shirts. Nothing to separate them. So I colored every gang
and then I came up with the concept for each gang."

Not only did this approach of pronounced differentiation transpire
to make the look of *The Warriors* highly stylish, it also made the various
gangs look galvanizingly like sports teams. It additionally by chance built
into the picture a continuing resonance. In an era long before the influence
of comic books had fed to any great extent into the movie industry, the tit-

ular gang ended up looking like superheroes while their rivals resembled supervillains. Another phenomenon that the *Warriors* wardrobe accidentally prefigured was video games. The gangs facing off in the picture now resemble the type of outlandish avatars to be seen on the screens of the type of personal computers that nobody in the late Seventies had any intimation would one day be owned by every household in the Western world.

In 1978, the 29-year-old Mannix had worked on commercials (and has continued to do so, racking up over 2,500), but was in the foothills of her motion-picture design career. In 1975, she provided wardrobe for the Peter Bogdanovich picture *At Long Last Love*. Frank Marshall had also worked on the film and it was he who suggested her for the costume design of *The Warriors*. "I loved Bobbie's creativeness and inventiveness," Marshall says. "She also was somebody who worked out of the box and was able to put together a great team and do it for a very small budget."

Mannix was "not at all" familiar with Sol Yurick's original novel and was just as innocent of the street milieu it—and its putative adaptation—depicted. "I was so naïve," says the native of Livingston, New Jersey. "I didn't even know gangs existed. I've lived a very sheltered life." A film about street gangs might be assumed to be quite a grungy, unglamorous assignment, but she says, "I didn't give it any thought until I was hired and it was time to get into the project."

Asked with whom of the *Warriors* production team she liaised, she says, "Totally with Walter." That liaison process would seem to have been an involved one. The June 1978 *Warriors* script revision contains almost no description of the gang uniforms, other than minor details like the Warriors wearing "vests," the Big Time Punks being in severe black, and the Dingos having "greased up arms" and "skin T-shirts." It doesn't even actually state that the Furies are dressed in baseball uniforms. Hill instead seems to have been relying on a process of improvisation and cross-fertilization. "We all had offices together," he explains. "So I would just go over to Bobbie's office. I'd be writing and Bobbie would be in there with the lady she worked with and Bobbie would say, 'How about this? How about that? I got an idea here for the vests.' We just worked it out as I was going. I don't believe in over-describing anything." Marshall recalls, "She and Walter would toss around [ideas] and she would bring sketches and designs and swatches and really a lot of opportunities and ideas to Walter. Things like the [Punks'] overalls and the rugby shirts—that was all her. Walter really wanted each gang to be really different so you would remember them visually and she was fantastic."

Regarding the titular group, Mannix says, "They have a gang name called the Warriors. Instead of going with some kind of army or navy uniform or some kind of Warrior that-way uniform, I went into [a] cowboy-Indian kind of thing. And they all have their individual character names. So that triggered certain elements that they should wear." Her work started before casting had been completed but the actors, once selected, inspired further design layering. "You have to, whenever you're building a character, consider the personality of the individual [actor] as well as the character that they're playing."

Mannix often obtained basics off the peg. "I bought pretty much everything, except I have a prototype vest for the Warriors," she recalls. "We were scouring the streets… It wasn't a big-budget show. It went mainly towards labor because it was three or four months of night shooting." Mannix doesn't remember feeling that the funds at her disposal were inadequate. Dorsey Wright, however, notes that Mannix's first design for the Warriors' vests was rejected by Paramount on cost grounds. "It would have been made out of leather and they were like, 'No, that's too intricate. We're not gonna pay for that,'" he says.

Mannix found pleather (leather-effect plastic) vests in downtown New York and decorated them with trim she obtained separately. The vests were designed to be worn open. They were also designed to be worn without shirts underneath, but she notes, "I think three of them didn't want to go shirtless. So James Remar had a tank top, but it went very well with the black leather wraps on his hands. Cowboy wore a t-shirt." "I wore a t-shirt because my chest was not completely hairy but it certainly would have made me look less like we were teenagers," explains Tom McKitterick. This issue clearly didn't trouble Michos, who was happy to parade his hirsuteness. Waites was shirted, but notes of his vest, "I chose to wear it buttoned." The fact that he was the only Warrior to wear his vest thus was deliberate on his part, to reflect the fact that his character was a cut above. Almost the equivalent of a collar and tie? "Exactly." For Brian Tyler, the bare-chest refuseniks probably made the right choice. "That happened to be a cold and wet summer," he notes. "So it was a little chilly for the time that we shot. I guess the good thing is we were doing so much running and fighting and practicing, that helped us stay warm." Marcelino Sánchez's sister Mayra recalls, "He did say that the weather was difficult, and that he always felt very cold because they were so underdressed. He was constantly very uncomfortable, and also, as a result, had colds and different physical

ailments." The Warriors' trousers were blue jeans or black or brown cor-
duroys, except for Rembrandt, who opted for flamboyantly red pants.
Shoes were generally sneakers/high tops ("baseball boots" in inaccurate
British nomenclature).

Despite being played by a black actor with a large afro, Cochise certainly had a very Native-American look. Notes David Harris, "The only
thing I didn't have on was a big Indian war bonnet. I did have the thing
on my head, and the feathers, and the necklaces and the belt and the
arm bracelets and all of that. We went as far as we can to make him look
like an American Indian. All the other guys basically have on vests and
black shirts. No one is as exotic as Cochise." Harris' distinctively sculpted
mouth shape—resembling a bow tie, with the top lip significantly bigger
than the bottom lip—complemented perfectly that exotic look. The Native American theme extended to the character's footwear. Harris: "He's
wearing Indian moccasins that go up almost to my knees and you string
them." They were handsome looking, but how were they for the sprinting
that was such a large part of the film? "They were cool. They were comfortable. I didn't think they were going to be, but we started doing our first
running scene, I said, 'Oh good, they're fine.'"

Although Hill's script specified a Stetson as the item of clothing
that gave Tom McKitterick's character his name, Mannix issued Cowboy a floppier affair than the headgear seen in the average Western. The
choice—again found in a New York store—initially dismayed McKitterick. "I thought, 'Well this is completely a punk hat,'" he says. "There was
nothing about that [that was] cool." In fact, McKitterick was initially underwhelmed by Mannix's efforts generally, finding her designs tacky. "Oh
my God—brown corduroys? I don't know about that." However, he came
round to her vision. "Cowboy's hat just seemed like, 'Well, this is what this
kid got his hands on. He's not going to have some sort of fancy Stetson'...
I might have grumbled a little bit at the beginning, but I think she did a
great job."

Ajax wore an earring, still sufficiently unusual for men in the late
Seventies that it's possible that Hill/Mannix may have been using it as a
shorthand for narcissism. Rembrandt sported a twisted red neckerchief
and Snow a wooden necklace. The latter also bore an afro that put even
Cochise's to shame. Tyler recalls, "When I came in for the auditions they
did tell me at some point, 'Don't cut your hair.' In '78, '79, afros were still
popular. The only thing they did was part it in the middle and [provide
a] headband."

The other characters' looks were fairly straightforward, with little added to the basic outfit. In fact, it could even be said with the likes of Ajax and Swan that, what with their neatly side-parted, clean-looking locks, they verged on conventional. Either way, Terry Michos remembers Michael Beck's appearance being an improvement on the first pass. "When he first came in, someone had done his hair a certain way: down across his face, more flattened and they had something around his head. And they said, 'No, that's not happening.' They pushed his hair back and made him look more rugged."

Like many of the film's gangs, the Warriors had a "patch," an identifying logo stitched onto the rear of their upper-body clothing. Theirs consisted of a flaming skull adorned in a Native American-style headdress. Above it was an arc-shaped banner bearing the legend "Warriors." The elaborate design is resplendent but feels incongruous, looking like it has been prepared and attached by a third party, most logically the gang members' mothers, something that might be said to rather undercut the Warriors' tough-guy aura. However, Dorsey Wright confirms, "The gangs in New York, we did have patches," adding, "God knows where we got that stuff from." Indeed, the Warriors' vests and patches in some ways look remarkably similar to those sported by the Reapers, a real-life New-York street gang memorably photographed by John Shearer in an August 1972 *Life* magazine feature.

Moreover, it has been pointed out down the years that the Warriors' patch bears a resemblance to the "Death's Head" logo of the Hells Angels, not known for being mommy's boys. Mannix, incidentally, says the Angels resemblance wasn't deliberate: "Didn't know the difference." Other people apparently did: the flaming skull in the Warriors logo was changed in merchandise that followed the film to a flaming snake.

Wright explains that, in real life, patches were in fact the only way gangs differentiated themselves. "No one wore makeup and loud clothing. It was mainly dungaree jackets—a jean jacket—with a patch on the back. That was every gang in New York City, no matter who you were. It wasn't face makeup or rags and stuff tied around your head. It was that patch, what we call colors. The only way you knew is that when they came into your neighborhood, from behind you would see the patch. And if there was more of you, if it was Black Spades territory and Savage Nomads came in, you'd tell them, just like in the film, 'You got to take that jacket off. You can't walk through my neighborhood wearing your colors.' Every gang understood that. So when I saw that in the film, I went, 'They got *that* right.'"

The *Warriors* patches were the handiwork of Rose Clements, an LA-based Englishwoman in her sixth decade, working from designs supplied by Mannix. "Rose used to be the embroider for Manwell & Nudie, who were the biggest rodeo tailors," Mannix notes. Just as Clements' flamboyant "Nudie Suits" beloved by the country & western crowd were impressively modernistic for such a senior figure, so she in no way betrayed her age with her stylish but often confrontational Warriors efforts. The work was also necessarily painstaking. Mannix: "Now they do everything on computer, but she did it on her hand-stitching machine."

Mannix says the nine Warriors actors were "very happy" with the concepts for their individual looks but readily admits, "The boys added some personal touches of their own... It was a group effort." She also notes, "I was working during the day, 'cause that's when the shops were working, the stores are open, and they were shooting at night. I couldn't be on the set all night and work all day. So a lot of things happened on the set or might have changed a little that I'm not aware of, because I couldn't be there to control it."

An example of the group-effort element is the modification of the appearance of the Warriors leader. The finished film saw Cleon's head memorably draped in dangling cloth held in place with a headband, the cloth's coloring resembling that of military desert camouflage. "That came from me telling Bobbie Mannix that a lot of gangs wore this headgear, so me and her devised this Arabian-looking thing," recalls Wright. "She came up with it more than I did, to give me more of a rough kind of look. There was a guy I knew. He was in a gang called the Javelins. His name was Bobby. He would wear 'do-rags' most of the time. With African-American hair, you brush it and then you put this rag on it to keep dirt and stuff from getting in your hair and then it starts making waves in your hair. It's more for hair styling than anything else." In the same vein, Remar says of Ajax's look, "The idea of the gloves was mine. They were just a regular pair of gloves with the fingers cut off. And I taped the wrists... The belt that I wore was my personal belt. The singlet that I had on was actually a dance leotard that I had left over that I put under there."

As for the film's most prominent female, Mannix says of Van Valkenburgh, "She was so easy to dress 'cause she's so tiny." While the script's direct visual description of Mercy was non-existent, Mannix would have understood that she was intended to be bewitching, and—once Van Valkenburgh was cast—knew the pulchritudinous material with which she was working. "We wanted her to be sexy," Mannix says. "We wanted her to show her stuff." To achieve this objective, Mannix issued Van Valkenburgh a pink, thin-strapped sleeveless shirt beneath which she would be patently bra-less. Her patterned, knee-length skirt, though, was less racy than functional. Mannix points out that it had a "slit up the front so she could run." It also had to facilitate the scene wherein a piece was ripped off it in order to fashion a petrol bomb. "We had to make a break-away. She needed multiples." Completely non-functional, though, were Mercy's ankle-strap, peep-toe pumps. In today's culture, it's not uncommon for young women to sport sneakers or even combat boots but in the late Seventies heels were the more realistic, if hardly practical, choice. "She ran in those high heels of hers—sometimes," says Mannix. "When you didn't see it, she'd have sneakers on."

As the Rogues were the picture's villains, it was natural that they be what Mannix describes as "probably the hardest—meaning edgy-looking—gang that we had." She dressed them in black leather, including hats and caps. The exception was leader Luther. "David wanted to look a little bit different from the others," explains Mannix. David Patrick Kelly and Mannix put together an ensemble that included a denim jacket, a sheriff's badge, and a piratical headband. "She was cool with it," says Kelly. "Bobbie was terrific and we really had a great rapport. She would kind of snicker and make fun of some of the other actors."

Kelly took his inspiration from documentary-cum-exhibition *You Do the Crime, You Do the Time*, in which French writer and filmmaker Martine Barrat enabled New York street gangs like the Roman Kings and the Ghetto Brothers to portray their own lives and experiences. "That came to the Whitney on Madison Avenue and that's where I saw her photographs and the documentary just before I began filming *The Warriors*," recalls Kelly, who was particularly struck by a photograph of two bearded, long-haired young men standing against a backdrop of urban desolation. Both wore brightly colored bandana headbands. "I don't think I showed it to her," says Kelly of Mannix. "I think I just suggested it to Frank, the costume supervisor, and he put it together for me." Not that Kelly was necessarily aiming for naturalism. He explains, "My headband was a kind of Japanese thing—Kurosawa and those things."

Kelly didn't adopt the facial growth of the men in the Barrat exhibition picture but by coincidence wound up with similar hair length. "Everybody was cropped off for CBGBs or looking like Travolta in *Saturday Night Fever* and I had this lo-o-ong hair," he says. "I would have much preferred short hair, but because of this *Working* show and this kind of forlorn hippie that I played in that, I was under orders to have my hair quite long." He received further orders from Walter Hill to keep it like that. "It just kept growing and growing and growing for the *Warriors* as the shooting went on. It was supposed to be just a month and it went on for three months... I always thought of myself as a man out of time." However, as with so many aspects of *The Warriors* that bore no relation to what was happening on contemporary streets, this then-throwback contributed to an overarching surrealism that is considered one of the film's chief attributes. "It worked out great 'cause it was so different."

Cyrus' all-black gang the Gramercy Riffs may have been highly disciplined and martial-arts steeped but they were made almost beautiful by Mannix. "They're actually women's coats and robes," she says of their orange satin karate jackets. Although the latter were store-bought, the voluminous-sleeved, hip-length patterned robe worn by their doomed leader Cyrus was specifically designed by Mannix, made from fabric she found in Greenwich Village. "It had a bit of a shimmer to it. It was cut velvet, and it had a wonderful pattern. So I just cut robes for him and he had drawstring black pants on." Although the robe might have seemed a little feminine for a tough-guy gang leader (notwithstanding the usual *Warriors* get-out-of-jail caveat about metaphor/futurism/heightened realism), it's appropriate in the sense that it evokes the sort of gown favored by charismatic religious or cult leaders who have the ability to hold audiences in thrall.

To some extent, the Riffs were actually more feminine looking than the Lizzies. "We wanted them to look a bit butch," says Mannix of the film's only female gang. This desire, however, didn't rule out a certain provocativeness. "Walter wanted these fishnet t-shirts, which we got and spray-painted different colors. He wanted their nipples purple and them to wear it just like that." The rather daring ensemble was stymied by the actresses concerned. "The girls in those days didn't want to show their stuff," says Mannix. "So they wore jackets and things over their t-shirts."

The fact that the Sharks/Punks have long hair and are dressed in blue denim overalls/dungarees (a change from the severe black the script proposed) suggests that the term "punk" is being used in its original, pre-CBGBs/Sex Pistols sense. In fact, *The Warriors* is remarkable considering its production timeframe in having no visible punk influence whatsoever. Hair is either hippie-long or coiffed, with no gel or spikes in sight. Even though punk was perceived at that point to be dying, in being utterly untouched by its fashions these gangs would have looked hilariously uncool to late-Seventies British youth and trendier American kids. However, Mannix insists that she was both conscious of and influenced by punk. "I have a lot of sketches that I don't see in the movie… The punks that I have on my sketch boards are spiked hair, big black eyes, tiger vests, hot pink." For different reasons, something else that failed to make the jump from Mannix's drawing board to celluloid was the Dingos. She recalls of the look she gave this ultimately jettisoned gay gang as, "Black leather, S&M, studs, silver accessories, handcuffs."

That the giant, skinheaded Turnbull ACs were amongst the most fearsome looking of the gangs wasn't necessarily entirely due to Mannix. "A lot of those guys brought their own stuff," she says. "I think some of them were real gang members." In their green t-shirts and blue jeans, the Orphans were the most ordinary-looking gang, something inspired by their name. "They had no money, no mothers and fathers," says Mannix in amusement. "So we give them t-shirts and we hand-painted 'Orphans' on the back, or silkscreened them."

At the absolutely opposite end of the scale were the Baseball Furies and the High-Hats, both of which groups wore elaborate facial make-up. The High-Hats' white pancake and mordant eyeliner, as well as their cylinder headgear, made them resemble mime artists. The Furies' facial decoration involved foundation set off by color-surrounded eyes and/ or visages of contrasting halves. "Creations that they'd never wear, ever," Mannix laughs. Not only does Mannix feel that the film's costumes were ones that real street gangs would not be seen dead in, she also says, "All the costumes were impractical… I didn't pay any attention to any of that. I was so naive." The classic example of gear that did anything but facilitate a rumble is the roller skates worn by the leader of the Big Time Punks. Yet Marshall demurs from Mannix's belief about lack of realism. "As outlandish as we would make them, later we would find a photo of a gang that was dressed all in leather like the Dingos or somebody that was on roller skates like the Sharks," he reveals. Meanwhile, Hill says, "The makeup stuff was really just part of the Seventies. Rock groups really broke the ground for that and people out in the street, especially at night, began to affect it. In New York we used to see people with outlandish makeup on while we were in prep for the movie."

Some of the gang costumes Mannix designed were intended to be seen for only a second or two, either in the montage sequence of youths making their way through subway tunnels or in fleeting glimpses while at the conclave. The latter also involved the poor visibility inherent in a night sequence. These gangs included the Boppers (a dapper black gang with bright mauve fedoras and vests), the Boyle Avenue Runners (black undershirts with red trim), the Electric Eliminators (bright yellow satin jackets with skull-and-lightning-bolts logo), the Gladiators (black vests and blue jeans), the Hurricanes (Hispanics whose straw hats actually bear the closest resemblance to anything worn by the Dominators in Yurick's novel), the Sports (black and yellow striped tops), the Moonrunners (silver satin jackets with a logo depicting a crescent moon stabbing a star), the Howitzers (a black gang in camouflage jackets), the Saracens (black undershirts with white trim), Satan's Mothers Motorcycle Club (sleeveless denim jackets over yellow t-shirts, logo depicting the devil's face), the Mongols (an oriental gang in loose-fitting tropical green and conical cloth hats), and the Van Cortlandt Rangers (black and white hooped shirts and fedoras). Mannix says she was having too much fun to find it upsetting that she was expending so much energy on designs destined for a miniscule amount of screen time.

Did Walter Hill turn down any of her designs? "Not really. It was so overwhelming. We had so much to do, we had to eat up every bit of imagination that we had." Mannix adds of the director, "The one thing great about Walter Hill is when he hires somebody, he lets you do whatever you are hired for. He certainly gives you guidelines in the beginning—you have many, many discussions—but then he lets us do our work."

That work is now regarded as iconic. Dorsey Wright simply says of Mannix's *Warriors* make-up and costume design, "This woman basically made this film."

"THREE WEEKS BEFORE we started shooting, we started working with Craig Baxley, because we were going to do all of our own fighting," says Beck.

Born in 1949, Baxley was a stunt coordinator working for the LA-based company Stunts Unlimited. He came onto the job when first choice Bobby Bass pulled out. Recalls Baxley, "Bobby didn't want to go out of town... He had a job in Los Angeles and the budget was not that much on *The Warriors* and when they told Bobby that he couldn't take any stuntman back to New York he was a little concerned because he knew they wanted the stunt coordinator to write and basically direct all the fights. Bobby's the kind of guy that likes to have his own guys. I actually didn't have a problem with it... He mentioned that I was available and they gave [me] a call the next day."

However, when he signed on Baxley found that he had his own issues with the project. "I met the stuntmen and I realized that they were basically a little long in the tooth. They weren't really up to the level of guys I would use... These were young gang members and these old guys just didn't want to hit the ground. They didn't want to fall, they didn't want to do anything. They just wanted to make the money. So I said, 'Forget this' and I went out and found these eight guys and trained them... Most of the guys I brought onto the film, they got their cards on the film. They weren't stuntmen and I ended up using them as the Furies, as the Punks. They were my nucleus. There was one guy, Jerry Hewitt, he was giving hot air balloon tours in New York, but he was a gymnast. This guy was just a natural so he was my go-to guy. He was the head Fury... There were a couple other guys that I thought had a lot of talent that I tried to use in a lot of different places." In this respect, he names in particular Eddie Hatch and Konrad Sheehan. Baxley adds, "The older stunt guys in New York, they were upset because it was the old boys' school. They thought every show that came into town..."

In addition to the training of the stuntmen playing the villains, Baxley's duties included coaching the people depicting their adversaries. He performed the two roles in parallel. "I had to train a cast that hadn't done anything except for Tom [Waites], who was the actual star of the movie. I basically had a little school for the actors as well as the stunt men... I had them every afternoon, learning how to do a picture fight. Basically, as I taught the new stunt guys back there how to do it, I taught these young actors how to do it." "They told us how to fight on a screen where you have to miss people's faces," says Terry Michos. "Otherwise you would hurt each other." Baxley: "I had six different punches, I had different styles, different way to cover a punch, different way to make sure it wasn't a miss. We'd do it in pretty quick succession." He found the Warriors cast receptive pupils. "They listened, they wanted to do it... It became second nature with them. I must say Michael and Jimmy Remar were amazing."

Baxley points out that part of what he was teaching his charges was how to control their bodies. "When you see a guy swing a bat and hit a home run, he's twisting his hips. There's certain ways you hit a golf ball. Well, there's certain ways you throw a jab, a cross, a roundhouse. I didn't like the way the old stunt guys did the fight, because everything was so broad. This one, I had a more aggressive style. Walter wanted it a little more broad, so I kind of met it halfway." As well as teaching fighting moves, Baxley instructed the cast in how to warm up before scenes so that they wouldn't pull muscles.

"I had them for two, three weeks," Baxley says. However, the universal recurring twin misgivings about *The Warriors'* small budget and tight schedule raise their joint head when he appends, "I didn't have enough time, to say the least… It was such a short, compressed schedule."

Some found the training process fun. Beck notes, "Having been an athlete I loved the physicality of it." "He was absolutely fabulous," says Tyler of Baxley. "I think one of the things that directors and producers have to do is they have to know who works well with people. He was a joy to work with." However, Tom McKitterick was miserable. "I don't think Craig was particularly happy with coaching me," says the movie's Cowboy. "I think he found me sort of stiff and I didn't really know how to improve the situation." "No," laughs Baxley. "That's his nature. He's a very sweet guy, too. I was always concerned that he was going to get hurt because he didn't commit himself a hundred per cent. When you throw a picture punch, if you drop your chin, you're going to extend further. If you keep your chin up, you're going to have a lot of authority if you're playing a hero or a good guy. But if you drop your chin and you lean forward, you're going to hit somebody in the head."

Baxley maintains that his "stunt coordinator" billing doesn't fully convey the breadth of his work on the picture. "I come from a very strong art background, illustrating storyboards and things like that. I wanted to be a production designer, but it didn't go that way." His artistic background made for a slightly different approach to the profession he did take up. "A lot of directors rely on a DP [Director of Photography] to set the shots, set the style, everything else, but for me when I do an action sequence, I see the sequence, I write the sequence, I shot-list. I just do it in cuts and then I put all the cuts together. That's what I did on *The Warriors*… I wrote all the fights in script form… When he saw what I wrote, Walter was like, 'Okay, where do you think the camera should be for this?' and I basically shot it like a second unit." Not only does Baxley feel Hill "didn't have the type of schedule" needed for him to personally realize the action sequences, he says, "I'm not sure he fully understood a lot of the movements. He knew that if I set it up, we could get it done really quick… Walter was very comfortable with me handling the fights for him because I'd written them and I'd trained the cast as well as the stunt men, so it was shorthand."

AS IS STANDARD for motion-picture production, rehearsals and shooting were preceded by a "table read," whereby the cast gathered in an informal, sedentary setting to collectively familiarize themselves with the script and iron out issues arising from it. This one took place on one of the upper floors of the Gulf + Western building, a structure next to Columbus Circle, Central Park West that was the property of Paramount's parent company. At this gathering, Thomas Waites would seem to have been a more bumptious presence than any of the other cast members.

"Tom was asking questions," recalls Kelly. "He said to Larry Gordon, 'Well, what's the purpose of this read-through?' And Larry Gordon said to him [menacing tone], 'To find out who we got to replace.'" Kelly says, "It wasn't just Tom—it was all of us being told to mind your P's and Q's." As proof of this, he points out that when he laughed at Gordon's remark, the producer turned his ire on him. "Larry Gordon looked at me and said, [menacing tone again], 'He's got a good laugh, doesn't he?' So he was reigning us in. He was making sure that we all knew that we had to toe the line, 'cause it was a big, uncontrollable set."

"You mean professional?" responds Gordon when asked if he was a hard ass on the project. "If they needed to be kept in line, I kept them in line. My job as a producer is to protect the production, protect the director. So if somebody is causing the production and/or the director trouble, then I have to try to stop it. So I don't know if that means hard ass but that's what I do for a living." "I didn't feel that," Waites says of the hard-ass suggestion. "Larry sort of sat back and just watched. He didn't give me any indication."

This writer can attest that Gordon is certainly a hard ass in the sense of being a slightly intimidatory interviewee (at one point Gordon commented, "So you don't know too much about *The Warriors*, do you?"). However, he is also both broadly courteous and prone to acts of kindness, the latter including persuading on my behalf reluctant interviewees to take part in this book.

"I got along very well with the cast," Gordon says. "They were very professional for beginners." However, he also says, "I don't remember having a lot of trouble except with one particular person." That one person was the man playing Fox. For all the denials of both men, the exchange between Gordon and Waites can't help but seem in retrospect like a harbinger of trouble to come.

FORBIDDEN CITY

FILMING OF *THE WARRIORS* began on June 26, 1978.

"They really didn't greenlight the movie until after we were shooting," claims Lawrence Gordon. "I was the last person on the movie to be made pay-or-play and we had a big fight about that too, me and Eisner. They wouldn't accept we were making a movie 'til after we were shooting. It's hard to believe. They kept dragging their feet about, 'Okay if you don't cut this, if you don't cut that budget, blah blah,' and we're actually shooting before they said, 'Okay, go ahead.'" But the production must have had at least some studio financing to commence photography? "Oh, we did, of course. But they still could have stopped us. They weren't in for that much money. They haven't committed to a lot of things they have to commit to."

The Warriors shoot could be said to have proceeded as uncertainly as it started. Hill would describe it as "horrendously tough." The director was speaking in retrospect, but Dorsey Wright obtained a similar feeling of being under the cosh from the get-go. "Nobody had any confidence in *The Warriors*," he says. "That's the feeling you got just being around the film. Everything seemed like this is going to be a heavy lift. I didn't see too many smiles. I saw people actually doing work. I saw people thinking about what they were doing. These guys were serious. So you knew that, 'Okay, kind of tone down being goofy, and do your damn job.' Whereas on *Hair*, the budget was ridiculous and I don't think anybody was paying it any attention, so there was lots of times we were just shooting the goddamn breeze and I'm standing around watching money burn." The fact that Wright's time on *The Warriors* was shorter than that of the rest of the main cast doesn't invalidate his point of view, not least because

93

the seriousness/horrendousness of the *Warriors* shoot would by common consensus only increase exponentially.

The problems started with "crewing up." *The Warriors* was not only an almost complete location shoot, but it involved sixty straight "days" of night shooting. Hill noted at the time that he was strongly attracted to night scenes, talking of the way gloom makes things take on different connotations and provides dramatic possibilities that the glare of day-light doesn't offer. Yet while it led to aesthetically pleasing results, night shooting was one of the reasons why *The Warriors* was a project that was the last choice for film-industry personnel looking for employment. Hill lists the other reasons the production had difficulties obtaining staff: "We were paying scale. There were five or six other movies being made in New York that summer. Also our movie frankly didn't sound so great: we didn't have any big movie stars; I was not a famous filmmaker." The upshot was, "Almost anybody that was one of the crafts would rather work on another movie than ours."

The first things shot by the crew that had been assembled with such difficulty were Coney Island scenes, including passages depicting the Warriors and Cleon's girlfriend hanging in their home turf. Said scenes occurred at either end of the *Warriors* narrative but, because they were all in daylight and all at the same locale, were filmed in one bloc. Only the final Coney Island scene—the beach confrontation—was held back in the schedule, and that for very specific reasons.

Aside from this opening clump, though, *The Warriors* was unusual in that it was not a movie whose shooting order paid no regard to a scene's intended place in the final cut. "It just laid out that way," says Hill of his decision to execute a broadly sequential shoot. He adds, "I was very con-scious of the fact that I had very inexperienced actors. I wanted to keep it very much within the notions of the way that the story played out, 'cause I thought that was much better for them and their performances. They wouldn't get thrown off."

"That was when I got a really good look at what this gang was sup-posed to look like," Wright says of these first shots. "When they had them all lined up, you start looking at each other, measuring each other so far as, 'Okay, I can believe this guy.' There's a whole machismo thing going on. I believed James Remar the moment I saw him. Regardless of color, I was like, 'Yeah, if I was caught in a situation, I'd want him with me.' David Harris I liked. He was kinda on the thin side, but he at least had that look and that cockiness about him. Michael works. Beck didn't come off to me as some guy from the sticks. It's like, 'Okay, he did some research.' I knew James Remar did research like there was no tomorrow." And dare one ask which colleagues he didn't think looked like tough guys? Wright, as is his wont, laughs heartily. "Well, Marcelino Sánchez. Very nice guy. In a real gang? No, he wouldn't have made it. Not at all. Cowboy—no, not at all."

The *Warriors* shoot immediately ran into a problem that was perhaps inevitable for this particular project: the collision of fictional and real-life street gangs. Coney Island was then the preserve of an Hispanic crew called Homicide Incorporated who quickly made it clear that they didn't want another gang—even a fictional one—parading its colors on their turf. Recalls Marshall, "Our police liaison asked us to have the cast take their vests off every time we went to lunch or dinner so they wouldn't be mistaken for a real gang." This anecdote may come from the end of the shoot when more scenes were shot in Coney Island, but Wright recalls a problem right at the beginning.

"There was a bath house and it said 'Homicide Incorporated' in big letters," he says. "That's how you tag your territory. Well, these guys from California, the art department, thought it would be nice to put 'The Warriors' over it. So at night, they went over that tag." The "Warriors" graffiti in question—placed high up on the wall of the building, huge in size, bright red in color, and bulbous and downwards slanting in design—was certainly striking. Not everyone was impressed, though. "In the morning, all these guys from Homicide Incorporated showed up," recalls Wright. "'Who the fuck went over our tag?' You could get beat or killed for doing shit like that. They came to the trailers. Me, James, a few of us came out and I had to let the guy know right away: 'Whoa, I'm an actor. There's no such gang as the Warriors.' He wanted to know who the fuck did it. So I said 'See those guys near the beach? That's who did it.' They marched down there to them, and I guess Walter Hill and Larry Gordon talked them into, 'You want to be in a movie?' Because all these guys wound up eventually as extras in the conclave."

The die was set for something that would be a motif of this production: employment of real-life gangbangers. Sometimes, such retention would not even involve trade off-cum-blackmail. "Sylvia Fay, who did the extra casting, was going to projects in the city, finding guys that looked like gang members and hiring them," recalls Wright. "So these guys were coming into wardrobe, putting on, you know, Moon Runner jackets. They were real gang members that she picked up and said, 'You want to make $50 a day and some lunch money?'"

Ironically, the graffiti in question was never seen in the finished movie because of a decision to excise from the film all the early daytime Coney Island scenes. However, as a result of the cast being assembled to pose for the camera in front of it, it was prominent in publicity photographs.

Another scene shot was a roll call/exposition scene similar to one in the Shaber first draft. Harris: "He tells me and Ajax, 'Heavy muscle.' He tells Snow, 'You got the stuff?'—the music box. He tells Rembrandt, 'You ready to mark everything?' He told us all what our position is." "Walter Hill's original [scene] to introduce the characters he had taken from a Kurosawa film, *Yojimbo*," explains Beck "All those characters were introduced in that Japanese film by their personality or what they were skilled at as fighters."

What Swan was skilled at, of course, was knife-throwing. Swan was depicted expertly spearing with his Bowie passing pieces of paper. Beck conscientiously practiced so that he would look convincing. "I remember in my apartment in New York putting a big wooden plank on the wall and throwing this knife, 'cause I didn't want a stunt double to do it. And I got actually pretty good at it. So on the day that we shot, they had a knife-throwing guy in there, but I did better than him. Man, I was sticking it every time." "I sit there and I watched him," recalls Wright. "I thought, 'That's gonna be a cool shot.'" Although Wright is generally benignly scathing about the lack of verisimilitude in *The Warriors*, he does say, "One thing that was basically true was back in the Seventies there weren't a lot of guns in gangs. There were knives. K55s. 007s. They were cheap knives that you can get at any hardware store back then for three or four dollars. So almost everybody had a knife. You were rich if you got a gun." (This fact may at the time of Yurick's novel have given greater resonance to the Dominators bringing to the conclave a gift for Ismael in the shape of a .22 pistol.)

Moving into the city, a scene was shot in Brooklyn depicting the Warriors walking uneasily toward the conclave through Mongols turf. "That was all shot down in Chinatown," says David Harris. The script states the passage to be taking place at dusk, but "Cochise" recalls the sun to still be high in the sky when they shot it. Notes Wright, "Another weird-looking gang." From what he says, they clearly thought the same of the Warriors, but for the reason of the latter's unrealistic variety of ethnicities. Wright: "All of the extras in New York were the same way when they saw the Warriors gang. If you notice, almost every gang in that film when it comes to race are almost the same race. Like with the Mongols—

they're all Asian. So when they said 'Cut,' they were like, 'What is it with your gang?'"

It was during the shooting of this scene that Wright first became aware that he was in the presence of an actor who was pure method. "Me and Remar went to Burger King to go get something to eat," he recalls. "Now I got the satin jacket on. It was our movie jacket. It still said 'Warriors' on the back, but I'm not walking around with that vest shit on. We're in Brooklyn. I know where I'm at. But he is wearing his entire outfit. He could care less. So I'm standing in line and you're waiting for your service and he starts now with this, 'The war chief is waiting' routine. I'm going, 'What the fuck is wrong with this guy?' I've never encountered a method actor before. Somebody had to let me know what he was doing. 'This is what method actors do. They don't drop it.' You have to respect the guy that's doing this in a rough neighborhood. You can get your ass kicked." "I wore the persona of Ajax around a lot," confirms Remar. "I just didn't feel scared at that time." Was that the ignorance of youth? "Sure. It's not something that I'd do now."

Problems with gangs increased as the shoot moved into the city. "We shot on the streets all over the city at nights and a lot of time on subways and undesirable sections," Lawrence Gordon says. "We had to have police protection and we still had some problems." Although the producers tried to keep their project quiet, word would always get around. "We were walking down a street—I don't know if it was in Queens—and it just kept getting more volatile," recalls Michos. "All of a sudden people started getting upset that we had colors on and things like that... First people started looking, and then more people came, and then *more* people came, and then people started shouting and screaming, and then guys that looked like gang members started showing up... We had to shut down shooting and leave. That was the first time I ever really realized, 'Boy, this is more real to them'... It was a scene that never ended up in the film." In Harlem, the failure to invite local gang members to be extras led to threats being made on the lives of Gordon, Hill, and Marshall, leading to the necessity for constant police protection. During a lunch break, thousands of dollars' worth of equipment was wrecked in a whirlwind visit by rowdies. There was also a lot of palms-greasing necessary to stop gangs disrupting the shoot. Lawrence Gordon recalls, "The only time that I really took fear not just for my life but for the production was when the police a couple of times said, 'Do what they want to do because we can't control this group.' We had police with us and the police said, 'Don't worry about this bunch, they're nothing,' but there were a couple of times when the police were concerned. So when the police were concerned, it was time for me to get concerned. A couple of times we had to make a deal." An NYPD contact would advise Marshall whom to pay off. "They were basically being taxed," observes Wright. "'If you're gonna shoot in my neighborhood, you gonna give me something or I'm going to mess up your shot or take your shit.'" Linked to this issue is a strangers-in-a-strange-land factor. Wright: "These guys came from LA with this backlot set routine in their mind that, 'Ooh, we can just go to New York and do certain things and shoot whatever we want.' No! How did you sit in LA at a big table? How did you plan this out? That you were just going to come into the ghetto and shoot this film and everybody's gonna be happy about it?" Gordon adds, "It wasn't great sums of money. And we found ways to cover it, make sure we could handle it. The studio knew about it."

Even putting gangs aside, Seventies New York was Seventies New York. A Joel Weiss scene on Avenue A was canceled due to a double homicide up the block, a take of an Orphans scene was ruined by a screaming police siren as cops chased a robbery car, and—recalls Craig Baxley— "A generator driver got shot in the head."

Tom McKitterick recalls a night in Brooklyn involving a perfect storm of problems. "We were under the intersection, two elevated trains above us, and we could never get a sound take. We kept doing it and doing it. The trains kept passing overhead. It's like: 'Alright, ready'—and then all of a sudden some gaffer says, 'Oh, this light's out of place.' They were very exacting about the lighting and whatnot. On that incident people were throwing some bottles off the roof. It was just incredible." It's not clear if he is referring to the same evening on which crew have recalled being urinated on from above. It's also not clear whether the illumination problems were the same ones referred to by others wherein the traditionally ultra-bright movie apparatus turned off the light-sensitive switches on the street lamps, involving devising a laborious solution that required taping paper over each light cell.

Some things, though, went mercifully smoothly. The subway scenes were arranged through the aegis of the Community Relations Department of the City of New York Transit Authority, even though its personnel weren't enamored of some aspects of the script. The stations, trains, and contacts they provided were, of course, essential to the film. "I went over the script with them," says Marshall. "I had a very good relationship with the guy who ran things then, Dennis Wendling. He was a young guy and he appreciated the fact that it really wasn't about what was going on *per se* but it was a metaphor." Nonetheless, it seems significant that nothing like the opening scene of the Shaber script—where members of the protagonist gang are to be found defacing a subway car—is to be found in the finished film. (Rembrandt saves his spray-can talents for one of the upright slabs in the graveyard.)

For the first time ever, a production was allowed to film uninterrupted across entire nights on moving NYC trains. The Authority made available for this purpose the Hoyt–Schermerhorn station, which had an unused track. "We shot a lot there," says Marshall. "That was like a set had been built for us. We had this one station that was closed that we could then run trains in and out of. That worked perfectly for us." "We would ride back and forth all night," says Michos. "They would switch the posters on one side and then, when we drove back, they would move all the posters on the other side so it looked like we were going in the same direction."

ALTHOUGH THE *WARRIORS* ACTORS broadly understood what they were signing up for in terms of hours and activity, this didn't make the reality any less disorienting and taxing.

"You're sleeping all day and you have to get up by two and be on the set by four to be picked up by five," recalls Thomas Waites. "It was the exact opposite of life and it was five days a week." The cast would congregate in the late afternoon at the Gulf + Western building. "We would arrive there, five or six on a day, and it was usually bright light, and then we would shoot all night," says Michos. "We would have these banquets at, like, one o'clock in the morning where they would bring in chicken masala, the whole shebang, and they'd bring in wine sometimes. We would eat like a horse, but we were all running so much that it never affected us… We would drive home and the sun was coming up and all the hookers would be on the street. We would get dropped off and we'd sleep in the day, except for a couple of weeks of day-for-night, where you can shoot in the day because it's inside. It was a very grueling shoot. I didn't realize it 'til I looked back on it when I was older, because we were young and hungry and it was our first film."

"When I shot *The Warriors*, I came in the movie at, like, 123 pounds," reflects Harris. "By the time I finished I think I was 119. Because all we'd do was run and fight." Although the storyline of *The Warriors* was clearly far from a static, drawing-room piece, Beck admits, "It probably was more arduous than any of us thought it was going to be before we started." Waites is almost audibly wincing as he recalls that arduousness: "You have no idea. I don't know how much of it they actually used but it was take after take after take, five o'clock in the morning, six o'clock in the morning, running, running, running, running, running, running." It was not just vigorous but tedious. McKitterick: "Many of the shoots were pretty much the same action. We'd run into place, everybody says a line, we wrapped." Remar notes, "We had a lot of running sequences that really had to be pieced together. So we'd be running in different sections all over the place. There's a couple of them where they had to time it just right where we're running down the street and it's on a long lens and the Baseball Furies come up over the rise. That took a few to time out properly. So we could look forward to spending the night running… It was summer and we were all pretty sweaty from start to finish."

Van Valkenburgh wasn't particularly dismayed by the movie's physicality. "I don't think I gave that a second thought," she says easily. "I was so thrilled to make a movie that my brain was not thinking about anything except the adventure that I had been afforded. It's intoxicating to be working in a set with a bunch of great guys and you just spend your time thinking about how to please everybody and how to have a really fulfilling adventure. The only reason it was complicated was that my shoes were not the greatest for running, so it required some stamina. Fortunately, I was younger in those days." Extraordinarily, she fell over only once. Even more extraordinarily, "I wasn't even wearing my high heels. I should have been. They put me in a strange pair of espadrilles that night. I think I would have been better off with those gigantic pumps."

Perhaps amazingly, some of the Warriors were despite this topsy-turvy and highly physical schedule working out in their downtime. This was not due to Craig Baxley, who had given them no fitness regime. "The workout they were getting every day with me, they didn't need to go to the gym," he reasons. "It's like a boxer when a boxer is fighting: that's his workout." Beck, however, was one of the film's cast who spent some of his free hours in the gym, in his case arriving there at around 2.30 in the afternoon. Admittedly, some of this was down to vanity: as he was bare-chested and bare-armed throughout, it would potentially have been embarrassing if he wasn't noticeably ripped. Brian Tyler, meanwhile, notes that his own good physical shape gave him an advantage. "At the time I was into martial arts, so it worked out well," he says. "It wasn't a lot for me to be up at five, six o'clock in the morning and go work out and just stay in shape."

Other leisure-time pursuits were less high-minded than gym visits. "This was Studio 54 time, this was cocaine time," says Michos. "Everybody was partying." The Vermin actor, though, wasn't a participant in the hedonism. "We were close, but... they didn't really take me with them to that," he says. "I'm a person of faith, even back then... I would tell these guys about God all the time on the set." Even so, Michos admits that his Christianity at that time wasn't of the purest stripe. "The girls were always a problem for me." Another example of his susceptibility to temptation was quite possibly the very fact of him signing up for the movie in the first place. He isn't one of those people who claims that he saw from the get-go that *The Warriors* was going to be more surreal than down-and-dirty ("I thought it would be more like a gang movie"). However, he put aside any misgivings. "Truthfully, I wanted to be an actor and I just separated it. You could call [it] hypocritical. I know that's what it was. I just said, 'I'm not turning down a role.'"

That the *Warriors* cast were happy to see each other when off duty was a sign of how instant was their collective chemistry. "We gelled," says Harris. "We liked each other. We came together as this group called the Warriors." This fraternizing extended to their director. Harris: "He liked the guys. We were his Warriors, his teenagers. Walter was real cool with the guys." When Harris celebrated his birthday, Hill and the cast members came over to his house to share cake.

There was another exception to this tight-knit scenario. Of Tom McKitterick, Harris says, "He never hung around with us after shooting. He just went his own way." "I'm a solitary person," McKitterick admits.

Meanwhile, Van Valkenburgh had muscled in on a camaraderie that it might be said she didn't technically have a right to be part of. Although she wasn't actually required until a month into filming, she decided to be permanently on set. Partly this was to acclimatize herself to night shooting, partly because "it was so amazing to hang out and watch everything happening... It was just so amazing to be around New York in the middle of the night when you wouldn't normally feel safe."

Luckily for the physically taxed Warriors actors, Hill turned out to not be a multiple-takes director. "Walter's direction was pretty lean, dialogue and everything else," says Beck. "I really enjoyed working with him but I always felt with Walter that if you were doing what he wanted you to do, then he didn't say anything to you. He just kind of let you alone. So you didn't really get a whole lot of direction unless you were moving in a direction that he wanted changed. I must have been on the right line because I don't remember Walter giving me a whole lot of direction about anything other than physically where he wanted me to be." Says Waites of Hill, "I think he figured, 'Well, I did my job in casting the right guys.'"

"He didn't over-direct us, but he knew just how to direct us," says Michos. "He allowed us to find little nuances in the characters to make them ours without going too far off, 'cause he didn't want anyone to be flamboyant. We were basically supposed to be just a group of people where no one really over-stood out. But he allowed us to create characters and if you look, the characters are unique for how limited and stoic the dialogue was." Brian Tyler: "If it didn't flow, he told you, but if it did flow, he let that expand." Not that Hill's at-a-distance approach should be inferred as sloppiness. "He was a very conscientious director," says McKitterick. "He looked over everything." Michos also observes of Hill, "He was always calm. He'd say things like, 'Come on, guys, come on,' but he was very, very measured. He would laugh a little bit, we talked, but I never got a sense that he was worried about much." "He's such a kind man and a wonderful director," offers Harris.

As for the director himself, Hill describes his approach as, "'Show me what you're going to do with it and then I'll give you some guidance, and then we'll shoot.' In other words, I'm a movie director, not an acting coach."

THE EARLIEST SHOT major "city" scene in the film was the gathering in the graveyard, wherein the Warriors try to get their bearings and establish a new hierarchy after the break-up of the conclave and the loss of their leader. As the gang start discussing their predicament, they don't talk over each other but speak in turn, and furthermore from screen-left to screen-right. This is not the only example of such utter non-naturalism the viewer will see.

Meanwhile, for Michos the passage reflected real life. "If you look at the scene very closely, you'll see that most of us were trying to figure out who we were." The scene was additionally one that enabled him to differentiate his character from the other members of the gang. "We're all talking the same. I said to myself, 'This is not going to work for me, I've got to find a way out.' I remembered this old cartoon called *Hercules* and in the series there was this character who was half-man and half-horse and he'd go, 'Herc! Herc!' He'd say everything twice in a high voice, especially when he got excited. I said, 'Whenever Vermin gets excited, I'm going to make him talk in a high voice and repeat things twice, and I'm going to make him more comedic.' It was a chance that I took. So you'll see me saying, 'We're gonna get japped here, we're gonna get japped,' or 'Hurt me, hurt me,' or 'I like it, I like it.' And it worked, 'cause my part got bigger... I just kept getting more lines."

A similar expansion happened to the Snow character, although in this case it was not via the machinations of the actor. The June '78 *Warriors* script had seen the man then known as Snowball be given two lines toward the end of the narrative, but the role was still clearly intended to be a minimalist one. This was something by which Tyler was not worried. "My job is to interpret the script the way the creators wanted it to be," he says. "If it was one word, one line, ten lines, then that's what it was." However, it so happens that he was ultimately given a slightly more active role, in terms of both action and dialogue (the latter indeed amounting in the released film to ten lines). "I had a little bit more—especially in that bathroom scene—as far as physical fighting. Same thing with the dialogue. When we split up in various parts of the city, it just looked and flowed better if I had more lines."

Following the decision hashed out in the graveyard that the second-in-command should assume leadership responsibilities, Swan proceeds to lead his men through the unfamiliar streets. These streets were not merely mean but slick. "It's an old trick from film noir," notes Hill. "We were doing big wet-downs right from day one." This tried and tested method of creating glimmering atmospherics was given a helping hand by the familiarity with the city of director of photography Andrew Laszlo. Born in Hungary in 1926, Laszlo worked as an apprentice cameraman before emigrating to the United States in 1947. His already extensive list of credits included movies *The Night They Raided Minsky's*, *Popi*, *The Owl and the Pussycat*, *Class of '44*, and *Thieves* and TV shows *Washington Behind Closed Doors* and *The Dain Curse*. A Long Island resident, Laszlo knew the chances were slim of a New York summer passing without a downpour. Accordingly, he suggested that not just a selection of the city scenes should feature wet streets but every one of them, thus sidestepping potential continuity issues. "There was a rainstorm that happened right after the conclave and so that justified the streets being wet for the whole movie," notes Remar. Consequently, reviews of *The Warriors*, whether good or bad, almost universally commented approvingly on the evocativeness and beauty of the film's gleaming, neon-dappled ambience. Some in fact have postulated that only an uninformed outsider like Californian Hill could have conjured such an otherworldly vista. As Beck notes, "That's never what New York City looks like: you don't have wet, empty streets."

Laszlo's expertise with color and picture composition would certainly be highly influential on *The Warriors'* singular look. For instance, knowing that the view beyond the subway cars' windows could not be corrected because of the in-situ carriage lights, he mixed it with multiple other colors to create an illuminatory hodgepodge. Although utterly unnaturalistic, it both achieved its practical objectives and as a byproduct created a surreal effect pleasing to the eye. The same principle applies to another Laszlo improvisation, although it is one that might also be said to verge on comical. When the Warriors were chased by the Furies through Riverside Park, it was found that the camera was losing them in the darkness. The normal way to solve this problem would be to put up lights out of shot. Unfortunately, there was no such thing as out-of-shot in this context: with each take involving running at least half a mile, the lights apparatus would at some point be exposed. Pre-computer generated imagery, there was no logical way to alleviate the situation. Laszlo—presumably also conscious of the limited time available to him in this rushed, impoverished shoot—decided simply to clip drugstore lights in tree branches. Somehow it worked, either because people thought it was part of the overarchingly surreal optics of the movie, assumed they were the lights of apartment buildings beyond the trees, or merely didn't notice.

The next significant street sequence in the narrative involved the Warriors fleeing from the Turnbull ACs (who are—bizarrely for skinheads but par for the course for this movie—a mixture of races). The Turnbulls give chase to the Warriors in their gaudy bus, their malevolent forms hanging off the vehicle, weapons at the ready, as their prey pelt for the safety of an elevated subway station. The averagely hirsute Craig Baxley unexpectedly found himself becoming bald for the duration. He recalls, "That night we were scheduled to shoot it, the production manager said, 'We can't do this gag. None of them are stuntmen and we'd have to have a stuntman drive it, not the guy that owns it.' I said, 'Well, he won't let anyone drive his bus.' So Walter said, 'Go talk to the guy.' So I want to talk to him and he finally agreed that if I drove it, he would let the company use the bus with all the guys hanging off it. So I went and put on a skullcap."

The Turnbulls sequence is presaged by a scene wherein the Warriors are shown lurking in the shadows near the "elevated," discussing the wisdom of making for the platform before a train is in view. There is nothing naturalistic about a passage that is choreographed to the last detail, physically and verbally. The Warriors are not clumped together but stretched back in a photogenic line of precisely overlapping trim torsos and grim faces. As in the graveyard, there is some conveniently non-interrupted dialogue. "Walter had apprenticed with Sam Peckinpah so you see the kind of Mount Rushmore lined-up profiles of the dudes," notes David Patrick Kelly. The scene sums up what might be termed the delicious falsity of *The Warriors*. Such photogenic and sequential scenarios are simply not part of real life but they engender a narrative slickness and compositional poetry so enjoyable that the viewer is liable to respond to accusations of lack of realism with, "Who cares?"

The night of the filming of the scene in which the Warriors hold off the Orphans by way of a Molotov cocktail will live long in the cast's memories, but emphatically not for good reasons. "Manhattan was a tough, tough place to be doing that," says Baxley. "There were people throwing stuff off the top of the roofs down on the crew." However, that was the least of the problems that night. "I was not real keen on the effects man we had on the show," says Baxley. Baxley watched said crewmember rigging the effect that would result in the car going up in flames. "He had a door on a cable and I asked him what he had in the car. He told me. I said, 'Man, are you kidding? Is that cable big enough?' He said, 'Listen, I think I know what I'm doing'… I went up to him probably three or four times, asking him. I said, 'Are you sure?'… Well, when he blew it, the door went flying like a hundred feet past the crew."

Recalls Michos, "They put so much TNT into that car, I'm telling you when that thing blew off, our bodies rocked. I was pushed two or three feet." Van Valkenburgh—fearless on other potentially dangerous occasions—says she found the night "truly terrifying." She recalls, "I don't think it was adequately explained to us how intense that was going to be… Tom and I were the last to run by the car and it was petrifying, absolutely petrifying. The sound effects of glass coming down through the sky was just a mortifying feeling 'cause I kept expecting things to be impaled in my arms. It was just crazy."

Frank Marshall asserts that the actors were more "scared by the sounds than anything" and that "nobody got hurt." However, it seems significant that Brian Tyler on this occasion takes the side of the cast. As might be expected of a man who went on to a career as a policeman, Tyler believes absolutely in the chain of command, repeatedly declining to question anything about the *Warriors* script or production, stating over and over that it was his job to do what the director said and to be "flexible." However, he insists, "It was a dangerous night." That cop career is also something that suggests he's hardly likely to exaggerate peril. "You got a bomb going off near you. You think it's going to do one thing and it does something a lot bigger," he says. "You felt it. You feel the heat, the percussion blast. It was dangerous." "The cast had every right to be concerned," says Baxley, adding of the effects man, "I was very upset with him."

The actors were sufficiently shaken that a clear-the-air meeting was felt necessary. "Frank Marshall came in to talk to all of us and he came in with a soldier's helmet on," says Michos. "It sort of lightened the thing and everyone laughed. There was some resolution where they gave us more hazard pay."

One would imagine that this incident would be grist to the mill of Thomas Waites. During the shoot he rarely missed an opportunity to pick a fight with the producers. For instance, he demanded an extra trailer for the Warriors actors. "He had done another film, he was a little more ahead of us," says Michos. "He knew more of that. I didn't think much about it because I just was so glad being on there, and it worked for my character." "They shoved all eight of us into one freakin' trailer," says Waites. "I was like, 'Come on, man. You don't even have air conditioning in here. There's eight men getting dressed? This isn't fair.' They were trying to be cheapskates. I think they ended up giving us two trailers... In that instance, I believe I was right." (That figure of eight would in fact rise to nine when one evening Van Valkenburgh found her usual dressing space flooded with extras and, invited in by the Warriors actors, stayed.) He is the first to admit that other objections he made were not so reasonable. For instance, he unexpectedly created a point of contention out of the fact that he was the only Warrior with a buttoned vest. "On a different night, I chose to wear it unbuttoned," he recalls. "The continuity person said, 'You have to button your vest.' I was like, 'Well, I may have unbuttoned it in between scenes.' 'No, you have to button your vest.' 'But don't I have the freedom to decide that maybe my character...?' Instead of just keeping my mouth shut and buttoning the vest, I made an issue of it." Curiously, though, Waites turns out to have had no issue with the explosion scene. "I thought it was great," he says. "I had no complaints about that."

At the opposite end of the dramatic scale to the car explosion was, for Van Valkenburgh, the confrontation with the Baseball Furies. Mercy wasn't present in their scenes, but the actress bore witness to them in her usual interested-observer role. The bat-wielding gang instilled her first major doubts about the project. "The night that the Furies came up out of their little dugout brownstone thing in that make-up, I thought, 'What movie are we making?'" she recalls. With no description of the Furies in the script, this was her first intimation that they looked more like Kiss than the New York Yankees. "I was very confused because we all took what we were doing very seriously and suddenly we've got this fantasy gang coming out. 'Oh my goodness, they're going to laugh at us now. Nobody's going to take this seriously. Anybody in a real gang's going to think we're all idiots.' I really was doing one-eighty at that point. I was like, 'I don't understand at all what's going on.' Now, it didn't take away from anything I was doing—I continued to have a great time—but I was dubious about the effect that we were going to have."

The script now dictated that the reason the Warriors turned to fight the Furies was not Ajax wanting to rumble but the fact that Cowboy gets winded. The reality was different. "I could have done that all night long," says McKitterick. "My whole life, I've been fit." The Warriors versus the Furies was a battle royale, possibly the most iconic scene of the movie. "He didn't just want to make an action movie," Marshall said of Hill in the extras of the *Warriors Ultimate Director's Cut* DVD. "Each fight sequence was choreographed in a different way to represent a different thing… They were choreographed to be almost like a ballet, like a dance." In the case of the Warriors-Furies face off—whether under the aegis of Baxley, Hill, or both—the viewer was treated to something reminiscent of the sword fights in Kurosawa's *Seven Samurai*, although enacted with wood instead of steel. "The baseball-bat fight's kind of out there," laughs Remar.

In fact it was Remar who gave it its *coup de grace* with a piece of improvised dialogue. In motion pictures, multiple changes are made to dialog and action during the process of shooting, many of them by actors. As the previous comments of Michos indicate, this is sometimes down to players simply wanting to assert themselves, even if a byproduct of this can be that the character and relevant scene is improved. Remar, though, says his decision to proffer something not found on a screenplay page was "a purely collaborative moment." He recalls, "I wasn't trying to fix the scene… I said, 'Walter, the guy looks like a lollipop.' He said, 'Let's call him a popsicle.'" Feeling his character to be "kind of a prick" with a "mouth on him," Remar devised a comment that he felt Ajax would come out with if confronted by such apparitions. The script's prosaic lines of defiance, "Come on, I'll waste all of you mothers. Come on, you fuckers," became instead the zinger, "I'll shove that bat up your ass and turn you into a popsicle!"

Meanwhile, the way that Ajax's Fury adversary (Jerry Hewitt) physically responds to this colorful invective demonstrates that spouses of crew can also make valuable contributes. Explains Baxley, "Jerry did the whole thing, flipping the bat around. Walter wanted to almost be comedic. My wife actually came up with that move. I thought that was a fun move." This twirling of a ball-bat like a samurai sword was another thing that gave the scene a Kurosawa air. In another change from the script, the scene ends with all four Warriors appropriating bats.

In the passages with the female gang (who now directly declare themselves to be named the Lizzies), Cowboy—as a consequence of having been relocated to the Furies scene—is no longer present, with Cochise taking his place alongside Vermin and Rembrandt. For anyone who might suspect that the name Lizzies was a coy variant of "Lezzies," Hill's direction seemed to be aiming to make things clearer. Two of the female gang members—a black woman with pulled-back hair and a white girl with distinctively crimped blonde tresses—dance suggestively together in a way not evident in the script.

Mayra Sánchez is surprised to be told that her brother's character was perceived by Walter Hill to be gay. "However, now that you mention it, it was apparent that Rembrandt was very unhappy in that scene," she says. "He just seems like he has such disdain for what's going on. He's totally disinterested in hanging out with those girls. So that would make sense if there was a very subtle representation there of that."

Harris was tickled by the post-modern nature of one of his pieces of dialogue. He recalls, "[Rembrandt] goes, 'Hey guys, we should be leaving here.' I go, 'Yeah, in a minute man. A little break in the action.'" Meanwhile, Michos provided another piece of extemporization. He recalls, "This girl, Dee Dee Benrey, I'm flirting with her in the scene but I turn and I walk away with the leader of the Lizzies and I sit down and I say to her, 'Looks like you're the winner.'" Michos recollects the climax of the sequence with somewhat less pleasure. "I remember jumping over that couch. Probably ten, fifteen takes diving over the couch and landed on my bare arms."

When Cochise was depicted smashing a chair over the head of a Lizzie intent on wasting him and his friends, the performer who took the hit was stuntwoman Victoria Vanderkloot. Although the chair was not liable to cause injury—it was made from featherlight balsa wood that broke on impact—Harris points out of the rationale of using Vanderkloot, "She knew how to sell that." "I basically got her SAG card on that," says Baxley of Vanderkloot. "She became a stunt person on that film and went on to do quite a bit after that."

When the Warriors trio make their hurried, couch-cresting escape, Cochise lays waste to the door. "Walter shot that at high speed which gives it a very special effect," says Harris. "That door basically exploded when I went through it." The scene in the finished film sees yet again a relocation in the narrative of the point where the Warriors become aware that they have been framed: it is now Rembrandt who informs them this following a Lizzie purring to him, "So you're the famous Warriors—the guys that shot Cyrus."

For Remar, the night on which he acted being captured by the undercover police officer was intense. With Ajax the only Warrior in the scene and Hill realizing it was going to take at least a day (i.e., night) to capture, the rest of the Warriors were dismissed. Finding himself the only principal actor on set on his last night of shooting, Remar was left feeling a little overwhelmed. "It was a difficult scene to shoot," says Hill. "Oddly enough, 'cause it was in some ways a simple scene, although emotionally it's not an easy, straightforward scene." Hill has subsequently worked with Remar extensively and feels he has an insight into his psyche. "It was his last scene, and he also hated to lose. He very much internalizes his parts and the idea that Ajax became vulnerable in that sense and entrapped was very difficult for him." Remar admits that he felt melancholy. "It's a sad scene. You're leaving this family that you bonded with and the character's being carted off to jail. I didn't want to leave. I wanted to keep shooting. I wanted to be in the movie 'til the end."

By coincidence, Mercedes Ruehl, the thespian playing the female cop, had the first name that David Shaber had originally intended for Mercy. Notes McKitterick of Ruehl, "She was a stuntwoman and that was perhaps her first scene as an actress." "She was not comfortable," says Hill. "It's very difficult on actors to come in sometimes and just do a one-day scene. She was very unsure of herself and we had to do a lot of talking, and I'm never very pleased by that... So it was a complicated night."

With what Remar terms the "intertwined" situation of his character being removed from the narrative and him dispatched from the shoot, the upside was that the actor was able to make use of his own feelings. "He was my character," he says. "I took it very personally." Remar's performance of the scene in his audition had been impressive, even startling. Now, though, he pulled out all the stops, depicting Ajax's reaction to the cuffs being slapped on him as in turns bewildered, furious, defiant, and finally defeated. For McKitterick, it meant that, despite the circumstances, the audience ended up feeling sorry for the character, for Ajax's behavior in the scene was actually the only glimmer in the film of the nastiness of the gang in Yurick's book. Minor stuff aside—pushing commuters out of their path as they run desperately for trains or standing on train seats—the Warriors do nothing anti-social except for this scene. As Harris notes, "He goes, 'Maybe you're all turning faggots. I'm gonna go get some.' 'Cause he's stupid. Then he's going, 'Oh, I like it rough' and he's going to basically rape her. That's the only time you see one of the Warriors out of line." "Jamie just hit the mark on that beautifully," McKitterick says. "That was the power of his performance—it was many things at one time. He nailed that."

Michos wasn't impressed by the aftermath of the arrest in the narrative. "That scene was weird to me," he muses. "We said, 'Cops got Ajax,' and 'I bet he went out swinging.' It didn't fit for me. We might have said, 'Well, what the eff those cops do, those effers?' It seemed more soft than I think the Warriors would have been." Hill had a different misgiving. "I think the biggest mistake that I made script-wise was having Ajax be captured by the cops," he says. "I think the movie would have been more satisfying if Ajax had completed the trip back to Coney Island. I'm not disappointed in the scene. As everything I've done with James Remar, I think he did a wonderful job. But I think from an audience satisfaction [perspective], they really missed him not being able to go the distance." Remar says he shared in this feeling, at least then. "That was the challenge: to get back home," he reasons. "The movie is based on an odyssey and Ajax was a character in the odyssey. We're based on Xenophon's March of the Ten Thousand, but it's a hero out of Achilles. Some of these guys fall down and die and it's always sad."

Mercedes Ruehl *has* gone the distance, career-wise. "She's a very fine actress who's had a good career," says Hill. Notes the stage savvy McKitterick, "She's had a great career in the theatre." Ruehl hasn't done too badly in movies either, in 1992 picking up a Best Supporting Actress Oscar for her role in *The Fisher King*.

CENTERPIECE CHAOS

THE WARRIORS IS A MOVIE whose centerpiece, unusually, occurs close to the beginning of its narrative, namely the conclave. Yet while the conclave takes place early on in the story, and although much of the film was shot in narrative sequence, the scene wasn't shot until late on.

Thomas Waites recalls that he worked seven weeks on the film and estimates that the conclave scenes were shot in the sixth or seventh week. In fact, it might have been both of those weeks, as David Patrick Kelly recalls, "The conclave I think took two weeks. It was supposed to be shorter than that."

Although the conclave was portrayed as occurring, as in the book, in Van Cortlandt Park, the shooting location was in fact ten miles across town in Riverside Park. "That area where they did the conclave is a kiddie's park," says Wright. "The section where Cyrus is making his speech, that's where those sprinklers go off and the little kids run around inside the little gated area. It's not impressive at all." However, he understood the reason for the relocation. "Logistically, to shoot that in Van Cortlandt with Bronx gangs around, you're going to have a problem. You're going to need a lot more police protection than on 72nd Street, which is a very affluent neighborhood. And one side of the park is the expressway, is the West Side Drive. You don't have to worry about people jumping out of their cars to see what's going on." He also admits that by motion-picture smoke and mirrors, "they made it seem like it was a really huge, big deal. I mean, we had a lot of extras."

111

"We had a thousand kids there," confirms Marshall. "It was pretty crazy." Many of the "kids" with whom Hill and co filled the park were not SAG-card carriers. "I would say more than half of those guys were real gang members," says Wright. The "undocumented" extras recruited from Coney Island and the local Riverside Drive Park neighborhood naturally had real-life affiliations and the fact that they came dressed in their own costumes and "colors" was handy for the budget.

Although gang members were no more immune than any other members of the general public to the allure of being immortalized in a movie, the novelty and glamor quickly wore off for some as they came to apprehend that filming could be hard work. Notes Kelly, "We'd show up about five in the afternoon and stay 'til seven the next morning." For civilians who weren't on the opposite-of-life sleep schedule that the *Warriors* cast and crew were, this could be taxing. "One night you got like 1500 people, the next night you got 600," Harris says. "They had to be there a long time... To keep people coming back, they had raffles where they're raffling off color TVs and all these things. They were going into community services or putting up flyers all over the city, 'Shooting *The Warriors*, you're going to get "X" amount of dollars plus a boxed lunch."

The conclave scene is the one part of the movie whose filming was observed by the author who had given rise to the entire project. After signing terms with Lawrence Gordon, Sol Yurick said he had heard nothing about the progress of the picture. "When the movie was in production, there was a piece in the newspaper about Gordon coming to New York to start shooting," recalled Yurick. The article mentioned the hotel at which Gordon was staying. "So I called him up, introduced myself. And he didn't know who I was." "This is total garbage," says Gordon. "That's total bullshit... The only time I recall speaking to Sol Yurick is when I made him an offer." Yurick recalled of the phone conversation that he was taken aback at Gordon's defensiveness as the producer launched into a speech about how an action movie was different to a novel. When Yurick explained that he would just like to see some of the filming, he said he was invited to Riverside Park.

When he got there the next evening, he was, on one level, mightily impressed. He later wrote, "I was overwhelmed and thought that here was my imagination concretized, industrialized, and populated with living people." Yurick's pleasure didn't last long. Introducing himself to Walter Hill, he found himself on the receiving end of much the same type of defensive spiel as Gordon had come out with. Perhaps it was similar to what

Hill told this author, although the director was reasonable in tone and philosophy: "It's the old thing: he's got a book and the movie's a movie. I've never understood why anybody thinks the movies are supposed to be like the books anyway. They're different. The book speaks for itself and the movie speaks for itself." Hill also points out, "I met him right in the middle of the chaos of trying to shoot that sequence and we spoke briefly. I was told later he thought that I was not properly respectful to him... I was just quite busy."

Although the presence of real gang members may have granted the conclave sequence authenticity, it also led to some discomfort for the actors. Recalls Michos, "Real gangs would say, 'You guys think you're tough, man?' And we would say, 'Oh, no, no, no, we're just actors—we want to learn from you guys' and all that." Wright: "It was best really to keep your mouth shut and just shoot." "There were some kids that were kind of scary," recalls Kelly. "They came up to me and said, 'Who you, the sheriff?'—'cause I had my little badge on my vest." Kelly recalls he didn't dare say anything back to his tormentors and was thankful for the presence of the stunt coordinator. "Craig happened to be standing right there and he moved in and said, 'David, you okay?' and they moved on. I just remember him being there keeping people safe." Beck has recalled instances of gang members wanting to challenge the cast and getting their "clocks cleaned" by security for their troubles.

Even despite the presence of these street toughs, the conclave shoot was the point where Michael Beck finally had his suspicions confirmed that this was not going to be a realistic movie. He'd first come to wonder about this "early on in some of the staging of scenes—just physically where he placed us." He says, "Andy Laszlo was a great guy and I'd look through the lens, 'cause I was always trying to learn more about the whole aspect of filmmaking. I would see some of the set-ups we had and I would just go, 'Oh, okay. I see what this is looking like. This is not *Rebel Without a Cause*. This is not some naturalistic [film].' And by the time we got to seeing how gangs were depicted... If you lived in New York City at that time and you saw any gangs on the street, they didn't look anything like what any of us looked like... Back then, most street gangs probably looked more like the Orphans. They were not dressed up. You could tell street gangs not [by] how they dressed but their attitude... By the time you saw the conclave gangs, you went, 'Well, we're doing some kind of surrealistic comic-book movie here.' Those visual things that Walter brought to the picture, his whole way of seeing it, they were not indicated in any way on the page."

Craig Baxley had been anticipating a far grittier movie in general. "I expected the film to go in several different directions it never did... It was just the tone of it I was concerned about. That it might come off as being silly... *The Wanderers* was being made at the same time and that was more of a realistic character study of troubled kids and everything else, which I thought was good. I thought this maybe could have used some of that sort of character studying."

Shooting the sequence could have gone wrong for pretty much the same reasons that the conclave did in either the original book or in its current film adaptation. Michos observes, "Any one person could have done something similar to the actual movie. Somebody could have taken out a gun or done something to hurt one of us. But it never crossed my mind. I felt almost naively safe." Wright adjudges the fact that things proceeded broadly peaceably as "amazing." He observes, "You got guys there that do have a beef with each other but they're letting it go because you want to be on film. To me, that's strange. We should have had a bunch of cameras in the Seventies shooting movies all through New York City and there'd have been no gangs. They all want to be actors."

In fact, some problems caused during the conclave shoot emanated less from street toughs than from the well-to-do local denizens. "You're in an area that's all expensive five-story walk-ups and brownstone," says Wright. "At a certain time at night we couldn't even cheer anymore because you're in a neighborhood where they say, 'Excuse me, it's ten o'clock. Stop making noise.' So we would just mime the cheer. During the day you actually do the 'Yaaay!' and at night all you heard was the bracelets, the whatever, or the ruffle of clothing. Nobody was screaming. They'd have us kicked out of there."

There was at least one fewer real-life gang member at Riverside Park than the producers were expecting. Unfortunately, that person was the single most important component of the sequence. "We lost our first Cyrus," notes Marshall. "The original Cyrus was a real gang member who just disappeared." Neither Marshall nor Hill remember this man's name, but both are effusive about his screen potential. "He was the real thing," Marshall says. "He did a reading for us. He was fantastic." "He was an interesting guy," says Hill. "He had been in gangs. He had been in prison. He was also a playwright. He had written something that had had some kind of off-off Broadway significance... I'm not sure if it was a one-man performance or a regular play—it had run its course before I was there—but he was quite the toast of critical opinion… He *loved* the idea of the gangs getting together and running the place."

"We didn't even know the guy had disappeared for quite a while," reflects Hill. "We only discovered that he had fallen off the face of the earth a few days before it shot." A hurried recasting process took place. This unknown personage may well have nursed regret over his no-show for the rest of his life. "At the last moment we found Roger Hill, who was great," says Marshall. Some will even consider that an understatement. For many, the performance of this last-minute replacement is the high point of the entire picture.

Born in 1952, New York City native Roger Hill (no relation to his new director) graduated from City College. Walter Hill notes of the anonymous first choice that he had "an interesting look" but that "he was a small man and he was not as good-looking as Roger." The latter's appearance was in fact also miraculously apposite. Although Roger Hill had a very Anglo name, his appearance bespoke exotic genes. Chris W. Hill, his son, says of his father, "He identified as African American," but reveals, "We're African American mixed with European." Hill's dual heritage is revealed in flowing locks not normally associated with blacks. The combination of that and his olive-looking skin almost eerily suggested that Hill's ancestors hailed from the Persia that the historical Cyrus trod. (The exotic look, of course, was completed by Mannix's gown-like costume.) This was the first of the pieces of good fortune attending the recasting. The second slab of serendipity was Roger Hill's immense talent.

Chris W. Hill notes, "He was primarily a theatre actor… He had been doing off-Broadway Shakespeare for a number of years… He had just done Hamlet right before *The Warriors*. Which explains why he did that character the way he did it. Roger did that as a theatre actor more than a film actor. Maybe that's what they were looking for when they cast him: that sort of big speaking-to-the-back-row-of-the-theatre type of performance."

"He had a lot of dialogue and he was scared to death that he wasn't going to be ready," says the director. "I had played Hamlet three months earlier, so that was preparation enough," Roger Hill later told warriorsmovie.co.uk. "The monologue came naturally because of this." He told the same site, "All the words belong to the screenwriter and Walter Hill. My contribution was delivery of the lines and physical vocabulary." Roger Hill certainly throws himself into the performance, flinging back his arms, thrusting forward his chest, placing exquisite, sibilant contempt in the line "our little piece of turf," and incrementally raising the pitch of emotion in the refrain, "Can you dig it!"

"I was there on set when they shot his scene, in a stroller," says Chris. "I don't remember it 'cause I was a baby. I was somewhere by the crew. We actually lived right near there… I'm sure it was not nerve wracking for him on any level. Both my parents are from the projects in the Bronx. There was a lot of real lived experience in him playing that character. So they did not feel out of place in that crowd. And he was certainly no stranger to performing in a theatre before crowds. I think that was a perfect role for him. That's what he loved to do. That's how he was in the theatre as well. He was a brilliant actor and he could grab an audience and he had a booming voice. He was intense on stage and as a father. He was just a very intense man."

Not only was the observing Yurick impressed that someone was sufficiently knowledgeable about Xenophon to choose to name the Riffs' leader Cyrus, he was fascinated at how the producers dealt with the message said character conveyed. He had himself imagined Ismael's ideas filtering through the crowd in a pass-it-on manner rather than as a declamation audible to everyone. However, the substance and delivery of the speech appalled the author and destroyed for him the very worth of the finished film. "At that point, it began to fall apart for me because the person who acts Cyrus was absolutely terrible," he said. "It was just bad acting. Very bad acting. There was no real rhetorical or inspirational quality." Nobody had more of a right than Yurick to a view about either the movie or Cyrus' speech. However, his disdain for Roger Hill's performance—and aforementioned amusement at its central catchphrase—are minority opinions.

Dorsey Wright finds it "extremely odd" that the decision was originally taken to recruit somebody with no acting experience for such a major role. Although he allows, "There are people who have not taken an acting lesson who are just charismatic people," he says, "If he was better than Roger, he must have been amazing person." Not that, initially, Wright was impressed himself. "Every actor, they want to know who the hell is playing Cyrus," he recalls. "I mean, it's a big part." He was underwhelmed when Roger Hill stepped onto the wooden platform from which Cyrus delivers his peroration. "I know him," he says. "You know how you see actors around?… I'm like, 'Oh, this is going to be interesting.'" Wright's skepticism shortly turned to delight as Hill began, as he puts it, "burning up the fucking set." He explains, "There are very few actors that I get lost in the moment when they're doing their routine. He was one of them. Those shots they got of me smiling—I could remember where the camera was and I could care less. I was looking at another actor and I was going, 'This guy is fucking good.' He started running off those lines. It was like, 'Yo, let's just keep shooting all night long'... I hadn't heard the story about some real gang member until after he did maybe his second or third take. Then it was going around, 'Hey, there was this other guy,' and I was like, 'Thank God he didn't show the fuck up.'"

Roger Hill also enthralled those who might ordinarily prefer their declamations to be less flowery. By common consensus, he had the genuine gang members before him ready to take the city for real. "If you look at what he did, he was doing Hamlet, only street," says David Harris. "'Ca-a-a-n you count, suckers!' Everything the guy was doing was brilliant. 'Our little piece of turf.' He was magnetic. I could see people following him. That character was supposed to be very charismatic, that could pull all these gangs together and make it into one gang to take over the city, and he had that kind of charisma to do that." Wright: "You get ten per cent of it sitting in the movie theatre, watching that on film. Being there while he's doing it, you look at this guy going, 'Fuck! Where's my knife! I'm ready to kick everybody's ass!' To where afterwards the first cheers and stuff were real cheers. Everybody felt it. It's like, 'Oh, shit. This is real.' And he fed off it, because the more takes he did, the better he got into, 'Yeah, I'm just going to miss [this] section, I'm going to tweak this a little bit.'... There's times in films and on stage where you're in a magical moment. You're looking at this actor going, 'God, I'm glad to be on this project. I'm so happy to be here.' It's like, 'This is what it's about. This is the heavyweight championship fight.' You want to be in those moments, and [Roger] Hill made one of those moments."

When Wright came on the project, he had been amused by the script's antediluvian terminology for fights and ambushes. "'We're gonna bop.' 'We're gonna get japped.' I'm, like, 'Do you know how old that shit is?'" Meanwhile, "Can you dig it?" would have been more appropriate to the Sixties timeframe and hippie environment of *Hair*, the film he had recently finished shooting. Roger Hill's mesmerizing quadruple deployment of that phrase—head thrown back, arms spread wide, to the backdrop of roaring extras—turned a potentially embarrassing anachronism into a resonant war-cry, transforming a flower-power relic into an endlessly quoted and imitated piece of movie dialogue, not to mention a piece of shorthand for *The Warriors* itself. David Patrick Kelly notes of Cyrus' speech, "I knew it was stylized. It wasn't Malcolm X or anything like that." Even so, as Kelly lyrically summed it up in the *Ultimate Director's Cut* DVD, "It was this great kind of faux messianic speech and resonated forever."

CYRUS' RHETORIC, of course, doesn't inspire the quasi-revolution he wishes for because of the fact that he is mown down. Craig Baxley found himself getting another unexpected role after proposing a more dramatic demise for Cyrus than the director had originally envisaged. "He was just going to have him get shot and drop on the platform," recalls Baxley. "I said, 'Let's have him get shot and go backwards off the platform and, like, drop twelve feet through a breakaway platform into three or four Judo mats. Walter said, 'God, be incredible. I'd love to see that.'" However, Baxley bumped up against the same problem with New York stuntmen he had encountered at the beginning, only exacerbated by the fact that the performer was required to have a similar skin tone to Roger Hill. Baxley: "There was no African-American stuntman in New York that would do it. So I found Alan Oliney, who was in Stunts Unlimited. Alan had doubled Eddie Murphy in *Beverly Hills Cop* hanging off the truck for that whole sequence. He was an all-round gymnast. He said he'd come back and do it for me. Two days before we were scheduled to shoot it, the production man, John Stark, said, 'We can't afford to bring him [over].' I said, 'Well, wait a minute—Walter wants this gag.' He says, 'Well, you go tell Walter.' So I went and told Walter. Walter looked at me and said, 'Well, you sold me on this gag. I want this gag done.' Now this is so politically wrong: I basically went and put on the clothes and they did my hair and darkened me down and I did the fall."

The fact that the substantial non-white element of the crowd wasn't perturbed by the "politically wrong" nature of what Baxley was doing may well have been another benefit of Roger Hill's mesmerizing performance. "When I came out dressed as Cyrus in front of those thousands of real gang members, I didn't know what was going to happen," Baxley recalls. "Here I am, a Caucasian guy with blue eyes and I've got Afro sheen in my hair and I'm all darkened down and wearing this big robe. I decided I wasn't going to look up until I got to the platform." His fears were groundless. "They're all cheering, 'Cyrus! Cyrus! Cyrus!' but we're not even rolling cameras. It was crazy."

The depiction of hell breaking loose upon the arrival at the conclave of Johnny Law was cannily crafted by the film's assistant director. David O. Sosna arranged the gang members in concentric circles, each ring of which would run in the opposite direction to their immediate neighbors. The only instruction each individual needed to remember was to follow the person in front of him. Judicious zooms and edits created the desired impression of bedlam. An important motivational presence during this process was the stunt coordinator. "Craig Baxley was constantly running around... cranking up the energy on it, which is hard to do with a lot of paid extras", recalls Kelly. "Every night out there to get all these people going in the right direction, he had to be the cheerleader. People were fatigued and there wasn't a lot of places to rest."

Kelly, of course, had his own crucial role, involving the pointing of a finger and the yelled mantra, "The Warriors did it!" "And now I become aware of David Patrick Kelly," says Wright. "Who I find out really quick is another method actor. And I'm like, 'This guy is insane.' David wouldn't interact with any of the Warriors because he wanted to keep his whole persona up: 'I don't like these guys.' So anytime they were on set together, he would eat elsewhere and wouldn't sit down and conversate with them. That's like, okay. When you watch the film, you go, 'Okay, this is one of the people who actually keeps the film going. He's a real interesting person.'" And another actor burning up the set? "Most definitely. He's eating up scenery in every shot, and he knows what he's doing. I tried not to eat up scenery because I didn't have that much confidence in what I was doing. And the guys that I was working with, a lot of them had never done a movie before. I just realized, 'Okay, when I'm with Beck or when I'm with Remar, we can do that,' because I felt that they had that energy. You know who to turn it on with, otherwise they will eat you alive. But to like do it all the way?"

Like Cyrus, the character of Cleon departed from the narrative during the conclave passage, quite possibly suffering the same fate as the Riffs leader. The scene marked the final installment of Wright's staccato Warriors schedule. "I had a contract for eight weeks," he explains. After initial shooting, his presumably deceased character wasn't needed for the post-conclave scenes and he temporarily departed the scene. "I was on a break for a while because they were shooting other things. I was auditioning. I had gotten another film, and we were doing readings and doing wardrobe and stuff for that too. So it was like, 'Okay, run back and do this conclave thing with *The Warriors.*'"

Wright's final scene was a memorable one: his character fending off Luther, Cropsey and Gramercy Riff-members before finally succumbing to sheer weight of numbers. For all Craig Baxley's efforts in teaching him how to fight without hurting his fellow actors, it was to no avail when Joel

Weiss—literally—overstepped the mark. Wright: "You have a mark you're supposed to hit. You're going by the depth of the screen, so everything looks like it's closer than what it is and you have to hit a mark so that you're far enough from my fist when I swing there's no way in the world it's going to hit you. Your job as an actor is just to do the reaction, with your neck or your face. But he overstepped the mark, he got closer than he was supposed to, and I punched him in the face. I went, 'Ooh, I'm sorry!' And Walter Hill was, like, 'What the hell are you doing! He didn't even go down!' It was like, 'Fuck, you should have known to just keep going with that.' When we shot it again, he made sure. And David Patrick Kelly made sure he was *way* from that mark. He made sure you will not be hitting me in the face with that elbow."

As the clock ticked down to twelve on the night this scene was being shot, somewhat farcical events took place. "At midnight, I belong to Orion Films," says Wright. As such, a limousine had been sent to pick him up from the *Warriors* set to transport him to the shooting location of *Hotel New Hampshire*. There was still talk of a chance, however, that his schedule on *The Warriors* could be extended. "I'm sitting on the hood of a limousine while they're talking about what they're going to do," recalls Wright. "Are they going to renegotiate this contract? Are you going to try and keep me longer? It came down to no, get in the car and go. Next thing I know I was at the airport heading to Tadoussac, Canada. If I thought my character was going to come back, not with their budget, it wasn't. People say, 'Did Cleon die?' I really don't know. I just know my time was up. They weren't gonna renegotiate… When the crowd jumps Cleon after they do the karate kick and then they all circle around him and they start elbowing him, if you look closely, there's nothing in the middle… I was already heading to the airport."

As he made his way to the Canadian border, Wright's feelings about the project he had just departed were not ecstatic ones. "To me, it had a promise of being something great and then I thought later on, 'Ah, this is going to be a small film. This isn't going to work'… I didn't have any expectations of this film. Because of my expectations of what a gang movie should be like. This, I really didn't understand. It was too comical and you got this interracial thing going on." What he viewed as the comical aspect derived from the "Hollywood version" of street gangs involving "top hats" and "face paint." He says, "Who the hell is coming out of their house with face paint on? I don't care how bad your gang is, you will get your ass kicked."

At some point before his departure, Wright had engaged in night-time reshoots of some of the dialogue from the previously filmed day-time scenes, plus some new segments. This was due to a crucial piece of advice offered to the director by editor David Holden. Holden told Hill that the movie would be more powerful if the Coney Island scenes at the beginning were jettisoned, not because they were substandard in any way but because their exclusion would make for a more atmo-spheric film. It would mean that the only non-nighttime scenes were the ones at the end showing the Warriors arriving at the sanctuary of their home turf, thus lending them a degree of symbolism. As Van Valken-burgh notes, "It wouldn't have much punch if it starts in the daylight and ended in the daylight. Daylight is their freedom, daylight is their victory at the end."

Hill accepted the logic. "They were editing the movie simultane-ously with our shooting," says Beck. "Somewhere through that process of shooting that summer, he saw that everything we shot for the first two-and-a-half weeks wasn't going to work, that this movie needed to start in the darkness." Says Hill, "I think when we were getting ready to make the movie and starting to shoot the film, I hadn't really committed—and I'd be the first to say it's my fault—to how special the movie needed to be. There was still some ambivalence and it was more conventional. When we looked at everything cut together that had been shot, I think it was the most obvious thing in the world was just to get rid of all that and give it that sense of dynamism hopefully that it has at the beginning."

As a consequence of the new policy, the word "conclave" is only men-tioned once in the finished film, as opposed to four times in the June '78 script. This was never going to cause harm. However, lost along with the scenes was important expository dialogue. Accordingly, the actors were called back to shoot some night-time, information-conveying segments that would precede the trek to the conclave. Cleon's speech to his assem-bled gang as he explained the purpose of and restrictions surrounding the conclave was shot again, this time at night and in the shadow of the Won-der Wheel, the Ferris wheel that has long been a Coney Island landmark. "Except at the Wonder Wheel it's a close-up just on Cleon," says Wright. "It wasn't like they were all standing in a row in the day scene. It was a completely different shot. That's where it threw me, because I'm doing the lines and it kind of dawns on me, 'I've done these lines before. I don't know exactly what they're doing.'" Also shot in darkness, this time on the Coney Island train platform, were some pieces of gang dialogue.

Wright insists that the reshoots were done "almost immediately" after the daytime scenes. McKitterick agrees with him, saying, "The decision to shoot the film at night entirely was made pretty early on." This seems to have been a separate process to subway mosaic material. Recalls Beck, "We went back and shot all those little montage shots: being on a train, the little scene with Cleon saying something, Swan saying something to Rembrandt, and all those little pops that made that montage of the Warriors going to the conclave. All those things were shot probably in the last week of shooting. Walter told us at that point, 'I've rethought... We've been looking at the dailies and it just makes sense that this picture is a night picture.' We just did it. Actors generally are just concerned with their role and playing and fitting into the story and serving the script. Generally you're not looking at it in the big picture like a director is. So I don't know that we got it. We just said, 'Okay cool, tell me what I'm supposed to do and we'll shoot it.' I think when we saw the rough cut of it, that was the first time we went, 'Oh. Oh, okay. There is none of that daylight stuff there.'"

Andrew Laszlo insisted that some of the new inserts occurred simply because filming was one day halted by a torrential downpour and, to fill the time, Hill wrote and quickly shot some interplay wherein Cowboy was deployed to ask first Cochise, then Rembrandt what they knew about Cyrus ("Magic—whole lotta magic" and "He's the one and only" being the respective answers). "I'm in the foreground first on the right-hand side of the screen, then on the left," reflects McKitterick. "Walter put that scene in not only to advance the dialogue, but to establish something about Cowboy's personality. It had to do with Cowboy's good-naturedness and his balance... I was shedding light on the other characters basically...The only regret I had in seeing that scene is that the focus was so shallow I'm sort of a blur."

Although Cleon's heart-to-heart with his girlfriend was jettisoned, it did appear among the deleted material released as extras on the *Warriors Ultimate Directors' Cut* DVD (2005). However, strangely there are several filmed sections lost to both *The Warriors'* theatrical release and (so far) DVD bonus features, among which number the Brooklyn scene on Mongols turf and the segment wherein Swan nails pieces of paper with his blade.

The latter's omission from the theatrical release could be said to constitute a lack of continuity. As Beck points out, "The reason that Walter wanted to introduce Swan as a guy that was handy with a blade is obviously for the payoff when he throws the switchblade into Luther's arm."

Beck also offers that the daytime cuts lead to it being less clear that the members of the Warriors are part of a much larger gang: "Cleon does say 'Nine guys sent as ambassadors to this thing,' but you've got to really be paying attention and extrapolate from there." Harris cites another continuity problem deriving from the excisions. Referring to the graveyard scene, he observes, "Ajax says, 'I want to be leader. I want to take over,' and then [Swan] says, 'Make a move.' We all stop Ajax [by saying] 'Cleon said, "If anything happens, Swan—second in command."' In the beginning, all that stuff is said in the daytime on the boardwalk. Cleon is telling everybody their place. That stuff never made it into the film… so no one knows how Swan became War Chief."

Lawrence Gordon simply states, "No one ever from the time the movie sneaked to the time it was out at the theatres made a comment that they missed set-up. It was dead weight." "I've never talked to anybody who's said, 'I don't know what's going on,'" agrees Van Valkenburgh.

Thomas Waites opines of the rejigging of the movie, "I think that takes away from the story a little bit." He seems to be in a minority in the cast. Despite his comments above, Beck says, "I certainly agree wholeheartedly with Walter's decision to do it."

Roger Hill's son Chris went on to a career as a film editor. He observes, "Everything that I've ever worked on, they usually reshoot the first few minutes of the film once they've assembled it and they look at it. It's very hard to set a film up. You want to set up your story, set up the world, in just a few minutes. They did that masterfully in *The Warriors*. Just the subway shots and all the gangs getting on the subway and the sort of whisper chain of people talking about what they were about to go see. By the time you get to the speech, you know the world you're in, you have fully set the stage."

For some, the cuts Hill made to the front end of the narrative had a culturally agreeable upshot: it so happens that in the final edit the first face on screen is a black one. Cleon can be seen telling his comrades, "It's still on, and we're going. Cyrus sent an emissary this afternoon to make sure…"

The changes also had another accidental effect, this one conceptually beneficial. The script had the gang arriving at the conclave without having yet been shown on trains. This would surely have constituted a considerable thematic mistake for a movie predicated on the salvation proffered by New York's subway system.

Unfortunately such luck seems to have been the exception, not the rule, with *The Warriors*.

MAN DOWN

THERE MAY BE ANOTHER reason why Walter Hill did not give Sol Yurick the level of considerateness the latter felt he deserved. Thomas Waites recalls the conclave shoot as a "very high-pressure situation." He is not only talking about the logistics involved.

Waites explains of the first non-logistic issue, "The executives from the studio started flying out to find out why we were over budget and behind schedule." *The Warriors* was Hill's first experience of either living or working in the Big Apple, and it showed. "Frank and I didn't realize how short the work day was going to be," reflects Hill. "I'm usually quite a fast shooter... We were used to California: you work twelve, thirteen hours a day making a film. So much of our film—probably 95% of it—was outside and we were shooting in the summer." Not only did the Big Apple sun go down late and come up early, but the contract-stipulated crew lunch hour ate into the precious few hours of darkness. Moreover, there was a dispersal problem. Hill: "The New York contract in those days, you broke an hour for lunch and the crew would go off to nearby places and buy their own lunch. In other words, the catered lunch that is usual in Hollywood wasn't a mandatory part of the contract." This was not the end of the scheduling issues. "We had young actors that were not used to working and we had some very tough locations. And we also got run off of a lot of locations where we had to scramble around, find another one. Also, we lucked into the rainiest summer in New York in fifty years or some goddamn thing." Michos also feels that the production team didn't take into account the "logistics of navigating" a "more compact and busy" city. Hill says the upshot of all this was, "We were only getting about a half a day of work done off what [we] estimated we were going to be able to do in a day."

"There was a lot of friction with the studio back in Los Angeles," admits Hill. "Of course, they're more result oriented. They don't care that much about our problems. 'Hey, come on, you guys are over-skedge.' There was a lot of discomfort." "Michael Eisner came to New York," says Lawrence Gordon. "We were at least in the middle of shooting, maybe more. He didn't come for us, he was in New York for business and he came to visit me on the set... He was in my trailer. I said, 'Michael, this is why we're behind. Look at what's going on out here.' People were jeering, all kind of stuff was going on. It was pouring rain." Hill insists, "At the end when all the bills came in, it turned out we hadn't spent nearly as much money as they said we were spending." However, he acknowledges that it was more difficult to adjudge the final tally at the time. "It wasn't so much the budget, it's the schedule. Time is money in the end. They always [said], 'You're three days over, you're five days. When's this gonna end? When are you gonna catch up?'" As the man who would later produce *Waterworld*, Gordon knows something about exceeding assigned finances. "We weren't that much over budget," he says of *The Warriors*. "Not for anybody to get crazy." However, he also says, "You have to understand, Paramount was a very tough studio. You had Barry Diller, Michael Eisner, Don Simpson, Jeff Katzenberg. They were tough. We had no stars in our movie, so they could beat us up. If we'd had Bob Redford in the movie, they would have left us alone, probably. But when a studio can beat you up, they tend to beat you up."

"There were a lot of curveballs thrown our way," muses Frank Marshall. "And that actually made it pretty exciting and interesting for me: how do we solve these problems? That's what I love to do as a producer." It's difficult to imagine that Hill was quite as philosophical as Marshall about the situation, not least after July 28, 1978. On that day—almost precisely a month after the Warriors began shooting—his new movie was released. *The Driver* didn't exactly replicate the box-office success that the Gordon-Hill-Marshall team had achieved with *Hard Times*. The lack of interest from the Stateside public (the only audiences Hollywood deemed to matter at that point in history) was compounded by the disgust of critics, who felt this movie about a getaway driver too clever by half in its showy toying with minimalist, brooding noir conventions (Ryan O'Neal's title character is both unnamed and virtually silent). It is devastating for a filmmaker at the best of times when a project on which he has toiled is an across-the-board failure. Yet the tumult of *The Warriors'* rapid and troubled shoot didn't even grant Hill an opportunity to lick his wounds.

Says Hill of the derision that engulfed him over *The Driver*, "I went to work, and said, 'I'm just going to go ahead and direct the movie. If somebody asks me about it, I'll talk to them.' But I was hoping that the cast didn't lose their faith in me. You're certainly sensitive to these things, but at the same time, everybody's trying to do their job. I remember saying something I think to Frank about it. And Frank said, 'Oh Christ, most of 'em haven't even read the reviews.' It was something I wondered about, but it just didn't turn out to be an issue at all. I would say this: if you are going to be upset about what other people think of your work, if this is traumatizing to you, then this is the wrong profession. I always knew that I was in it for good and you have your high moments, you have some low moments." Gordon: "We weren't happy about it, but we're professionals so you just got to keep going. You don't stop." Hill adds, "The odd thing about *The Driver* is that now whenever it seems to come up it's usually presented to me in a positive way. The years have been kind to it." Back in '78, however, that critical reappraisal was in an unimaginable future and Hill admits he was left wondering whether the film's reception heralded the end of his career. "I was thinking, 'It's a good thing I'm shooting something right now, because I still got a shot here.'"

Remarkably, everyone questioned about Hill's demeanor during the *Warriors* shoot testifies to a preternatural calm. David Harris represents the consensus when he says, "I never, ever saw Walter down or frowning or look like something is really bothering him." McKitterick says, "I could tell he was under a tremendous amount of stress, but he [is a] remarkable person. Really, really remarkable and I don't think anybody other than Thomas Waites had any problems with him."

McKitterick's comment unwittingly serves to raise the issue of whether there is a link between Hill's disappointment about *The Driver*'s reception and Waites' fate. It was during the "very high-pressure situation" of the shooting of the conclave that Waites chose, of all times, to give Hill another headache by remonstrating with him about what he was filming.

As previously mentioned, Waites had already made his presence known on the *Warriors* set in ways not designed to endear him to producers of a project whose budget was at stretching point from the very start. While the trailer intervention was reasonable enough, the same cannot really be said for other gripes that Waites articulated. "He was complaining about a lot of things," Terry Michos recalls. Says Frank Marshall, "He was kind of full of himself and asking for close-ups and things like that." In the midst of the chaos of the conclave shoot, Waites himself says he began "bitching and moaning" about misgivings he had about the way the movie was developing. "I was like, 'There's too much violence,' and 'This isn't the movie that we agreed to make.'" Whereas several of his colleagues had come to the conclusion that the film was more cartoon than cruel, Waites was unsettled by the feeling that Hill was constructing something exploitatively brutal. "I guess I didn't realize that the violence was as graphic," he says. "It was clearly my mistake... I did read the script and I did work on the script with him, but as an idealizing young man I was hoping that it would be more romantic than violent." As far as Waites was concerned, he had signed up for a love story, specifically that between the Fox and Mercy. "We ended up going off together. Our whole mentality was, 'This violence is wrong and there's gotta be another way to live.' The implication was that our love would be a much healthier alternative than what we were experiencing and what we were involved in. It happened very shortly after we picked her up and we started to almost separate from the rest of the group... It changed significantly to my mind... It was just one violent episode after another." He accepts that this was not an alteration down to rewrites. "It would be more stylistically." He states, "I myself don't believe in violence. I wish there were no such thing as war and the violence we have in our country and our culture is horrible, it's abhorrent."

Waites' heightened queasiness about violence seems to stem from his tough upbringing in Levittown, a Pennsylvanian working-class neighborhood where kudos was obtained by hurting people. "If you went to that part of the world at this particular moment in time, you would want to get out as quickly as you got in," he reflects. "I was running with a bad [crew]. It was called the Bristol Terrace Gang... I became a good fighter for a little guy. Nose broken three times. Teeth chipped. In fact, Paramount had to fix my teeth for *The Warriors*." "I really hurt a guy one night," Waites recalled to the *Village Voice*'s Jackson Connor in 2015. "I picked this guy up and threw him down and heard this girl say, 'He's really tough!' That went right to my suffering, depleted ego. I thought, 'That's what I'm going to be. That's what I'm going to do well: fuck people up.'"

Finding a different kind of validation in high-school drama class saved Waites from that fate. "I knew in the back of my mind, 'I have got to find a way out of here,'" he says. "I thought it was going to be sports, but I got into a serious car accident." His injuries might have ruled out a sports career but opened the door to another. "I got addicted to Demerol. I had very severe pain in the beginning. But what I did as the weeks went by is I would pull the emergency cord for the nurse to come and give me a shot of Demerol and I would act like I was in pain. So the doctor came in the next day and he's like, 'He shouldn't be getting this much Demerol. What's going on?' And then they both looked at me and the nurse went, 'You want to be an actor' and a light went off over my head. For the first time in my life I started to perceive reality differently than fighting in the streets...

"On the crutches going from sophomore year to junior year, I was like, 'Well, how am I going to pick up chicks if I can't fight or play sports?' I saw everyone going to the drama club and I went, 'Well, let me try that.' So I auditioned for a play called *Don't Drink The Water* by Woody Allen. I played the Russian KGB agent. Then I auditioned for the musical *Cabaret*, and got Joel Grey, the MC. And then I did another play after that. Then I auditioned for Juilliard."

His tryout for entry to New York City's famous performing arts conservatory was greatly assisted by the fact that Waites had been mesmerized when he took in a screening of Franco Zeffirelli's permissive-era interpretation of *Romeo and Juliet* (1968). "I memorized the entire balcony scene, both characters. That was what I used to audition for Juilliard."

When it came to the *Warriors* trailer dispute, Waites says, "I went through the proper channels. I went to the second AD [assistant director], who went to the first AD." He accepts that his complaints about the tone of the film were not similarly done by the book. "I should have gone home, called my agent and said, 'Listen, you got to call them and tell them this isn't the movie that Walter and I agreed to make,'" he says. "Instead of doing that, I just kept bothering him." Waites feels that his unhelpful behavior in the already fraught atmosphere of the conclave shoot was the tipping point in Hill's patience with him. "I gave the director a hard time and after about six or seven weeks he said, 'That's enough'... Not that Walter isn't a good guy or even an amenable director to actors' ideas, but I just picked the absolute worst moment to approach the guy... To have this actor going up to you before every take and, 'Well, wait a minute, what about this?' and 'What about that?' I think that night have been the moment, but I can't be certain."

Firing Waites was not a simple proposition. It first had to be cleared with Paramount. Telling a studio-financier that a production that is nearly two months into filming and which is well behind schedule proposes to jettison its leading man was, as Hill observes, "a difficult moment." "It was a real test of a producer and Larry was up to it," he says. He explains, "I always liked Larry to do all the interfacing with the studio because I knew that I wasn't going to say the right thing." Another reason for Hill's reticence is that he and Paramount president Michael Eisner were not exactly bosom buddies. "Walter never liked him," says Gordon. "There were a couple of things that happened, which I won't go into. It didn't involve *The Warriors*, it involved other movies. Walter did not like what Michael had to say. They didn't fight or anything. He didn't like his notes." As for himself, Gordon says that he was "very good friends" with Eisner and adds, "I was also very friendly with Don Simpson." If it wasn't for these good relations, he admits that the task with which he was faced "would have been harder."

Of the bombshell proposition he lobbed Paramount's way, Gordon notes, "They could have said, 'Absolutely not.' I didn't have the right to spend their money." He found, though, that the studio understood his predicament. "It took some discussion. It wasn't like, 'I'm gonna fire Thomas Waites, goodbye.' I believe Michael and Simpson were on the phone and we discussed it and we explained what we were going to do... They already knew we were having problems... They thought it was very interesting that we could be able to do that. They wanted to be assured we could pull it off, which they were."

"I fired him," Gordon says. "It's something we agreed had to be done for the good of the movie and we worked out how to do it and we did it." Hill, though, is somewhat less matter of fact about the turn of events. "That's a painful subject," he says. "I don't think I was getting through to him. I think we weren't communicating with him very well and his performance was suffering and I thought it might be better for the film if we ended it in some hopefully graceful way. I felt badly about it then, I feel badly about it now. I'm sure it was a real blow to Tom and his career and was not a happy moment for me." The director echoes Gordon's overarching point, though, when he concludes, "But I think it was the right thing for the film."

A message was received by Waites' agent Jeff Hunter one Saturday afternoon. It was then promptly relayed to the actor. Says Waites, "Never forget it as long as I live: 'They don't want you back.' I said, 'What? Where?' He said, 'On the set of the film. They don't want you back'... I couldn't have been more shocked. I was stunned. Nobody gave me a warning, no one called my agent. It was a bolt from the blue. It was like, '*Wha-a-at?*'"

"That's what happens when you start getting high on yourself," says Dorsey Wright of the departure of his colleague. However, Wright does admit that he was shocked when he heard that Waites had been dismissed. "Because he was great to talk to, because he had a lot of knowl-edge. He knew what he was doing. He understood his craft." Some, like Michos, have attributed Waites' assertiveness to his greater experience compared to most of the rest of the cast. However, it's interesting to note that although Waites and Wright were at pretty much identical stages in their respective careers—both had made a movie before and both would shortly make another—their attitudes were diametrically opposed. "My thing with directors, and even to the lighting man, is, 'Find out what they need, go and do it, and get out of the way,'" says Wright. "I learned that from *Hair*. Miloš Forman taught me a lot. I didn't know what a mark was, I knew nothing. By the time I came to *The Warriors*, I was a seasoned pro on hit your mark, know your damn lines, get out of the way. Some people fall into that I'm-a-star routine and it's like, "Scuse me, if we're digging ditches, are you the best ditch digger? We're making a *movie*. There are a lot of people in this movie. Stop rocking the boat. That means nothing off set.' I looked at it as a job. Some people look at it as, 'I'm special.' Special what? You're a person that can remember some lines and you can emote. Don't get it twisted. The director and everybody else has other things on their mind… You could blow a million dollars for that one day, just doing some dumb shit or catching an attitude… That precedes you to the next film. They'll know, 'Oh, he's a prima donna.'"

All surely reasonable (even if it has to be said that Wright is, par-adoxically, self-aggrandizing in his humility). Yet Hill actually dissents from what is otherwise the consensus that Waites' bumptiousness was the major problem. While he concedes, "There was some of that horseshit," he insists his major issue was, "It just wasn't happening on screen." He elaborates, "One of the things that drives you crazy is he came in, he read beautifully, and then when we went to make the movie it just wasn't there anymore."

Waites seems shocked to hear this. "That upsets me terribly, because I'm not doing my job," the actor says. "I just wish he told me… If I wasn't delivering the kind of performance he wanted, I wish he would have spo-ken to me and I would have tried to improve it. I would have fought like hell to keep my job."

Although Gordon says of Waites, "His performance was not that good because he wasn't happy," he also reveals, "We had another problem, too. His agent would not give us an option on him. We had options on everybody else and I kept negotiating with the agent and he kept say-ing, 'You're not going to get an option.' So besides having issues, we also couldn't close the deal. It wasn't as much of a concern for Walter as it was for me, but he knew about it. He knew that was part of our decision." However, this wasn't a dealbreaker. Gordon: "If Walter had been thrilled with his performance, we wouldn't have replaced him."

Hill adds, "Also I think he was not in good shape, shall we say? Emotionally or maybe physically." Those who detect an insinuation of intoxicant use might not be too far off the mark. Waites does say, "There were drugs in the equation, but who was doing them and when they were doing them didn't have anything to do with my interactions with Walter... Did I do coke a few nights? Yeah, I did. So did a lot of people." However, he lays the blame in a similar area. "I was born an alcoholic... They were going to kick me out of Juilliard too because of my behavior. When you're an alcoholic, you don't have to be drinking for your behavior to be noticeable to other people. You become difficult. You become grandiose. You become incommunicative. You become irascible and unpleasant... I was never drinking on the set, ever. But I'm sure I drank the night before. I could have. And I'm sure that my behavior was affected by my drinking."

Some might suspect that Hill's behavior—his drastic reaction to the Waites issue—was affected by that derisive reception to his new film. Can the director say with his hand on his heart that, if it were not for the trauma he was going through because of *The Driver*'s failure, he would have taken the extreme step he did? "Oh, I can say that. It had nothing to do with *The Driver* and the reception of *The Driver*. I don't think there's one goddamn thing in the movie that has anything to do with the reception of *The Driver*." Hill does say, though, "Maybe it represents a failure on my part that I wasn't able to get through to him better. If [I] were Elia Kazan I'd have probably gone over and lived in his apartment and become part of his life and gotten through to him somehow. I'm not like that."

As well as suffering the trauma of losing a huge career break, there was personal anguish for Waites analogous to that experienced by a pupil expelled from school. "I loved those people," he says. "I felt like my family had been ripped away from me." In the midst of his shock and upset, however, there was a glimmer of comfort in the form of the sensitivity Hill showed him. "I called Walter at his hotel," Waites remembers. Although he asserts that the director didn't take responsibility for events ("He made it sound like Paramount wanted me gone"), Waites does give Hill immense credit for being willing to speak to him at all. "Being a gentleman, he took the call. A lot of guys in that position would just be like, 'Well look, he knows he's fired, what's he need me for?' He said, 'You alright?' I said, 'Yeah, I'm really upset.' He said, 'Well, that's the way it is and just hold onto yourself'... He just was a man about it."

Yet neither that small kindness nor the fact of landing some good roles subsequently prevented Waites going into a personal freefall. "Mostly I just wept," he says. "Mostly I just was full of remorse. I wish I'd gotten sober then. That would have been a good decision, but I didn't. That certainly gave me a good excuse to go to the bar and cry on the bartender shoulder... I immediately went into psychotherapy. I joined a karate class that I stayed in for ten years to work on my discipline. I was broken."

Beck had been cringingly watching Waites' unraveling relationship with Hill and Gordon during the shoot. "You would had to have been not having your eyes open to see early on in the picture that there was a lot of tension there," he says. "You just kind of go, 'Oh man, don't do that, you're going to get these people really pissed off at you'... He made it really difficult for them. Trust me on that... So it didn't come as a complete surprise that there was a reaction. I think we were all taken aback that it was as severe as it was."

As to the way the news was broken, he recalls, "We got called to a little meeting out in the middle of the set. Walter Hill and Larry Gordon and Frank Marshall were there and they said, 'This is what's happened. Tom Waites has been removed from the movie and Swan is going to go in this direction with Mercy.' They just went through the whole thing and left us to deal with it."

It was at this point that Hill's stratagem of awarding roles in *The Warriors* on the basis of which actors were liable to bond like a real gang briefly looked like backfiring. The all-for-one ethos by which the thespians had indeed become suffused prompted an eruption of defiance. "We all took a personal offence because, 'Hey, you can't get rid of one of us,'" Beck recalls. "That was the initial reaction. We all went back to the motor home and sat and talked about it and got pissed off." The defiance, however, died down almost as quickly as it had flared. Explains Beck, "The general consensus was that there's not really anything we can do about it. We'd better just move on and try to make this movie work."

THAT HILL TOOK the time to take Waites' bewildered call is all the more remarkable considering the extra workload and stress the director had piled on his own shoulders by firing the actor. "I've been doing this a long, long time," reflects Gordon. "Walter and I did seven movies together. We've never written anybody out of a movie in the middle of shooting. That's almost unheard of. In fact, I don't even know if anybody's ever done it."

The reasons why are obvious. If the actor is present in a good deal of shot footage, junking the existing scenes is prohibitively expensive in terms of both wasted material and potential reshoots. It is also aesthetically and practicably problematic: audiences will wonder why on earth a character has suddenly disappeared from the narrative. These problems are of course made all the worse if a picture is both low-budget and over-budget. That Gordon and Hill had felt compelled to jettison Waites despite being cognizant of all this is perhaps a measure of just how difficult they had found him to be. Hill acknowledges that if it hadn't been for the fact that the picture had been shot unusually sequentially, Waites' firing wouldn't even have been a feasible option.

The director now had the task of providing a rationale for the Warriors leader to no longer be visible. It was decided to exploit the strand of the plot that showed the police on the lookout for the Warriors: Fox would fall to his death beneath a subway train while grappling with one of the boys in blue. "I came up with that," says Craig Baxley. "One day Walter just said, 'I'm going to kill him.' I thought he was physically saying I'm going to kill him. He said, 'No, I got to kill him in the movie. I don't want him in this movie anymore. Come up with something.' It was a very easy thing to do. Sonny Landham was an extra at the time. I kicked him out of the extras and made him a cop." A camera assistant who resembled Waites from behind was called into supplementary service. Baxley: "Basically I had no stuntmen and this guy had a red natural. I said, 'Have you ever done a stunt before?' and he said, 'No.' I said, 'Here's what I want to do. I want to turn the third rail off. This policeman, I'm going to throw a bat at this guy. Another policeman's gonna grab you and throw you off. And I'm going to put a big catcher down there, a big pad. You could fall twenty feet into it. You're only going to drop three feet.' He said, 'I'm fine with that.' We got him in the clothes and we threw him off into this pad, and then we took the pad out of there. Blocked the camera off when we did the stunt and then let the car come through and we just jump-cut it." "

"It looked terrible," asserts Waites. "Nothing against the guy that did it. But an actor acts with his whole body." Not only does Waites feel there was a certain lifelessness about the individual in question even before the wheels of the train notionally hit him, he also claims, "You can see the pad that the guy landed on." Waites adds, "I kind of wished that they would have said to me, 'Okay look, this isn't going to work out with you. Would you do your death scene?'" However, he does admit, "I was such a conceited little prick I probably would have said no."

Regardless of any deficiencies in technique, the insertion into the narrative of Fox's death doesn't come across as particularly contrived. However, neither does it have any special poignancy, even though presented in slow motion. As nobody witnesses it—Mercy makes a run for it as Fox is rolling over the ground with the cop—there are no cutaways to shocked comrades' faces, while the post-mortem about it amounts to Swan asking Mercy, "Where's the Fox?" and receiving the reply, "A cop grabbed him." Even if Mercy's next line—"He didn't have a chance"—had not been cut, it wouldn't have much redeemed the inquest's sheer lack of pathos. Offers Michos, "There must have been some subliminal, 'I'm done with this guy.'"

Solving the problem of how to lose the Fox didn't mark the end of Hill's problems but created new ones. Filming the death scene turned out to incapacitate Van Valkenburgh. Explains the actress of the crew member who from a certain angle resembled Waites, "We had to do a shot of us running down the platform of the subway station. He was a sweetheart, but he was a camera assistant and shy and we tripped up. I fell down and landed on my right wrist and fractured it and was hauled off to the hospital and put into a cast [up to my] armpit and was not even able to work for a month." "So we really had to rewrite things," observes Marshall.

Even before Van Valkenburgh's misfortune, though, devising Fox's death scene was only the beginning of the changes to the narrative now required. Asked if the production lost any days of shooting to accommodate rewriting, Hill laughs. "No. Didn't have 'em to lose. Did not have them to lose." He elucidates, "I'd rewrite in the hotel during the day. We'd shoot all night and then I'd sleep and then I'd write a while and I'd write on the weekends. It was hectic." He adds, "The film I think has its merits and everything, but I'm in a lot of ways glad I don't have to make it again."

Tom McKitterick has a recollection of Hill's mooted solution to the significant structural problems facing him that seems quite bizarre. Says the Cowboy actor, "Walter brought me into the trailer and said, 'How about if you get Mercy?'" McKitterick's ultimate response seems in its own way no less bizarre. Although he had found his character to be rather sketchy, his confidence had been bolstered by a sequence that enabled him to give Cowboy some substance. "There was a scene between Swan and me and Vermin where I had a big close-up. Basically, Swan was speaking to us about tactics and Vermin was being challenging. I had no lines in it.

I just looked at Swan and I turned slowly and looked at Vermin and then I looked back at Swan and my only inner dialogue is, 'He's the man—Vermin.' That's I think what my character was: it's some type of balance... Walter had told me not to move my head so fast, move slower, 'This is not the stage,' and the things that he told me I did. If you're getting a tight close-up like that, don't blink, just look, and act the thoughts inside you... The next day, Andrew [Laszlo] and everybody said, 'Phenomenal. That was great.'" The scene never made it to the final cut, but it left McKitterick feeling of Hill's proposed change, "I knew I could do it."

However, at the same time he was befuddled by Hill's suggestion. He recalls, "It was terribly confusing. I was like, 'Why me? This doesn't make any sense'... I hadn't played the scenes like I wanted her. I just assumed that she was gonna go with the head of the gang." When asked what response he verbally articulated to Hill, McKitterick responds, "I don't remember saying much. I said, 'Yeah, I guess so.'" In retrospect, he says that he should have asked for a drink and to see some "dailies," industry parlance for the footage of each day's shooting (UK equivalent: "rushes").

For his part, Hill seems bewildered by McKitterick's recollection. "It may have been he misunderstood my remarks or something," says Hill. "I cannot imagine any such moment. He seems to be positing the idea that I was insane. I don't know—I certainly have no memory of this."

McKitterick adds of Hill, "Right before the scene with the Furies— the big chase—that evening he said he'd have to let me go. I don't know how that stood in relationship to when he offered me the role of the romantic lead. I think the firing came first. It [was] all to do with Thomas being fired and how to tell the story. No reason was given and I didn't really ask. I was crushed, of course. But I felt, 'Well, this is the movies.' I could tell that he was scrambling to try to reshape the movie. I had an understanding that he was improvising a script. Every day practically we shot it was transforming itself and I was very sympathetic with what he was doing. I knew he was an artist. I guess I knew that the studio was pressuring it." He recalls that his disappointment didn't last long: his firing was reversed as swiftly and mysteriously as it had been enacted. "I was hired again by the end of the evening," he says. "When I was reengaged I said, 'Whoof.'" Again, the director's recollection is diametrically opposed to McKitterick's. "I have no memory of firing him." Moreover, Hill can't imagine why he would in the circumstances. "[It] was amazing that we got away with the Tom Waites situation, but the continuity situation..."

Told of McKitterick's recollection of Hill making an overture to become his leading man, Michael Beck makes a sound of amusement. "I've never heard that until now," he says. "Can you imagine? On the night that Larry Gordon and Walter Hill told us [that Waites had been fired], Larry in the same breath said that the new storyline was with Swan and Mercy." McKitterick concedes that the way Hill ultimately did decide to solve his narrative problems with the Swan and Mercy through-line seems in retrospect "a no-brainer."

It was no-brainer, though, that may have made Hill feel he was chasing his own tail. After all the work done in transferring much of Hinton's dialogue and action to the Fox, he was now compelled to undo it all. Hinton's successor Swan now became a much more central character, being given the keynote scenes with Mercy in the tunnel and on the subway train when the prom couples appear.

Although in the finished film, Mercy is treated more roughly by the Warriors than in the script, unlike in the script she goes with them willingly, not as a hostage. The rejigging of scenes meant that she and Swan end up in the tunnel when a cop spots them at 96th St Station after Swan makes his way there from the park where the honeytrap cop was situated and she follows him.

Despite the change in the person to whom she is addressing it, Mercy's live-for-today speech remains pretty much the same. Stating that sometimes she remembers who she "gets" on Friday and Saturday nights, sometimes not, she snarls, "I want something now. This is the life I got left." Despite the defiance of the peroration, many will find it sad. Did Van Valkenburgh view her character as a tragic person? "I don't think I was going that route," she reasons. "I personally like to try and embrace the qualities that fortify the person that I'm trying to play. If you start judging them, then you're distancing yourself. You can't really be inside the person [if] you're going to have some sort of attitude about them that would come from a third-party place. Somebody else might look at her and go, 'Oh, she's a tart, she's a whore, she's this or that,' but I could justify—and that speech helped—where she's coming from. If you're living that kind of a life and you're kind of on the edge, it's hard to have romantic fantasies about what life's going to be like five years from then. And I think that also her way of connecting intimately with people was on this physical plane. I think she wasn't totally connecting to the emotional life the way we might think about doing that today: just putting something a little richer, a little more meaningful into our emotions. It's just a wariness about how much vulnerability you're going to exhibit around the people you hang with, so her way of getting close was in the physical expression. A lot of people are like that. So I needed to be gentle about that. In the tunnel, there was that one moment where he walks away from her after the big kiss and I think that's like one moment of vulnerability that slipped out for one second. But you got to keep your guard up or people will take you down."

The kiss between Mercy and Swan directly following her speech was photogenically shot against a passing train. Today, the shot could be convincingly simulated with nothing but computer graphics, but in the late Seventies it involved something close to a military operation, with crew issuing instructions into walkie-talkies in order to coordinate the passing train and the coalescing sets of lips. Meanwhile, the ever-inventive Laszlo had another idea. Noticing how in these dim conditions light could be seen flashing off the city's new-style aluminum subway cars, he decided to capture the unusual effect. Illumination was shone into the tunnel at an angle so that it would reflect back into the camera. "I was fascinated with how they timed that out," says Van Valkenburgh. "It was the express train from the Kennedy Airport into the city, so it was a very particular train. I was so busy trying to make sure I knew what I was doing and not screwing up our end of the deal that I wasn't absorbing all the technical details, so I didn't ask a lot of questions. It constantly thrilled me how meticulous they were about setting us up so we were right there when the train goes by. There's so much stuff that they do 'post-' these days, all that digital magic, that it's lovely to see anything that really happened in the moment that wasn't fucked with, that was real."

Filming in pitch-black conditions with a train thundering by mere yards away must presumably be an unnerving experience but Van Valkenburgh says, "I don't remember being frightened at all… I wonder why I wasn't… I guess I really trusted that everybody had figured out what they were doing. We were all set up in that one tunnel, so either it was a tunnel that wasn't being used or we were all crazy. And the other train, it was different track and it was divided by a lot of whatever the intense architectural structure is under there—all the giant pillars and things that support the system—so it was on the other side. And we're young, we're making a movie. All of it becomes weirdly thrilling. It was just one of those mad adventures."

Some seem to feel that the tableaux of two faces kissing in the gloom as a train thunders and glimmers by would not have been nearly as evocative if Waites had been one of the participants. There has, in fact, been some suggestion that the Fox-Mercy love scenes being transferred to Swan and Mercy was not the consequence of Waites' firing but the very cause of it. Marshall says of the dailies prior to Waites' dismissal, "The main thing was on the screen. Swan was just popping every day and you say to yourself, 'Well, why wouldn't Mercy want to be with Swan? He's the most charismatic of the Warriors.' So we rewrote the script and wrote him out of the rest of the movie." "I don't remember it that way," says Waites. "I don't remember it having anything to do with chemistry and I remember it having everything to do with my being a pain in the ass. I certainly felt that I had chemistry. I felt very attracted to her as a man. I'm sure that that translated to a certain extent." "I don't know that's fair," Hill says regarding the alleged lack of chemistry between Van Valkenburgh and Waites. "We really didn't shoot the scenes between them. We really hadn't gotten into it. It wasn't like we shot the scenes between Thomas and Deborah and then found them insufficient and therefore had to make certain decisions. These decisions were made before those scenes were shot. As to whether or not they were getting along professionally behind the scenes I really couldn't say. I did feel that Tom was putting himself in a position that he didn't seem to be relating to *anybody* in the cast."

Regardless of how much Waites' dismissal was related to his lack of chemistry with the leading lady, David Harris never felt it made much sense for Waites—all curly red hair and sometimes hangdog face—to have the movie's starring role. "He's a wonderful character kind of actor, but he's not Tom Cruise, he's not Brad Pitt," he says. "Michael Beck is Tom Cruise forty years ago. He had that whole Hollywood look."

Beck offers, "We had already played the scene where Mercy has the confrontation with us with the Orphans and then follows us and I reach down and tear off her skirt and make a wick for the thing, and even in that little scene there was some sexual tension going on between Deborah and I." Not that it was going on in real life. Beck: "I made a habit early on in my acting career not to have flings with my leading ladies. It just always seemed like it was asking for trouble." He does add of him and Van Valkenburgh, "We became lifelong friends." He also notes, "Walter said to me—I don't know whether it was so much a justification—'I feel good about this change because I can already see on what we shot there's a lot of chemistry between you and Deborah, so this makes sense.' They already had in dailies things that showed them that it was going to work to go down this road. When you're making a movie, some of that stuff is just organic." Van Valkenburgh: "It turned out to be a very tumultuous shift… They realized that Michael and I just naturally had a chemistry on screen so there wasn't a problem switching my romantic loyalties to another member of the gang. Initially our two characters weren't connected at all. His character was actually supposed to go off and have this treacherous adventure with another gang that isn't even in the movie anymore. The whole movie had some other stuff going on that just evaporated into thin air."

Indeed. "It was very hard to keep track of the script," says McKitterick, "because every day we would be given new pages which were in a different color—pink, yellow, orange—and you inserted those into the script. The original script which we had been presented at the top of the shooting was, forget about it." As Swan now had so much new action, it seems logical that it was concluded that it would be difficult to include the Dingos scenes without unbalancing or even making a nonsense of the narrative. McKitterick certainly thinks so, saying, "You couldn't tell the story that way."

Walter Hill demurs. "I think what we really lost scenes about was the fact we were overschedule," he says, and includes the passages involving the Dingos in this reasoning. "We never got a chance to shoot it," he says of the gay-gang scenes. "It was money. It was perceived to be an expensive scene. To have shot it we needed not only the scene itself, but we needed the capture scene and the rejoining scene and things like that. So it was a big economic chunk, and the story made sense without it."

Either way, Beck notes, "The Dingos were sent home and I'm sure they were not happy." McKitterick can confirm that. "My friend John Snyder had originally been assigned the role of the head of the gang who captured Swan," he says. "John was so looking forward to that role." Another actor scheduled to be a Dingo probably got over his setback: his name was Kevin Bacon.

The only reason one doesn't automatically accept as gospel Hill's explanation for the jettisoning of the Dingos scenes is that he has no recollection of the presence in the script of another dropped passage, namely the shoot-out with the penny-arcade sheriff at Union Square Station. Yurick was always convinced this scene was shot, citing the presence of the cowboy mannequin in the background of a solitary frame of the movie. However, Marshall says, "I don't remember it at all, so I know it wasn't filmed." "It was never shot," Beck backs up Marshall. A potential explanation for its absence is that if the scene became yet another tableau inherited by Swan from Fox, it would make the former just a little too prominent in the proceedings. Beck offers his own rationale: "Probably Swan, the stoic that he was, would not have been a character to have put a dime in the slot." A simpler possible explanation is, once again, the cost and time factor.

Whatever the reason, for Yurick, the omission of this scene was symptomatic of his unhappiness with the film's interpretation of his source material. "I saw all kinds of little lapses and things like that," he said, one example of which being that he hadn't chosen to set the book's proceedings on the Fourth of July for no reason but that the film had jettisoned that timeframe. He stated the value of the duel to be, "a commentary on the confrontation between law and order, even in its game form. How you lose."

AT THE OUTSET of shooting, Vermin was intended to be shot dead by the Lizzies and Cochise to be fatally dumped by the Baseball Furies in the Hudson River, albeit offscreen. In the released film, both characters make it back to Coney Island. Amusingly, both actors think it was their own brilliance that secured their respective characters a reprieve.

"I think Walter liked what I was doing, this character was so appealing," reasons David Harris. "You don't want to get rid of Cochise. Cochise has got to make it back to Coney Island. He was just so—this is my opinion—electrifying. Had a great look. I think what I did with the character was really good." Terry Michos feels his colleague's salvation was down to a different reason: "Paramount kept saying, 'This is too violent.' Cochise got killed when they threw him in the river and they said, 'No way this is going to happen.' The whole film got toned down." Of Vermin's salvation, meanwhile, Michos offers, "I changed my character to be comedic, and it really ran through the whole film. Every time I go to one of these conventions and it's a question-and-answer, people always say, 'You're the funny guy, I related to you.' Michael will always say, David will always say, 'Terry is the comic relief in a somewhat violent film.' I think that's one of the reasons I stayed on, because I made a switch in the character."

Neither Gordon nor Hill recall any edict being relayed from Paramount about limiting the casualties. "I was in constant fighting with the studio about the budget, but as far as creative is concerned, they didn't pay that much attention to the movie," says Gordon. "Maybe I just had grown dissatisfied with that idea," Hill says of the two characters' deaths. "The script was always being worked on to some degree." Could it be the case that, having got rid of Fox, he just felt he needed to keep the numbers of the gang up? "Yeah, that may well have been." As to the theory on the parts of both Michos and Harris that they stayed in the picture because of the quality of their performances, Hill says, "Well, that's fair enough. Obviously, I did feel they were good enough to keep 'em in the movie."

As with the jettisoning of the early daytime scenes, it's remarkable how the narrative of *The Warriors* emerged unscathed from all the rejigging and rewriting caused by Waites' firing. Just about the only discernible casualty is the rationale for the Rogues' pursuit of the Warriors. As the only witness in the Warriors' ranks to Luther's crime is now deceased, there seems no reason for Luther's crew to follow them to Coney Island. The Rogues might be suspicious that Fox had told the others, but this is not stated. Moreover, dialogue citing that Fox witnessed the slaying was dropped.

When it comes to the biggest plot change—the loss of Fox—the $64,000 dollar question is: did it have an artistically enhancing, damaging, or neutral effect? "It strengthened the movie," avers Gordon. Hill is more ambivalent. "I think it strengthened the movie in the sense that the guy that Beck played was a more logical leader and had a stronger core about him," he says. However, he adds, "The scenes between Deborah's character with Beck that had been Tom, I'm not sure they were better. They had to be rewritten in a way that was more succinct and a little more elemental, but you can't compare something that is with something that might have been. Might-have-been always wins." He further adds, though, "I was very happy with the way it worked out."

"Who knows?" says Beck. "It certainly was a different movie in the script than what turned out, but you sometimes have to look at things and go, 'Maybe that was the way this thing was supposed to work out,' because this movie to me is quite phenomenal. None of us knew anything at that point anyway, and nobody ever knows that they're making a movie that's going to become a cult classic. Would it have had the same impact had it been the movie that was in the script? Those are unanswerable questions."

Not for Waites. "I think it weakened it," he says. Asserting that the shooting script was "much more interesting," he reasons, "You can tell, I'm sure, by speaking to me that I have a certain facility for expressing myself, or language to some extent. If you could exploit that and make that be the hero—that the intelligence or the Shakespeare in the story wins—I think that's a far stronger, more interesting message than the young, good-looking, Aryan god with the knife in his hand... I think

Sol Yurick's 1965 novel *The Warriors* provided the source material for the film of the same name but was markedly different to it in tone and structure.

David Shaber, whose first draft film-script adaptation of *The Warriors* contained several of the iconic scenes for which the movie is revered.
(Courtesy of Sam Shaber)

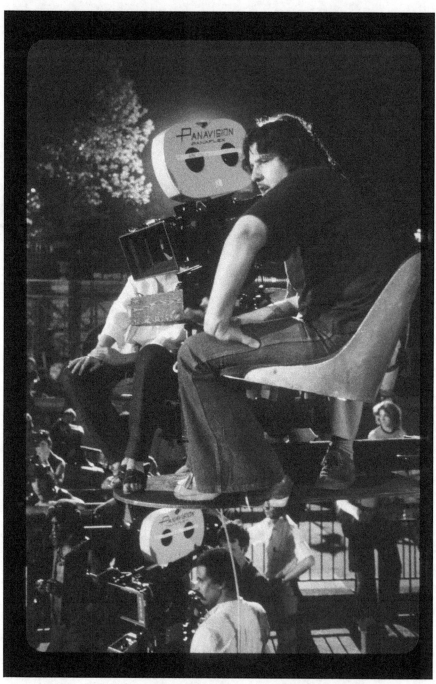

Walter Hill, who—post-Shaber—fulfilled on *The Warriors* the hyphenate role of writer-director. © Paramount Pictures Corp. All Rights Reserved.

Hill shows Lisa Maurer—an actress playing a member of the all-female gang the Lizzies—how to waste a Warrior. © Paramount Pictures Corp. All Rights Reserved.

Hill and Michael Beck (Swan) rehearsing the film's famous rumble with the Baseball Furies. In the middle stands Andrew Laszlo, the production's influential cinematographer. © Paramount Pictures Corp. All Rights Reserved.

The Furies fight is clearly getting to an exhausted Beck.

Hill directing on a platform of the New-York subway system that would be such a central component of the Warriors narrative.

Hill discusses a scene with Marcelino Sánchez (Rembrandt) and David Harris (Cochise). © Paramount Pictures Corp. All Rights Reserved.

The Warriors' executive producer Frank Marshall on set. The car on which he sits is the one blown up by the Warriors by means of a Molotov cocktail in an incident that caused much rancor among the cast. (Courtesy of Frank Marshall)

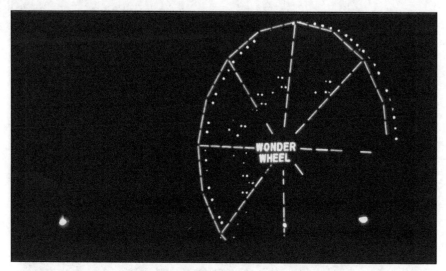

The Wonder Wheel. This fixture of the Coney-Island skyline was used to open *The Warriors*.

An unintended consequence of the decision to cut from the film all its early daytime scenes was that the first face seen on screen was that of Cleon (Dorsey Wright). However, he disappears at the quarter-hour mark.

Roger Hill mesmerizingly played Cyrus. His cry of "Can you dig it?" became one of the film's immortal catchphrases. © Paramount Pictures Corp. All Rights Reserved.

The post-Cleon Warriors as seen in one of Walter Hill's stylized "Mount Rushmore" line-ups. L-R: Snow (Brian Tyler), Ajax (James Remar), Vermin (Terry Michos), Cowboy (Tom McKitterick), Cochise (David Harris), Rembrandt (Marcelino Sánchez), Fox (Thomas G. Waites), and Swan (Michael Beck). © Paramount Pictures Corp. All Rights Reserved.

The memorable kiss between Swan and Mercy in a dark subway tunnel was visually beautiful but its filming had to be planned like a military operation. © Paramount Pictures Corp. All Rights Reserved.

Luther, played by David Patrick Kelly, taunts the Warriors with the phrase "Come out to play!" It provided the second of the picture's endlessly quoted lines. © Paramount Pictures Corp. All Rights Reserved.

Examples of the Rotoscoped transition scenes, designed to resemble comic-book panels, seen in *The Warriors Ultimate Director's Cut*. © Paramount Pictures Corp. All Rights Reserved.

Shooting the "prom couples" scene, in which an ashamed Mercy (Deborah Van Valkenburgh) makes to smarten herself up under the scrutiny of well-to-do fellow train passengers but is stopped by an aggrieved Swan. The iconic passage is suffused with pathos and class-consciousness. © Paramount Pictures Corp. All Rights Reserved.

The "one-sheet" for *The Warriors* (left). Illustrated by David Jarvis, it was chilling and controversial. The poster displayed at UK cinemas (right) seemed designed to appear far less provocative. © Paramount Pictures Corp. All Rights Reserved.

Walter Hill. (Photo by Nicolas Aproux; courtesy of Walter Hill))

Lawrence Gordon, the producer
who came across the Warriors
property on a bookstore spinner.
(Courtesy Lawrence Gordon
Productions)

Frank Marshall, now one of the industry's leading producers. (Courtesy of Frank Marshall)

Craig Baxley was The Warriors' stunt coordinator but feels at times that he was a de facto second unit director on the production. (Courtesy of Craig Baxley)

Bobbie Mannix's colorful costume designs are to a large extent responsible for *The Warriors'* iconic status. (Courtesy of Bobbie Mannix)

Barry DeVorzon provided the picture an innovative and menacing score. (Courtesy of Barry DeVorzon)

Kenny Vance was responsible for the film's additional music. (Courtesy of Kenny Vance)

Michael "Swan" Beck. (Courtesy of Michael Beck)

Thomas G. "Fox" Waites.
(Photo by and courtesy of
Tess Steinkolk)

James "Ajax" Remar.
(Courtesy of Steven Siebert)

Dorsey "Cleon" Wright.
(Courtesy of Terry Michos)

David "Cochise" Harris.
(Courtesy of David
Harris)

Brian "Snow" Tyler.
(Courtesy of Brian Tyler)

Tom "Cowboy" McKitterick.
(Courtesy of Tom
McKitterick)

Terry "Vermin" Michos. (Courtesy of Terry Michos)

Deborah "Mercy" Van Valkenburgh. (Courtesy of Deborah Van Valkenburgh)

David Patrick "Luther" Kelly. (Photo by Zen Lael; courtesy of David Patrick Kelly)

Roger "Cyrus" Hill (1952-2014), with son Chris. (Courtesy of Chris W. Hill)

Marcelino "Rembrandt" Sánchez (1957-86), with sister Mayra.
(Courtesy of Mayra Sánchez)

it was Pauline Kael said the movie becomes much less interesting after Thomas Waites gets killed. I think she's right. As much of a comic book as it is, if you don't care about the main character, you're not going to care about the movie."

Waites is given ammunition for his belief by the loss of Fox's philosophizing when the Warriors arrive back at Coney Island. Some of this material was given to Swan, but some of it was simply jettisoned, including—crucially—Fox's comment to Rembrandt, "Don't let go of your spray can. It's your passport in case you want to get out." The absence of the latter is a particular pity because it was possibly the only moment of real tenderness between any of the endlessly backbiting Warriors. Although Hill's memory is hazy on some things, he has clear recall of why he took this decision, one that goes back to his most fundamental change to David Shaber's template. "The affection between the characters, I liked that idea, but I didn't like the suggestion that there was a middle-class alternative," he says. "I never could find a way to do the line without suggesting that the characters might want to go on and lead bourgeois lives." "I dispute that," says Waites. "I would prefer that, just like I got out of fucking Bristol with Shakespeare, everybody feels like there's a chance. That you're not stuck in this ghetto. There's a way out aside from drugs and fighting. But I'm more reflecting my own personality. It's not my movie… Shit, film is a director's medium."

FOLLOWING THE BAPTISM of fire at the conclave that was his inauguration in the shoot, David Patrick Kelly filmed the scenes in which he and his Rogues colleagues try to facilitate, via the now somewhat primitive-seeming 20th century means of telephone conversations and radio broadcasts, the capture of the Warriors.

It was during this period that the fibs of Joel Weiss, the man playing Luther's lieutenant, caught up with him. It's long been known by actors that if they are asked by a casting director the equivalent of, "Can you ride a horse?" they simply answer in the affirmative and—if it's not true—worry about it after the contract has been signed. It was the job of Weiss' character Cropsey to drive the hearse that constituted (as Kelly has termed it) "the Roguemobile." "He told us he could drive," says Marshall. "The first night he got there, he crashed the car 'cause he didn't have a driver's license." "I remember him struggling a couple times to get it into gear," laughs Kelly. "It was automatic…. I think there were some testy words when he was not quite accurate on the marks when he had to drive up quickly and park. He had to take a couple of swipes on it." Weiss has remembered almost being arrested during the shooting of the candy-store scene because he drove out into open traffic. The testy words, therefore, are understandable: the troubled *Warriors* shoot now had yet another problem to overcome. Weiss was taken for secret driving lessons under the 3rd Avenue L Train.

Kelly remembers that the Roguemobile was uncomfortable enough without Weiss' white-knuckle stewardship. "He's the only one who had a seat," he says. "I was on apple boxes and the rest were just in the hole back there."

"They kept very busy while I was healing," notes Van Valkenburgh. Eventually, though, Hill ran out of ways to work around the Mercy character and had to find a way for her to reappear regardless of Van Valkenburgh's continued infirmity. "Walter's so fast," says Van Valkenburgh. "His imagination will just keep coming up with stuff. He inserted this scene where I acquire this blue jacket. That covered up the splint that was on my arm and then we resumed shooting." Said scene—the one in which Mercy follows Swan into 96th St—is a masterclass in rationalizing away plotholes with quickfire dialogue, glib motivation, and the dismissal of inconvenient facts:

> Mercy: Hey wait! There's still cops all over the place.
> Swan: Where's the Fox?
> Mercy: A cop grabbed him.
> Swan: So how come you hung around?
> Mercy: I don't know.
> Swan: Where'd you get the coat?
> Mercy: You ask a lot of questions.
> Swan: Don't give me that.
> Mercy: I stole it. Cops are looking for somebody in a pink top.

Despite Hill's ingenuity-cum-barefaced cheek, fate was not yet finished with toying with him.

"We were rehearsing another scene and everything went great and Walter shouted 'Action!' and we started to shoot the scene and a baseball bat came up too soon," recalls Van Valkenburgh. "I ducked but it hit me in the forehead and split my head open. I was just a magnet for accident." Hill presumably wasn't in the mood to reflect on the irony of the fact that, despite this being a film in which the cast performed their own stunts, the only injuries accrued resulted from non-stunt related mishaps. Van Valkenburgh: "At that point, I think everybody was running for the valium. We had a plastic surgeon fix that up and we disguised my wound and we just kept going. From that point it was just, 'We going on, no matter what!'"

After abandoning Mercy in the tunnel, Swan makes his way to Union Square Station. Mercy follows him, and the remaining Warriors materialize too. When the group take refuge in the men's room from the hovering Punks (as they are termed in the credits), the man playing their roller-skating leader should logically have been Baxley. He had appeared as one of the players in *Rollerball*, the 1975 movie about a future sport redolent of a sort of murderous version of hockey. In addition was the cost factor. "Absolutely" hamstrung by the amount of money available to him, Baxley—as well as driving the bus for the Turnbull ACs and doubling as Cyrus—had been obliged to take several other roles. "I was a Punk and I did five or six other things on the film that you couldn't tell it was me. I just tried to fit in wherever I could because I didn't have the people." However, this was one role in the movie Baxley did not take. "That was Konrad," he says. "I was doing so much and Konrad said, 'I can skate.'"

The preamble to the bathroom fight saw another moment of improvisation. Michos recalls, "Deb said, 'Hey, wait, I can't go in there, that's the men's room' and I go, 'Are you kidding?' I knew that the scene, it wasn't finished. There was another beat, 'cause it wasn't strong enough. So I just intuitively grabbed her and yanked her in the bathroom. People in the audience, the house came down."

When the Punks follow the Warriors into the toilet, the mayhem on screen was achieved with delicacy and intricacy. "Choreography in a very tight space with a bunch of people," notes Brian Tyler. "It's different when you're in the park and you got a whole lot of room to play around with and you're basically shooting one character against another and then you move everything and you shoot these other two characters fighting." For Michos it was almost agonizing. "It took over a week, I'm sure, to shoot the bathroom scene, which was ninety seconds or something on film," he says. "It took a long, long time. We'd have to turn the camera on [with] almost every punch. Every move was marked out very clearly and slowly. I was a stage actor—a lot of energy and [used to going] from A to Z in the piece. We really had to have confidence that it was going to be pieced together."

The scene in the men's room was the only one in the picture not shot on location. Instead, a set was specially designed and built on Long Island. "That was out in Queens," recalls Tyler. "The entrance was in the train station and then the actual interior was a set [in] Astoria Studios." The cramped confines of a real public toilet would not have lent itself to the battle royale being envisaged by Hill and Baxley. Harris: "It had to be shot there because… you can pull walls out and put the walls back and do this and do that… and get the camera angles right and shoot from above." The "wild walls" were suggested by Baxley, who explains, "I got with the production designer when they were designing the set. I made sure that I could throw somebody through the door and be inside the stall with the commode with a camera in there."

For McKitterick, the scene summed up a recurring problem. "I was a hard job for Craig," he says. "I kept breaking these balsa-wood bats 'cause… I was making contact when I didn't quite understand how the camera angle would cover me missing by four inches… I thought, 'Holy fuck—I've broken another one.'"

Baxley may have been worrying about other things. The finance-dictated multiplicity of roles of he and his crew had, so far, been mitigated by the fact that they could be made unrecognizable behind the likes of Fury make-up. In Astoria Studios, the situation reached breaking point. Baxley: "Walter said, 'I've seen all the guys so much. I gotta have some new faces.' So I talked him into letting me bring four new faces in from California."

That new quartet would be participating in a weird scenario. Almost all the violence in the movie was deliberately stylized, but the men's-room scene gave rise to a moment that seemed to take things onto the plane of outright fantasy: Vermin was seen literally flying through the air and crashing into a mirror. Remar speaks for many when he notes that this shot seems "out of the realm of possibility." Baxley, though, doesn't consider the scene way out. "It was basically a guy being picked up by a bigger man [and] thrown into a mirror, which I've seen happen in a bar fight I can't tell you how many times."

"People always ask me, 'Did you get thrown into the mirror?'" says Michos. Although the mirror was only a "breakaway," the answer is negative. "They [put] me on a small trampoline and I jumped and then they cut to the guy going into the mirror and falling off the sink." In fact, Baxley reveals that this is the only occasion in which one of the main actors was doubled. "I couldn't take a chance," he explains. "Part of your responsibility as a stunt coordinator or as a second-unit director is the safety of the crew and the cast and the stunt people. We did three or four spot trampoline gags in that fight and that one was five, six feet off the ground dropping onto a sink [and] onto the floor. So I had one of the guys I brought up from California do it."

The scene on the subway back to Coney Island involving the prom couples might now involve Swan and Mercy rather than Fox and Mercy but retained the same poignancy and class consciousness. As Harris puts it, "It was like, 'Okay, here comes the goody two-shoe kids come from the prom.' The Warriors have never been at no prom. Half of them never even got out of high school, or even went to high school. They're looking at Swan and Mercy and Mercy starts to fix her hair and Swan takes her hand and puts it down. Like: they're no better than us."

BACK TO CONEY

WHEN THE *WARRIORS* shoot returned to Coney Island for the film's final scenes, it marked the reappearance of David Patrick Kelly. "I was only supposed to be on this movie for a few weeks, but it extended from May or June to September," he reflects. "I was on retainer all those weeks, so I got all that extra dough... I probably shot just three weeks out of the whole thing." This might be said to be the only stroke of good fortune the actor experienced during the entire time *The Warriors* was being filmed.

For one thing, he had found his appearance was perceived in real life to be as villainous as it was intended to be in fiction. "It wasn't the mode. That had some occupational hazards that I didn't foresee." His other, related, issue was being both burgled and evicted. "I inadvertently got kicked out of my apartment for trying to look as slimy as I could," he recalls. "I lived in a tiny little apartment in SoHo and the people were a little bit scared." He suspects the hand in the break-in of a sinister neighbor named Rich. "One of the creepiest people I ever knew," he recalls. "This low-level gangster... I think he was his mid-thirties at the time... He was really something out of a Scorsese movie. He lived by himself with two little poodles and he would imitate me. I'd say, 'Hey Rich, how you doing?' He'd say [soft, sinister tones], 'Da-a-a-ve... Da-a-a-a-ave... Da-a-a-a-a-a-ve...' instead of replying. It was kind of scary. I don't know for sure, but I think Rich was involved in robbing my apartment and breaking down the door... If it wasn't Rich it was somebody else at the behest of the land-lord... The landlord asked me to leave... So I was just pedaling around the whole time we were filming *The Warriors*, staying at cheap hotels and waiting for my next day's call. We had no cell phones. I had to go to the payphone and call into the production manager and say, 'Am I on?'... I stayed at the McBurney Y, which has very cheap rooms and I could keep my bicycle in there... I stayed at hotel after hotel in New York and was not too friendly received... I remember staying at the Gramercy Park Hotel—that was a famous rock hotel back in the Seventies—and Warren Zevon came into the elevator and he just shook his head and walked off 'cause I was going up at the same time."

Unlike others, Kelly didn't take advantage of the option of being on set when he wasn't needed. "I remember a couple of the other people did," he says. "Jim Remar showed up for the final shootout, the confrontation on the beach and things like that. I remember production assistants trying to keep me off the set. They didn't know who I was... I just wanted to be the character, stay in it and show up at the time." For the same reason he stayed away when he wasn't needed, when Kelly was on set, he didn't do much mingling. Although he had disobeyed a staple of method acting by prejudging his character, in another respect he was sticking rigidly to method bible: he would have nothing to do with the cast members playing his antagonists for fear of contaminating his performance. "I knew if I started to get into conversations with people that it would be, 'Who's your agent?' and 'How d'you get this job?' Things were moving very swiftly and you had to stay up all night and Walter would add things or add a shot, so you had to try to stay in character. There's a limited time when you're making a movie and film acting is more than acting. You just have to be the character... I remember having nice conversations with Michael and Deborah and Remar after rehearsal, but I did try to maintain that." He says that on this cash-strapped project this was sometimes difficult. "We all dressed in one trailer." "I had one conversation with David," recalls Michos. "We were waiting. It was during the shooting of the final scene. We sat on a bench overlooking the ocean and we got to talk for about an hour, just about life, about where we came from, thoughts and things. It is true he did keep to himself very much. He really stayed in character. Jamie did too. James Remar really stayed in character for most of the film. Not as much. But David definitely did that. He was distant in a way, but I had one conversation with him that got me to see into him and he was very sweet."

Kelly does say of method, "I try not to let other people be affected by it. I'm not fond of people saying, 'I played a ballet dancer and I took two weeks of classes.'" He is clearly not insensitive to those fellow professionals who disdain his school of acting, something which raises the issue of whether some of the *Warriors* cast were upset about him being standoff-ish. "Well, I won't tell you who, but there's a guy to this day who won't speak to me," Kelly laughs. "I'll see him from time to time on the subway. He won't talk at all."

The Coney Island return gave rise to another of those pieces of inspired improvisation that are common to movies but cannot be legislated for. It involved the creation of a line that would become every bit as iconic as "Can you dig it?"

There is some dispute about its provenance, but it stemmed from the fact that Hill decided on the day of shooting that what he had written (or rewritten) lacked something, even if he wasn't quite sure what. The scene in question was the one wherein the Warriors, standing under the boardwalk, are challenged by the Rogues from their customized hearse, ultimately leading to the climactic beach showdown between the two parties. "We were just going to drive up and sort of look at each other, and Walter said, 'It needs more,'" Kelly recollects. "Something was cooking in Walter's head. He wanted it cool—like a Western stand-off. He didn't want explosions. He just wanted this face-off. But he couldn't just let it sit with us looking and them looking and then going to the beach." Hill: "I said, 'This goddamn scene is not working. Say something to them—we've got to figure something out.'" At this point, the memories of the two men diverge.

Hill says, "I got him thinking about it and then I had to run off and do some work at the camera about setting the shot. When I came back he said, 'How about this?'" Kelly remembers events thus: "He called me over. It was just me and him. He said, 'David, I want you to make something up.' I said, 'What?' He said, 'Sing them something.' I said, 'What should it be?' He said, 'I don't know.' And I think he said, 'Come out to play.'" Kelly walked away "aghast" because Hill knew nothing of his edgy CBGBs hinterland, the director's musical knowledge of the actor extending only so far as his performance in *Working* of "lyrical, folkie ballads." Recalls Kelly, "I said, 'What am I gonna do?' I was talking to myself now, wandering around. But I was excited too. I knew that it was an opportunity."

His first idea seems to have been a way to divert Hill from his singing suggestion. "I picked up two dead pigeons and brought them to Walter. He said, 'No, that's not gonna work.'" Kelly sought something else he might use as a prop. "They used to sell these midget beer bottles back then—I don't know if they still do." Rooting around beneath the Coney Island boardwalk unearthed what he was looking for. "I found three of those and from my days at the MoMA and stuff like that, I just started doing that.... It was part of this off-Broadway experimental thing and I clicked them " Clinking miniature bottles whose necks were slid over his fingers did indeed create an intriguing sonic effect, but it still needed accompanying words. It was at this point that Kelly's sinister and possibly burglarizing neighbor became a benefactor.

Kelly: "I said, 'I don't want to sing a lyrical thing.' And I remembered Rich and [how] he would do that taunting thing to me. It was so hateful and it was so just evil. I said, 'This is what I'm gonna do.' I don't think I even said it. I think I just did it... Probably half an hour to come up with all that. But nobody knew. Nobody saw it. It was all in my head." While Kelly didn't sing them as such, there was certainly a sing-songey quality– if menacingly so—to his words, "Wa-a-arriors—come out to pla-a-ay!" Repeated over and over, they quickly rose to a pitch in the vicinity of dementedness. "I was thinking of trying to sing... in a particular crazy way that would humiliate them," Kelly says. "We only did it twice. We did it once in rehearsal and then Walter said, 'Bring the bottles up slow... Start with them off-camera and then bring them up onto camera'... You heard them, and I started saying it and then you saw the bottles come up."

As all good method actors do, Kelly dug deep for the scene. "I was thinking of tragic bad things that had happened to me," he says. "I was homeless for the entire filming because of that guy I was imitating. That accounts for a great deal of the rage and anger." His solemnity was not matched by his colleagues. "All the guys in the back of the Cadillac there were cringing. And the sound guy was kind of moving his earphones back... I just think they were saying, 'What the fuck? What is this?' It was so out there." Meanwhile, some of the crew weren't even aware of the magnitude of what was occurring because they were distracted by the fact that they had found a money-stuffed woman's purse under the boardwalk. Kelly's performance did land where it was meant to, though. "Apparently, it was quite effective for the Warriors," says Kelly. "It gave them the creeps, as they admitted later."

Hill gives all the credit to Kelly. "It is absolutely a moment that David created and I'm very happy to have been there and if that's the line they remember most in the movie, that's fine with me." Perhaps not entirely seriously, Hill also says, "When you choose a good actor you've done something good as a director, and I was very clever in hiring David Patrick Kelly... I was smart enough not to change it. You create conditions for good things to happen and then hopefully you're smart—if something good happens you won't go in there and put your foot though it."

Kelly, meanwhile, thinks that the way the line was delivered was the culmination of his varied, multi-discipline career. "I think you can hear Dylan in that chant," he says. "Some of the rhythms of it… Somebody on Twitter pointed out that it's 'Dear Prudence' too: similar phraseology. Who knows? Who knows what's unconscious?… But the main thing was trying to do something original, emotionally true, and part of the times in which we were living." Those times, of course, involved a musical generation newer than that of Bob Dylan and the Beatles. Kelly is convinced that his CBGBs days inform the scene. So too his alternative theatre work. "Why is that the thing that has lasted for so long?" he muses. "In my humble opinion, it really has to do with this musical aspect of it and there are a lot of elements in that: there's experimental theatre and the clicking bottles and the way that I sang… All those club gigs and seeing people go crazy—Alan Vega and Suicide or Iggy [Pop] stomping through the crowd at Max's or some of the folks at CBGBs… The whole cultural muse that I was a part of and that I was participating in was nuts."

As for Rich, his real-life inspiration in downtown New York, Kelly says, "I think he's still down there." And completely unaware of his place in cinematic history? "Yes… I hope he never finds out. I doubt that he will. But maybe he'd be honored because the weird thing about that 'Come out to play' thing is that people always say, 'Oh, he's a weasel. He's a coward punk character, Luther,' and stuff like that, but there's something about it that they admire."

Because of the not entirely ecstatic on-set reception to his performance, Kelly admits, "I honestly didn't know if [Hill] would keep that in there." However, he was fairly confident about what he'd done. "Sometimes when you do something, you do have a feeling. I didn't have any idea about the iconic thing. I just had a feeling it would work."

In the film's final edit, the clinking bottles are initially only the aural backdrop to a longshot of the hearse. This adroit piece of direction/editing means that, at first, the audience doesn't quite understand the source of this odd noise, making for an almost eerie effect. Editor Freeman Davies, Jr. can take some credit for this, particularly as he extended the clinking sound longer than Kelly actually executed it.

Kelly is convinced that the only reason he was given this opportunity to improvise in the first place is because the troubled, distended shoot was in its final week. He says, "I think Walter was thrilled that he was almost done. The drama of Thomas, and him seeming draconian, allowed him to say, 'Well, I can be creative with acting. I wanna show that I can be inventive.' It was definitely a gesture to me for having been a good soldier, having been through the whole thing, delivered stuff that he really liked all the way along. This was the ending. You know: we're done after these two or three days of filming. And I think he sincerely liked the way I sang. We'd all known we had to mind our P's and Q's. We had to do what we were told. You have to admit this was unusual for him to say, 'Just make something up' and to give me that responsibility. His most crucial direction that he doesn't give himself credit for was to say, 'Sing them something.' 'Cause if you think about it, it's really bizarre in that moment."

Kelly has noted that "Can you dig it?" resonated forever. Remarkably, though, his own phrase did even better than that, the line surpassing Cyrus' dialogue in the stakes of becoming famous, iconic and employed by the public as a shorthand for the film. It should be said, though, that despite being much repeated, it's almost invariably repeated slightly incorrectly. Even people who might be expected to know better get it wrong: more than one cast member interviewed for this book was under the impression that it's "Warriors, come out *and* play." Ditto Lawrence Gordon. Rock band Twisted Sister released a 1985 album entitled *Come Out and Play* on which the misquoted phrase is repeated several times to the accompaniment of clicking bottles. "It really annoys me," says Kelly of the imprecisions.

Nowadays, no one seems in any doubt about the power of Kelly's performance, in either that scene or the movie as a whole. "He's a great actor," says Remar. "He gave a *tour de force* performance." While Beck concurs with that assertion, he also has an actor's weary resignation about villainy being by default more compelling than heroism. "Doesn't the bad guy always steal the show?" says *The Warriors'* main hero. "The bad guys, they're always better written, they always have the best lines." For his part, Kelly says, "My parents saw it in downtown Detroit and my mother's review was, 'You almost looked tough.' Who have I been compared to? Back then people said, Baryshnikov. Believe it or not, they said the young Harry Houdini. They said Kirk Douglas. So—villainous? I think it was the whole Gestalt there. I still hope to do my lovable character someday."

ALTHOUGH *THE WARRIORS* had for practical reasons been shot unusually chronologically, by the end of the shoot it had become necessary for political reasons that there be synchronicity of photography and narrative. The final scenes on the beach were held back in the timetable for the simple purpose of preventing the production being closed down. "I kept telling Walter that we had to save it until the end because we were over schedule," says Marshall. "I knew that the minute we shot the last scene of the movie that the studio would tell us that was it." "And it wasn't very hard for them to figure out my strategy," notes Hill of Paramount. "So it was really getting pretty hairy there at the end."

The beach on which the Warriors-Rogues confrontation occurred was portrayed as Coney Island, but in fact David Harris reveals, "It was Brighton Beach, up the road." When Luther and co follow the Warriors and Mercy there, the audience is treated to another "Mount Rushmore" line-up, the group staring defiantly at the Rogues in perfectly-spaced formation.

The confrontation scene was, for Harris, the culmination of some comically inept gunmanship in the movie. "It's funny, because when he throws the knife in his arm, it's like, 'How did that bullet miss him?' Like when the Lizzies are shooting at the Warriors, especially Terry. He's the last guy through the door and she's still shooting. Boy, there's some terrible shots. They didn't hit anybody."

The staging of the knife hurling would ordinarily have been Baxley's province, but the stunt coordinator says, "That's Walter... He was running out of time." Baxley was occupied with a stunt elsewhere. "The limousine was going to jump off an abutment and land on the beach and drive right up in front of the Warriors," he explains. "I was going to do that." However, the clock was against him as much as it was Hill. "We had it all worked out... The ramp was built, the car was rigged, everything else, and they ran out of time, so that stuff was never done."

The observant viewer will notice that the beach section sees Luther sporting a hooded sweatshirt in which he'd not previously been seen. Supplied by Bobbie Mannix, it was worn for a prosaic rather than aesthetic reason. "They had a huge prop arm," says Kelly. "Michael was just supposed to hit near the place and then this knife was supposed to pop out of it." Unfortunately, "The arm just did not work. We tried it two or three times. And then I said, 'I got an idea'... We ended up doing it old-school." Kelly fired Luther's gun and then quickly thrust a concealed half-knife prop into his arm while crumbling in agony, with some adroit cutting by the editors doing the rest. This quasi-farce had one prophetic result, Luther presaging by several decades an era in which a "hoodie" is a synonym for lout.

Kelly decided to have Luther responding very dramatically to the blade piercing his flesh. He was inspired by *Angels With Dirty Faces*, the 1938 gangster pic in which Rocky Sullivan (James Cagney) is implored by a priest to go to his execution like a coward so as to not provide a bad role model for other young men. After initially refusing, Sullivan does so, ostentatiously screaming and whining as he is dragged off to the electric chair. "I always remembered that," says Kelly. Although the script did dictate that Luther cry, he was once again dispensing with the Actor's Studio edict that a thespian should not judge his character. "I hope I don't seem like a moralist, but I decided that he was evil and that he was all braggadocio and that you should show that somewhere. That when he had the upper hand with his gun and there's backing by Mr. Boss he was cool, but when it comes down to it he was that guy crying like a baby on the beach."

When Swan retrieves his knife from Luther's limb, the script originally had him wiping it on his own pants leg. By the time the scene was shot, it had been changed to wiping it in Luther's abundant hair. This is one change that doesn't quite work, because for a second it seems for all the world as though Swan has scalped Luther, which leads to a moment of puzzlement on the viewer's part as to why the Rogue is still alive.

Kelly points out, "You never really know what happens to Luther. The Riffs come down and Luther is left with them." "I always was hoping that there would have been a final fight scene," says Michos. "But I think the way this ended had Walter Hill's stamp on it: less is more."

When it came to the final shot, Hill rejected the previous climax of Swan staring out to sea, while Paramount rejected his idea of the insertion of mock comic-book panels. Hill opted for a mellow longshot of the Warriors and Mercy all walking together down the beach, Swan and Mercy bringing up the rear holding hands. When the shot does eventually end, it's on a freeze frame. James Remar thought this the ultimate vindication of the decision to jettison the day scenes from the front of the picture. "It's a beautiful shot and it has more of an impact," he says.

It's perhaps easy for Remar to adjudge this an exquisite result because, although present, he wasn't involved in filming it. The participants found its execution excruciating. The walk down the beach was protracted so as to accommodate the closing titles being superimposed on it. A long, leisurely stroll along a beach during the summer months would have been perfectly pleasant but, the shoot having gone overschedule, summer had in real time given way to fall. "We were freezing," says Michos. "We had to walk that beach over and over." "Remember, all we have on is these little vests," says Harris. "Every time Walter said 'Cut,' I'd go, 'Costume!' and they came running to me with blankets and a heater."

Michos: "David Harris would come up to me after every take and say, 'Terry, you know what I'm gonna do when I get home? I'm gonna take a big, hot bath.' His body was shivering. And then the water came over my sneakers on one of the takes, but we had to go back and continue to do more takes and my feet were sopping wet." "It had been a long shoot and it was exhausting," says McKitterick. "It was just like, 'Please, let's get to the end of this.'" The only person having a good time that day seems to have been David Patrick Kelly. "I'm not much of a complainer," he says. "I come from a military-inspired family. A lot of art too, but being a good soldier was always part of the deal. We were on location, we had free food and things like that. It might have been cold and things, but it was always exciting."

"In my opinion, the movie has a rather limp ending," says Hill. "That was due to a lot of things... We shot it very, very quickly and I just thought it wasn't as fully developed as it could have been if I'd have had more time. It's all very argy bargy. I think I shot it all in about six or eight hours... There's just a lot of things that bother me... Had I had a little more time and a little better luck on the weather... There's a terrible mismatch with the waves. The waves change from before lunch and after lunch." Adding to Hill's problems was the morose belief as he and his colleagues packed the equipment away that he had a final shot that was next to useless but which could not be done over. "[With] Swan and Mercy going down the beach, Andy kept saying, 'We're losing the light, I'm wide open,'" Hill recalls. "We thought, 'God, it's going to be murky.'"

However, there was a sweet moment even in the midst of the stress and exhaustion. During the long last take, the actors were required to stay in character until they were dots on the horizon. Unable to hear instructions from the crew, they finally decided that they must be able to stop now and trudged back—whereupon Van Valkenburgh was presented with a dozen red roses by Hill and Marshall.

POST

IF THE BEGINNING of post-production on *The Warriors* can be defined as the moment the crew sat down to watch the last sequence they'd shot, it got off to a good start. The final scene featuring the walk to the far horizon on Brighton Beach turned out to not appear like it was shot at dusk after all. "We had more light than we thought," recalls Hill happily. "We went to dailies and it looks like noon."

Although shooting had wrapped, this didn't mean that the Warriors camp could relax: Paramount were acutely aware that in what would be a race to be first the other street-gang films were limbering up in the other lanes. "We were told we had to be in the theatres in February," says Hill. "So we had a very fast post-production and we had to make editorial decisions very quickly." "We brought in four editors," recalls Marshall. Along with Freeman Davies, Jr., recruited in this department were David Holden, Susan E. Morse, and Billy Weber. Marshall: "Each editor had two reels of the film and Walter would go around and look in on each editor in order for us to finish in time. Back in the days when we were on film, that was really difficult." "Editing took a lot longer in those days," confirms Hill. "You can edit much faster now than you could when we were working on that one, just as you can light much faster now that everything has gone digital."

Yet while *The Warriors* production team was physically and mentally exhausted, behind schedule, and facing a race to be first, there was still creativity going on. For instance, the deliberately artificial tenor of the film was intensified by the introduction of "wipes," scene transitions whereby a line would move across the screen, pulling in its wake a new scene. Common in cinema's middle period, they had long been dispensed with as overtly stylized-cum-corny, which was sort of the point. McKitterick: "I think it actually went with the spirit of the cartoon aspect of the movie. All very skillful on their part." "There was a lot of creativity in there," says Marshall of the editing period. "Right down to the close-up of the DJ. The close-up of her lips. We had wider shots of her, but it really seemed to be a motif that we could use to move *The Warriors* along."

The editing process also saw Hill issue the instruction that the narrative should "move, move, move, move." Slow moments were cut to the bone. However, Michos points out the difference between this dynamism and simple freneticism. "It has a great pace, but there wasn't fight after fight after fight after fight," he says. "He was very smart. The confidence that Walter Hill had to allow this film to unfold instead of just making it a high-energy action film at every scene—the tension between waiting and walking and waiting and a skirmish here, a skirmish there—really heightened the effect and made it more real. Drama is intensified life. He was able to get that. So people started to relate to and bond with characters. They would never do that today. Everything's faster."

Hill nipped and tucked, dropping several scenes, lines, and exchanges. Deletions included a night sequence wherein the agitated Warriors wander a park before arriving at the conclave, part of Cyrus' speech where he tells the assembled that they have been shucked by the courts and schools, the depiction of a report being made to the new Cyrus about failures of other gangs to deal with the Warriors, and a section at Union Square Station in which the others fill in Swan on what exactly happened to Ajax and finally communicate to him that the Warriors are suspected of shooting Cyrus. Some of the footage of the Rogues' car arriving in Coney Island was jettisoned, as was a part of the same Coney Island section wherein Vermin said, "I got an idea—let's run." As one of the key alterations to Shaber's original vision had been to render the Warriors more heroic, the retention of the latter line—which made them look like cowards, and furthermore on their own turf—would have made no sense. The line that confirms Cleon's death was also cut, leaving his fate ambiguous.

Hill decided to emphasize right at the beginning of the narrative both the locale and the nocturne ambience by inserting a shot of the Coney Island Wonder Wheel illuminated pink against the night sky. Following which was a symbolic shot of the D Sixth Avenue Express—colloquially, the "D train"—the rapid-transit service that runs between 205th Street in the Bronx to Stillwell Avenue in Coney Island.

ALL FILMS REQUIRE post-dubbing of some kind, usually to obtain a second crack at scenes compromised by a noisy atmosphere, replace unsatisfactorily delivered lines ("looping"), add sound effects like telephone peals and crowd noises, fix continuity errors, and tone down off-color language for alternate prints (in those days most commonly TV versions, but now encompassing airline iterations).

McKitterick says the shoot's persistent sound problems meant all his own takes were ruined. "I post-dubbed every line," he says. "The line readings were pretty much the same as I did before. I don't think it was to correct a performance thing." Meanwhile, with post-dubbing part of every film actor's contract, Thomas Waites was facing the embarrassing prospect of turning up for a soundstage session on a project from which he had been unceremoniously removed. "Frank Marshall was a really nice man," Waites recalls. "So, no, it wasn't humiliating for me. At the end of the day, I'm an actor. If there aren't artistic differences, it usually means the thing's no good." All of this sounds reasonable and temperate enough, but a couple of things suggest that Waites didn't feel that way at the time. Asked whether if Walter Hill hadn't been such a "gentleman," he would have gone back to do the post-production dubbing, Waites admits, "Probably not." Then there is his decision to exercise a right that is as much a staple of actors' film contracts as the post-wrap dubbing obligations. It followed Waites viewing a rough cut of the picture in around October 1978. "I had to go to a screening room. Somebody set up the camera. Just me sitting there by myself watching. I said, 'Okay, thank you' and left and then I called my agent the next day and I said, 'I don't like it'… I was so still in the throes of my own interior tumult that I had my name removed from the credits."

He admits, "I can't say with my hand on my heart that there wasn't an element of revenge… I thought, 'Well, I'll show them that they shouldn't have fired me.'" However, he also says, "You have to understand my mindset at the time… I thought I was going to be a big star. I was put under option by Paramount, three-picture deal. They don't even do that anymore. I had just done a movie with Al Pacino called *And Justice For All*. I went on to do some things on Broadway. My mindset was that if I ever do become what I expected to become, I didn't want to be associated with something that promoted violence."

THE *WARRIORS* AUDIO additions also, of course, included the soundtrack.

In a sense, there are two soundtracks to *The Warriors*. The incidental music, or underscore, was the work of Barry DeVorzon while the "additional music" (songs that the characters in the narrative can theoretically hear, such as records played by the DJ in her booth) was provided by Kenny Vance. "Originally, I was going to do it all," recalls DeVorzon. "Joel Silver, who was assisting Larry, suggested Kenny because he could go out there and negotiate deals. I agreed to that because having to go out and identify other recordings for the DJ to play was time-consuming and you had to negotiate, so I was happy that Kenny took that off my plate."

At some point, Vance's remit to license existing recordings was altered. "I wanted to buy the old songs and Paramount insisted that we do new versions of the songs that we used," says Hill. "Paramount thought that was too old-fashioned." The director is unsure if there was also a budgetary consideration. "I don't know what the song would have cost, nor do I know what it costs to record a new one. I was just told 'no'... There had been so many fights and they just basically said, 'You're not going to win this one.' They were under the impression that I had won a lot of them. I was not under such an impression." It has to be said that Hill doesn't seem to know much about the music in *The Warriors* beyond De-Vorzon's score. "I've only heard the music as it exists in the film," he says. "I know that they produced an album. It didn't come out for years." While it's true that *The Warriors'* soundtrack LP was delayed, it was only slightly. Moreover with the exception of one track, the non-score parts of it don't feature "re-dos" of oldies, as he seems to believe.

"What I was chosen to do was to make records that would fit in different themes for the movie," says Vance. Born in 1943, Vance was a former member of doo-wop outfit Jay and the Americans, the most famous of whose string of hits was the plaintive "Come a Little Bit Closer". In his new career as supervisor of motion-picture music, he reflects, "I was on a roll." He had fulfilled that task for the films *American Hot Wax* and *Animal House* (both 1978). As well as this function, his *Warriors* responsibilities included producing and compiling the soundtrack LP. Of De-Vorzon Vance says, "I met him and I was in the studio with him but never really collaborated with him." However, he did get to hear what DeVorzon was supplying: doomy synthesizer-led music that was a contrast to his more organic and soulful contributions. He doesn't feel that the two styles jarred. "That juxtaposition was what it needed."

With one exception, the tracks Vance produced were new songs commissioned by him from a variety of artists. "I remember going to the set many nights that Walter was doing the scenes and you actually felt that there was an ominous presence in there," he says. "I wanted to capture that... The people that I picked were the fringe people. Mandrill, Genya Ravan—they were all kind of tough, streetwise people that aligned themselves in my mind with what the film was about."

Walter Hill was Vance's "point man," but not a hands-on one. "I think he trusted the fact that I was going to do the job that I was hired for." Hill told him in which scenes songs should appear but "it wasn't that you got a lot of information from him about what he thought the music should be." Vance says, "I would send them clips: 'This is the skeleton of this. And this is that.' So they kind of knew what was happening."

Vance assembled some celebrated backing musicians for his tracks. "There was a thread through all of the source music and that was basically Paul Griffin on keyboards and Elliot Randall on guitar." Griffin had appeared on many classic records, including Bob Dylan's 1965 magnum opus *Highway 61 Revisited*. Randall was famed for his work with Steely Dan (Vance: "I discovered those guys and I produced them"). "Elliot plays this screeching guitar that, to me, underscored what the Warriors were all about," Vance notes.

Among the names listed on the soundtrack LP's inner sleeve was that of someone who was then on the cusp of fame: Luther Vandross. "I wanted to enhance some of the background parts and Luther was the first-call studio singer. He brought Ula Hedwig. She was one of the Harlettes with Bette Midler. This was a New York crowd of studio singers and, oh my God, what a sound. I figured I might as well join them, so I sang with them. It was thrilling. That sound is on the backgrounds of 'Echoes In My Mind', and I think 'Love Is A Fire' and 'Nowhere to Run.'"

"In Havana," written by Artie Ripp and Steve Nathanson, is performed by Vance and Ismael Miranda (the latter a man with, ironically, the same first name as the prototype Cyrus in Yurick's book). A joyous, salsa number, it is heard very low on the radio in the candy-store scene. "Echoes in My Mind" (written by Claude Cave II and Carlos, Louis, Dr. Richard, and Wilfredo Wilson) is performed by Mandrill. A piece of sleepy funk, it's heard in the DJ's booth when she's telling the listeners that she has been asked to relay a request from the Gramercy Riffs. "Love is a Fire", a torch ballad written by Johnny Vastano and Vinnie Poncia, is performed by Genya Ravan with Rouge and is heard on the jukebox in the Lizzies' apartment. Also heard in the Lizzies' pad is "You're Moving Too Slow," a pounding blues sung by Johnny Vastano and written by Eric Mercury and William Smith.

There is one song in *The Warriors* that, rather than serving as background music, is introduced by a character into the narrative to make a point, specifically the record on which the DJ places a stylus after declaring of the Warriors, "Here's a hit with them in mind." In the Shaber first draft, the song employed to set the gangs on the Dominators'/Warriors' tail is an imaginary record, "Remember My Name" by the Dead Dogs. The June '78 draft specifies merely a "rock number." With shooting wrapped, the crew were faced with the necessity of choosing an actual piece of music. The choice made was inspired. "As I recall, David Holden came up with the idea and put it in the work print," says Hill of the use of "Nowhere to Run." The song is superbly apposite but was spoiled for some by the fact that the single the DJ proceeds to play is fictional, being a new recording by Arnold McCuller. This version is played well and sung competently but the fact that it wasn't the treasured Martha and the Vandellas smash was inevitably going to disappoint many. Not the least of those people was Pauline Kael, who ensured to mention her disapproval in her famous *New Yorker* write-up of the film. "It pissed me off," says Vance, "because the truth is the record that I made had so much energy to it and even though the Martha and the Vandellas record is a great record I wanted to do something that was more aligned with our film. Obviously, she didn't get that aspect of it."

"The spectrum was a very New-York melting pot," says Vance of the variety of styles to be found in his tracks. "I was in alignment with what was happening in New York City streets at that time." Well, with one exception. Vance wasn't of the right generation to be cognizant of the punk scene spawned by CBGBs. "Well, yeah, for sure," he says with a sound of amusement. "If it was happening, I didn't really connect with it."

Vance says he knows nothing about "Night Run" by the Mersh Brothers, composed and arranged by Philip Marshall, a song heard in the DJ scene after the Baseball Furies fight but which doesn't appear on the soundtrack album. One part of the solution to that mystery seems to lie in the fact that Philip is brother to Frank Marshall.

"Nowhere to Run" excepted, most people who have seen *The Warriors* would be hard-pressed to identify or name any of the Vance-organized songs featured in it. Despite the hard work, stellar musicians, and listenable end product, his music was interpolated in the briefest of snatches, sometimes at low volume. "I just made the best records that I could at the time," shrugs Vance. "I didn't realize that was what was going to happen. When I heard, it was, 'Okay, I guess if anyone's interested, they could listen to the soundtrack album.'"

Born in 1936, Barry DeVorzon (frequently misspelled "De Vorzon") had been a songwriter since the late Fifties and a soundtrack composer since the turn of the Seventies. In between those two milestones, he'd managed to squeeze in the co-founding of Valiant Records. One of his nine soundtracks so far was Hill's directorial debut *Hard Times*. He also wrote music for the Hill-Gordon inaugurated TV show *Dog and Cat*. De-Vorzon wasn't, though, the standard score composer. "I couldn't compete with Johnny Williams or Jerry Goldsmith, but what I could do was approach a film using contemporary music, not just in the songs, but in the score itself," he says. "My whole background was in contemporary music—rock 'n' roll, pop music. At the time, television was jazzy, motion pictures was conventional classic background. They used pop songs in the motion pictures for the main title or end title." Although he admits that his specialism restricted the projects he was offered, he also says, "At the time, there weren't many people doing it, so it worked. Now today, of course, introducing contemporary music into motion pictures is quite common." In fact, he suspects that latter fact may be down to him. Of *The Warriors*, he says, "I think it was the first motion picture that was [entirely] scored with rock 'n' roll and synthesizers."

"Basically I told Barry, 'The movie's crazy—make it crazier,'" Hill states of his score instructions. Although DeVorzon was just as oblivious of punk as Vance, he was cutting-edge in the sense that he decided that the Hill brief would best be fulfilled by embracing nascent electronic keyboard technology. "It was about this street gang crossing New York and it was kind of surreal," says DeVorzon. "I thought using rock 'n' roll and synthesizers would match what Walter had in mind." Synthesizers were then rather primitive affairs, their tones limited to the mechanical, the oppressive, and the doomy. This, though, was precisely what attracted DeVorzon to the idea of deploying them on this project. "Made the Baseball Furies look even more sinister." Also attractive to him was just how novel synths were. "If you were a musician or composer or writer at that time, you were definitely interested in synths. They were bringing new sounds to music." Relatively new though synths were, it should be said that the Beatles had been experimenting with them as far back as *Abbey Road* (1969), and—of all people—the Monkees two years before that. Moreover, in 1971 Wendy Carlos via *A Clockwork Orange* pioneered scoring major motion pictures with synthesizer. Indeed, DeVorzon says, "I do remember liking that movie. That was not on my mind, but I'll bet you subconsciously it played a part."

Of his tools, he says, "I used the CS80, Yamaha, and a Moog." The crux of the synthesized parts of the *Warriors* score was a piece ultimately titled "Theme from 'The Warriors.'" A propulsive creation with a dark, churning, two-note underpinning, it's laced with blasts of electric guitar, features a counterpointing percolating keyboard, and is sprinkled with glittering shards of additional synthesizer. It appears at the beginning of the movie and then in different iterations throughout. "That's important in a score, for continuity," says DeVorzon. "You don't want a completely separate piece of music every time something happens on the screen."

DeVorzon recalls that this main title led to the only specific instruction Hill gave him on the project. The music is heard in the montage sequence featuring the expository dialogue that had been shot to compensate for the loss of the daytime scenes. DeVorzon: "You can't have that dialogue if you have a theme pounding through it, so I said, 'Walter, is there any way you can give up that dialogue? Because you're gonna hurt the impact of the theme.' He says, 'No man, I want that dialogue.' He's the boss, so when the dialogue scenes came up, everything would drop out, and the drum and the sustaining synth would just keep that feeling going, let the dialogue in, and then right after the dialogue I either changed key or hit it. It provided a dynamic that really worked out well. Whereas had I not done that, it's possible the theme would have become a little redundant. So Walter's insistence on this dialogue actually helped the main title."

DeVorzon recalls that during post-production Lawrence Gordon expressed concern about the fight between the Warriors and the Baseball Furies. "He felt that was just too graphic," says DeVorzon. "Especially when Sound Effects put in the bats making contact and all that stuff. That was a dramatic scene; I was going to stay out of it. He insisted that I add music to it. The reason being when you add music to a scene like that it takes away from the violence. It reminds people that they're watching a movie. And he was right. It took the edge off it. I wrote a new piece. It has nothing to do with the main title or the Baseball Furies chase, but it had elements of it." "I didn't ask him to do anything," demurs Gordon. "That's what he wrote. He scored the fight and then it was discussed maybe taking it out. And I was very much for leaving it in... Walter wasn't as bothered as I was by the rawness of no music there. If you saw it without the music, it's very, very rough... He was not happy about leaving the music in. I think he became happy but he wasn't in the beginning."

DeVorzon adds that his music for the men's-room section was something else again. "The bathroom scene was another very different kind of scene. Wasn't as in your face as 'The Fight'. It was eerier: the setup, with the kid on the roller skates."

The final element required for the *Warriors* soundtrack was a song over the end titles. For this component, DeVorzon decided to take advantage of his friendship with a famous musician. "When we were in post, Barry DeVorzon kept saying we were going to get a song from Joe Walsh," recalls Hill. "It was like, 'Would it happen?'" Potentially, Walsh's participation could considerably benefit the film's public profile. His hit 'Life's Been Good' had peaked at #12 on *Billboard* in the year of *The Warriors'* production. Meanwhile, the Eagles—membership of which might be termed his day job—were a commercial phenomenon courtesy of *Their Greatest Hits (1971–1975)* and *Hotel California*, two of the biggest-selling albums of all time, and that status was cemented at the end of the year of *The Warriors'* release by their multi-platinum LP *The Long Run*. "We started dubbing and we still had no song," says Hill. "The very last day when we were doing the last reel, Barry comes through the door and he holds up a little cassette and he says, 'I got something. Joe and I did it last night.'"

The pair had put together "In the City," a mid-tempo number of proletarian yearning rendered emotively by Walsh in his distinctive high voice. In terms of the demarcation of role among the creators, DeVorzon says, "The melody and the approach was the two of us but I probably had a little more to do with the lyric because I was more involved with what the picture was all about." The narrator of said lyric declares that although the streets of his neighborhood don't hold much pity, he knows there is something better "somewhere out there on that horizon." DeVorzon reasons of this theme, "The end of the picture had a hopeful feeling. For the most part they're in one piece and you just got the feeling that they were going to try to find something better. The bad guy got his and they were home."

"So we put the song up, and he played it to the film," says Hill. When the last bars died, the room looked expectantly at the director. Hill recalls his response as, "Well, it's a good song. But it's very kind of West Coast, and this is an East-Coast movie." "It didn't have a lot to do with the score itself," DeVorzon admits of a creation whose major chords and bright rock ambience were a departure from the portentous wodges of synth he had provided everywhere else. "It was its own animal." Recalls Hill, "I'm telling you, there wasn't a face in the room that wasn't like, 'Oh God, after all this shit, now we've got this problem.' Then I said, 'But I think we ought to use it. I think it works.' So we laid it in."

Although DeVorzon had obtained a go-ahead in advance for the creation of the film's closing number ("The studio had to negotiate with Joe Walsh. I had to notify everyone"), he unexpectedly found he had competition for the job. "Kenny promised he would just do the songs for the DJ, but I learned from the music editor that he had submitted a song for the end title," he recalls. Vance, however, insists that he was asked to submit a theme tune. "Walter didn't have that much input in it," he says. "Joel Silver was more into realizing that the music was important and he says, 'Use this guy. He's up and coming.'" Said up-and-comer was songwriter Desmond Child. Child would go on to become a hugely successful composer, his name attached to such earworms as "You Give Love a Bad Name", "Livin' on a Prayer", "Dude (Looks Like a Lady)", and "Livin' la Vida Loca". "I think this was his first chance of being mainstream," says Vance. After Vance met with Child, the latter came up with "Last of an Ancient Breed," which he also sang. Musically, it's a rock anthem in the overwrought, soaring vein of the material on Meat Loaf's *Bat Out of Hell*, released the year previous to *The Warriors'* production. Its lyric talks about poor men's sons standing their ground and its chorus prominently deploys the word "Warriors" (nowhere heard in "In the City"). Vance: "I don't know if they originally wanted it to open the movie, but it was definitely written specifically with mentioning the Warriors in mind and being *the* song of the movie."

DeVorzon says of the unforeseen rivalry, "That quite honestly didn't sit well with me. I told Larry and Walter, 'It's your choice.' And they chose Joe's and mine." In the film, "Last Of An Ancient Breed" is only heard briefly in the background in the DJ's booth when she informs listeners that the Warriors have got the better of the Orphans. Was that disappointing for Vance? "No. [I'm] always collaborative and I always felt like whatever's best, wherever they want, is fine with me as long as it serves the needs of the film. And at that time Joe Walsh was more of a name."

"And that turned out to be the song I guess that people remember," says Hill of "In the City". I ran into Joe Walsh years and years later and I said, 'I owe you a favor. I never got a chance to thank you, but I think you helped make the film better.'"

Once it was given the nod as the closing number and sonic back-drop to the long trek down the beach and freeze-frame, "In the City" was shown to be cued up by the DJ and dedicated to the gang, this time as a sort of apologia for the Warriors' maltreatment over the course of the previous night. The number provides a reasonable degree of pathos and feeling of resolution, as well as a sunny note to take the edge off a dark film. However, the fact that this "In the City" was not the fiery anthem of the same name recently made famous by UK punks the Jam but a mellow creation sung and co-written by a member of the type of band dismissed by the New Wave as dinosaurs only underlined the complete absence of punk influence in *The Warriors*.

It also brought to mind the fact that neither electronic music nor Eagles-member fare was the sort of thing one could imagine the cool young dudes within the Warriors' ranks putting on their cheap turntables. Was that ever a consideration for the director? Hill says no, although he doesn't give the impression that a lot of thought went into it. "Decisions were made very, very quickly," he shrugs. In fact, as befitting a streetwise musician, David Patrick Kelly took more of an interest in that depart-ment. "It was the year after all the American so-called punk bands had gotten their contracts," he reflects. In reference to one of those bands, Television, he says, "I wanted them to use—even though it was a year old—*Marquee Moon* as the soundtrack." DeVorzon offers that despite the broadly contemporary feel of the score, the intent was not to convey the idea that his contributions were the sort of music the characters depicted in the film would be grooving to. "You could probably make that point better with what the DJ was playing," he says. "I wasn't necessarily try-ing to be what was happening at the time... That music was background music to support the movie itself, using elements of rock 'n' roll and syn-theszers that they probably were listening to, but as songs. In other words, songs and a score are two different things."

"I don't remember being conscious of being under the gun or any deadline," says DeVorzon of his *Warriors* gig. "I had the right time to do it." However, he does admit to feeling a different kind of pressure when he had to present his finished work to Hill and co. He had laid out the bones of the score in the privacy of his home studio and the director and pro-ducers remained out of the loop even when he began recording for real. "They never heard it 'til we were on the dubbing stage... Now we're on the dubbing stage and I was on the spot. The picture had been edited. We had sound effects to work with, but what was the only thing no one has ever heard? That's the score... When you're on the stage, you not only hear the music, you look at it against what's happening on the screen... So I was nervous to say the least... It was a great relief to me that they liked what they were hearing."

"THERE WAS A LOT of short-tempered remarks and misunderstandings."

This is Walter Hill's impressionistic memory of the relations between Paramount and the *Warriors* camp during the picture's post-production process. Much of this seems to revolve around things Hill wanted to include in the movie but which the studio vetoed for reasons of budget, time, or—he seems to think—simple spite. He says, "The studio had said fine, those were all wonderful things, and then in post-production said, 'Oh no, no, we can't have any of this and that and the other thing.'"

The director had firm ideas about how the film should be framed for the viewer. "I said that I thought the movie was incomprehensible unless you understood it was in some kind of science-fiction mode and that it was in some way based on the Greek antecedents and that it was comic-book in its nature," Hill says. "I was convinced that, though the film had a lot of merit, the movie would not work without the proper frame that I wanted to give it." All his attempts to provide this context were stymied.

It was felt that the stentorian tones of Orson Welles would be perfect to read out the screen crawl included in the June '78 script that made obvious the story's echoing of *The Anabasis*. "He agreed to do it," says Hill of Welles. (This may have been a consequence of Marshall's work with Welles on the *Other Side of the Wind* project.) One might imagine that Paramount would be pleased at the gravitas that the great actor-director would have lent the project, but Hill recalls, "The studio said, 'We don't want him'—which was like, 'Christ, what does it take?'" The screen crawl was not used.

Another dispensed-with idea was Hill's plan to precede what he viewed as the film's chapters with annotated illustrations, the result of his "infatuation" with American comic books. That was also nixed at a higher level. Hill's desire to include at the beginning the legend "Sometime in the future" would have barely cost a dollar or taken five minutes to arrange. One report has it that it was vetoed because Paramount felt it uncomfortably similar to the already famous *Star Wars* preamble, "A long time ago in a galaxy far, far away."

These points of disagreement, however, were miniscule compared to the issue of Paramount's attitude to the film as a whole. "When I showed the movie to the studio, they hated it," says Hill. "They hated it all the way. They just didn't get it. They thought they were going to get a movie like *Saturday Night Fever*, a little more gang oriented. Working class Brooklyn to Manhattan and back. When they saw this comic-book fantasy they just said, 'What the hell is this?'"

Also unimpressed by the picture were the cast. This, though, was for a variety of different reasons. As traditional, cast and crew attended a screening of the rough cut. For Dorsey Wright, it had the potential to be a happy occasion because it was one on which he discovered that the first face to fill the screen was his and that the opening dialogue came from his mouth. "That's wild," notes Wright of this turn of events. He wasn't to enjoy the surprise for very long, courtesy of the diametrically opposite effect it had on his companion. During the shoot, he and Pamela Poitier had carried over their on-screen relationship into a film-set romance. Accordingly, the two arrived together at the Columbus Circle Gulf + Western building where the screening took place.

"As soon as she saw the Wonder Wheel, she got really upset 'cause she realized all her scenes were cut out," Wright recalls. "It was a shock to her." Wright still hadn't worked out the purpose of the night-time reshoots of the daytime Coney Island dialogue. Even so, "She got mad at me, thinking I was part of it... I'm sitting next to Pamela holding her hand and all of a sudden my fingers are being sqoze to where the blood isn't going through anymore. I realized, 'Oh my gosh, she is getting upset. She wants to know what happened to those shots.' And it's like, 'I'm the last person you need to ask... Nobody told her or me ahead of time. I guess they didn't even figure that we were seeing each other." Poitier was so distressed that Wright didn't get to take in the entirety of what was effectively his big-screen debut. "She was like, 'Yo, I want to leave.' I think the conclave thing had just came up. By then we both knew, 'You are not in this film.' There was no way in the world this movie is going to jump back."

The director and the producer were the next targets of Poitier's ire. "We were in the [aisle] and she got into it with Walter and Larry about what was going on... It became a whole routine of 'You cut me out!'" Unaware of Hill and co's decision to only feature daytime scenes at the close of the picture and the aesthetic motive thereof, Poitier—says Wright—assumed a political rationale for the occurrence, one engineered by the acclaimed star of the likes of *In The Heat of the Night* and *To Sir, With Love.* "She really thought it was her father. She was telling me a story about basically how Sidney didn't want her to use the last name in film, in her career. That she was supposed to work her way up from the bottom or whatever… I'm like, 'Okay, I'm not gonna argue that point. I'm not part of your family.'"

Although Hill has no recollection of any confrontation with Poitier (or, come to that, the rough-cut screening), he says of the decision, "I always felt badly about that. You basically made decisions, what you think are best for the film. Your ultimate loyalty has to be to that, and you have to make some painful decisions sometimes."

Hill's editing also provided a shock for Lynne Thigpen. The DJ had not just changed gender from Shaber's first draft but her role had been significantly expanded, her commentary now acting like a Greek chorus. She was even given the last line of the movie ("Now for that group out there that had such a hard time getting home: sorry about that. I guess the only thing we can do is play you a song"). However, at no point throughout the finished picture does the viewer see the character's face. As alluded to by Marshall, the director had made the decision to zoom in on the DJ's lips as she was uttering into the microphone honeyed threats to the Warriors. This was a perfectly standard filmmaking maneuver. Not so the director's decision to depict the character exclusively like that. Stylistically, it was a smart touch, lending the DJ a mysterious, even God-like, air. On a human level, it was brutal. "Lynne Thigpen sat with me at the screening," recalls Kelly. "She jumped a little bit." Although Thigpen had previously appeared on screen in TV movie *Fol-de-Rol* and the motion-picture version of *Godspell*, her role in *The Warriors* was a potentially life-changing one. It must, therefore, have been a devastating experience to realize she had effectively been anonymized and marginalized.

The rest of the cast had their own issues with what they were seeing. The young and inexperienced actors were expecting the kind of polished proposition they might witness at a commercial screening in a movie house. Beck says, "For ninety-five per cent of us, we'd never seen a rough cut of a picture. That was tough, because it's got temp music in it and it's got slugs for missing scenes and it's not color corrected. You're going, 'Oh, is that what this will look like?'" Michos: "It didn't really have all the bells and whistles in… We all walked out of there: 'Oh, what did we do? This is terrible. Oh my gosh.'" The shocked cast repaired to the Blarney Stone restaurant across the street from Gulf + Western, where, says Beck, "We all commiserated on this horrible movie that we had made."

Once again, though, David Patrick Kelly was an exception. He recalls enjoying himself. "They seemed kind of bummed out by it all," he says. "I was laughing a lot... I consoled Larry Gordon... Larry said, 'I think he has the spirit of this movie,' even though Larry said later that he was very worried that the movie was not gonna make it and stuff like that. I'm not saying I'm the only guy who got it or anything like that, but that's the way I felt."

Spirits were hardly raised by a preview of the film in Long Beach. "It was a disastrous screening," says Gordon. "We had a much older crowd." Recalls Hill, "It was not a success in the sense of the numbers were very good, because almost all the adults got up and walked out. But all the young people stayed and they quite liked it."

Perhaps the two men's recollections are so at odds because, as the producer, Gordon was liaising more closely with underwhelmed Paramount executives. Gordon: "They were very, very turned off with the screening because the crowd wasn't excited... I remember Frank Mancuso, who was the head of distribution, very important to the studio—he later ran the studio—saying, 'I just don't know about releasing this movie. Maybe we have to rethink it.' He was talking about releasing it almost like a black film or a gang film."

As is traditional, the members of the public for whom the screening was arranged were provided cards on which to write down comments. Hill isn't sure if anything was altered as a result of the feedback ("There must have been a couple of lines that changed, but I can't remember anything"). However, he notes, "The only thing that was a real bone of contention was that there was a line that I cut out. Usually it's you want to leave something in and they want to cut something out. But I had cut something out and Eisner insisted that the line come back. It was a line of Mercy's where she said her mom was on welfare or something. I thought this was too realistic. We fought about it and he insisted. He said he wouldn't even release the movie unless I put the line back in. So I put the line back in." Hill would seem to be referring to an element of Mercy's live-for-today discourse ("I see what's happening next door and down the block. Belly hanging down, five kids, cockroaches in the cupboard "). Hill recalls a review when the movie came out which cited the line as a false note. "I remember I took a copy of the review and I circled it and I sent it to Eisner."

Gordon says that, in any case, it wouldn't have been possible to make any substantial changes. "We were basically locked," he asserts. "And, truthfully, we wouldn't even know what to do, because we had the best movie we thought available."

In this utterly uncertain and unpromising climate, *The Warriors* was sent out into the wider world.

PROMOTION

WHATEVER MISGIVINGS PARAMOUNT may have had about *The Warriors*, they couldn't deny that Walter Hill had risen above both a tumultuous shoot and an acrimonious post-production to enable the studio to put it on the screens before its numerous potential rivals. It was the culmination of a sub-annum turnaround almost unknown in modern Hollywood. *The Warriors* moved from a green light in probably April 1978 to shooting by June 26 to theatrical release on Friday, February 9, 1979.

The final cut of *The Warriors* has an official running time of one hour, 34 minutes. Although its f-bomb quotient had plummeted from the June '78 script rewrite to the mid-teens, the Motion Picture Association of America designated the picture "Restricted" (those aged under seventeen had to be accompanied by an adult guardian). Being "R"-rated naturally limited the film's money-making potential, but the producers didn't consider dubbing out the profanities. Gordon reasoned to journalist David Bartholomew, "We are taking an R-rating on this film not because of the violence so much as the language, which to remain true to the story and characters is necessarily rough and authentic."

The studio, of course, was in a strange position regarding *The Warriors*. Its executives had already made clear their skepticism about the potential of the property, but they now had to set about the process of promotion in order to recoup costs and even make a profit.

As traditional, one of the planks of promotion was the printing of a Handbook of Production Information, then colloquially known—when the printed word was the predominant means of publicizing a product—as a "Press Book." In the case of *The Warriors*, it took the form of a spine-stapled, litho-printed magazine of 22 roughly 8" x 11" pages. It contained a cast list, preliminary technical credits, story synopsis, production anecdotes, cast biographies, a profile of Yurick's novel, and career summaries of Lawrence Gordon, Walter Hill, Andrew Laszlo, and Frank Marshall. It came with four hand-stapled inserts amounting to a further thirteen pages of text which, aside from a reproduction of a recent *Film Bulletin* article by David Bartholomew, was mostly comprised of more production anecdotes. A glossy still or two would probably also have been provided to journalists with the package.

Another intrinsic part of movie promotion is the "one-sheet," a film poster measuring 27 inches by 41 inches for display outside theatres running the movie (or in its lobbies as they prepare to). "I was in New York and the two heads of marketing at Paramount were in New York, and they called me over to show me the proposed one-sheets they wanted to use," recalls Gordon. "They showed me all these one-sheets that were terrible. I learned as head of production at AIP to always say, 'Show me what you didn't like.' I said, 'I want to see the stuff you turned down.' They showed me this poster and I said, 'That's the one we should go with.' And they were very, very angry. And besides that, they hated *The Warriors*… I just said, 'That's the one. That's what we should go with'… Walter loved it, too… They said, 'Are you out of your mind?'" "There were a couple others that I liked better," says Hill of Gordon's preferred poster. "I did like the typeface, though. They used our typeface from the film." (The poster was also not the favorite of several seen by Michael Beck, who via a remarkable coincidence happened to meet on the subway prior to the film's release the New York-based artist responsible for other designs.)

There is unanimity between producer and director on one thing about the poster. "You had nothing to say about the marketing," says Hill. "They kept you very much walled off." "We had no approval," confirms Gordon. "They could have told me to kiss their ass… Luckily, Eisner sided with me."

The hitherto rejected artwork had been provided by David Jarvis. A graduate of the Los Angeles Art Center College of Design, Jarvis had painted the posters for the Spaghetti Western *The Silent Stranger* and the soccer prisoner-of-war Sylvester Stallone vehicle *Escape to Victory*. He also rendered album-cover art, including *Hugo In Wonder-Land* by Hugo Montenegro, *Havana Daydreamin'* by Jimmy Buffet, and the Elvis Presley compilation *Welcome to My World*. His design was a major reason for *The Warriors* turning from a mere cinematic release into a phenomenon but was odd for more than one reason. In fact, on one level, it is quite easy to understand why the Paramount promotion department might have questioned the sanity of Gordon with regards to his partiality for his poster.

Jarvis had provided a vista ostensibly comprised of members of the film's various gangs. Although many one-sheets are impressionistic rather than strictly literal, this one took some jaw-dropping liberties with reality. Prominent in the composition is a figure clearly meant to be Swan but wearing a headband that said character never sported, a black male who wears the headdress of Cleon but has the facial features of Cochise, and a female dressed all in denim and wearing a cap who is possibly intended to represent Mercy but, aside from her aura of toughness, looks little like Van Valkenburgh's character. Behind and to the right of the Cleon-Cochise amalgam is a man whose face seems modelled on that of Tom McKitterick but who wears not Cowboy's Stetson but a yellow Arab keffiyeh. Two female figures further back in the composition wearing similar caps to the Mercy-esque figure and boasting curiously luminous eyes not only look identical to each other but seem to be modelled on Kate Klugman, one of the actresses in the Lizzies. On the far left of the picture, beside a Baseball Fury, is a formidable looking character with his hands on his hips and sporting sunglasses beneath a perfectly bald pate. "That's me," says the hirsute Terry Michos.

"They just took my hair off," continues Michos. "They must have taken it from a still. I never posed... They thought it was cooler. Maybe they liked my face. Maybe it was depicting something of the Turnbull ACs. They were trying to create a montage of the whole *Warriors*." Whatever the reason, he wasn't happy and says he told the powers-that-be, "You can't do that. I'm trying to get a career. I'm going to go to my agent." Their reaction? "They laughed. I was really upset about that, but I had to deal with it. I had no pull."

Dorsey Wright's shock at his first sight of the poster was compounded by him being in company. Driving with his mother, grandmother, and a friend, he suddenly spotted it on a billboard. "I pull over and park, tell my mother look up," he recalls. "She looks up. 'Oh, the movie you're in?' I say, 'Yeah.' They go, 'What the fuck? Where *you* at?' When your mother knows that's not you... My first comment was, 'Fuck—we all look alike?' But then I realized they did the same thing with Terry. It was a bad poster. I still look at it today and go, 'It made no damn sense.' None of us are actually on that poster. Beck is there but that's really not Beck. Maybe they thought, 'Look, this movie isn't going to go anywhere. Let's just throw anything together.'"

Where the illustrator wasn't being overly impressionistic, he seemed informed by whimsey. A bald-headed, mustachioed figure two rows behind Michos appears to be based on Burt Reynolds. Off his right shoulder is a head-cocked bald man who bears a close resemblance to David Carradine's Kwai Chang Caine in the flashback sequences of the TV show *Kung Fu.* Some illustrators make such jokey insertions on a "Wonder-if-anyone'll-notice" basis. From what Michos has heard, someone did notice. "Some later posters, those guys' faces were dotted out."

"Well, I didn't pay that much attention to it except for how it hit me," shrugs Gordon of the poster's nonsensical aspects. Yet regardless of the inaccuracies, eccentricities, and possibly superior alternatives, the Jarvis poster was not just striking but chilling. A profound air of menace suffuses it. The grimly staring gang members stretch into the distance. The Baseball Furies member standing off the Swanesque figure's right shoulder looks particularly intimidating, his disturbing garish make up accentuated by a scowl and a hoisted ball-bat.

The copy placed over the picture only intensified the unsettling aura. "THESE ARE THE ARMIES OF THE NIGHT," it declares in capital letters. The text below is lower case, but packs even more of a punch: "They are 100,000 strong. They outnumber the cops five to one. They could run New York City. Tonight they're all out to get the Warriors." As alluded to by Hill, beneath the picture was the film's logo, which rendered the Warriors' name in uneven, dripping lettering deliberately redolent of the type of spray-can graffiti to increasingly be found defacing walls across the nation. Taken as a whole, the poster spoke powerfully to the fear of moral decay that increasingly afflicted Western society, reflected in spiraling crime rates, obnoxious everyday behavior, and indeed violent and exploitative films, which—from its poster—this one gave every sign of being. All these problems had the greatest resonance in New York City.

The traumatic New Year's Eve subway mass-mugging incident related by Michos earlier in this text had a happy ending. "All of a sudden the train screeched to a stop, the doors flew open, and a bunch of police came in," he says. The *Warriors* poster, though, was positing—almost with relish—a scenario where such salvation was not possible. That street gangs were greater in number than the forces whose job it was to control them was exactly the type of notion to send a shudder through ordinary civilians. Yet while it might have been disturbing and even offensive, the poster was also alluring, and for the same reason as was Hollywood's increasingly gory and exploitative fare. People might be disapproving of and frightened by portrayals of violence, but they were also often intrigued and even excited by it.

Although Gordon says the *Warriors* camp "liked" and "approved" the poster's tagline, it also constituted a remnant of an abandoned plan by the studio to give the film a title he detested. "They wanted to change the title to *Armies of the Night*. I called Walter. We hated that title. And the only thing that saved us from not having this called *Armies of the Night* was Norman Mailer had written a book that had that in the title and they backed off."

Possibly the most crucial component of a film's promotional process is moving-media advertisements, in other words trailers and TV spots (the latter being commercials constituting very short versions of the trailer, usually running to around thirty seconds). For Hill, these changed everything. He recalls, "There was a guy back east that cut a trailer and that trailer really played well… The studio kept getting good feedback on the trailer… and the studio kept getting very good TV spots… When I saw the TV spots I thought, 'Jesus Christ, that'll shake somebody up and that'll get some people in the theatre'… That's the only thing that kept us alive, I think. Had it been other than that, I don't know if they'd have released it, they so disliked the movie."

The theatrical trailer for *The Warriors* featured the type of ominous, gravely voiceover then *de rigueur* for movie ads. "*These* are the armies of the *night*," a man urgently advised the viewer over a shot of the masses gathered at the conclave. Cyrus was shown impassionedly demanding, "Can you dig it! Can you dig it!" A litany in the same gravelly tones then soundtracked a visual montage of gangs: "The Furies. The Boppers. The High-Hats. The Lizzies. The Turnbull ACs. The Gramercy Riffs," and finally "And these are the Warriors."

One of the Lizzies was shown saying, "We know about the Warriors. They're a heavy outfit."

"They're from Coney Island," said the gravelly voice, now acting as a Greek chorus.

Mercy was then on screen saying, "The Warriors? You guys are the big dudes, huh?"

"Now they're in the Bronx," said the voiceover.

Cut to Swan announcing, "We're going back."

Gravelly voice: "Twenty-seven miles behind enemy lines."

Swan: "It's the only choice we got."

Gravelly voice: "Between them and safety stand 20,000 cops and a hundred thousand sworn enemies."

The fierce, sunglassed visage of New Cyrus (African-American actor Edward Sewer) was then seen demanding, "I want them all. I want all the Warriors."

In a final staccato flurry of melodrama, the gravelly voice stated:

"They've got one way out.
They've got one chance.
They've got one night.
The Warriors."

In its own way, *The Warriors'* trailer tweaked reality as much as did the film's poster. In the context of the actual film, the Lizzie comment is not a genuine tribute to the Warriors' toughness but rather flattery designed to relax them so as to facilitate vengeance, while Mercy's line was actually cut from the picture. Moreover, the trailer was clearly trying to suggest a level of darkness, menace, and violence that the movie simply doesn't possess.

Despite its inaccuracy, though, it was powerful and ominous and would have created in many viewers the same mixture of trepidation, disgust, and excitement as the one-sheet. Essentially, it was likely to make people want to see the film even if they hated themselves for that desire. "That trailer was frightening," says Michos. "There was a lot of commentary about that trailer. It sort of spoke of something that could happen. That's why we packed them in."

THE FILM POSTER'S BILLING block carried a piece of promotional cross-fertilization: "Read the Dell book." The release of the movie on which it was based had finally caused Yurick's novel to make it into paperback in his home country. The Dell release was naturally the archetypal movie "tie-in" edition, its cover making a virtue of its adaptation to the big screen ("Now an explosive movie from Paramount Pictures"), featuring stills from the production it had inspired. Its gaudily elaborate design was dominated by a sort of gutter-level coat of arms consisting of a graffiti-defaced metal shield backed not by a traditional heraldic component like crossed swords but a baseball bat and a length of chain. Set within the shield was a menacing color still of four Warriors staring at the camera lens, one of whom—Swan—was armed with a baseball bat.

Sandwiching the bulky, bright-red lettering of the book title was a sil-houette of a New York skyline and a drawing of running figures, two of them clearly a hands-held Swan and Mercy. The capitalized copy at the top read, "They are New York's toughest street gang. Cool is the name of their game. For keeps is how they play it." The taglines were consistent with the tone of the cover, but hardly with the movie: nobody would know from glancing at it that the Warriors were the ones menaced in the film, rather than the ones doing the menacing. But then, this wasn't a novelization of the movie but a reissue of the actual book that had inspired it. It would be fair to say that the copy was broadly consistent with the greater savagery of the film's prose antecedent. The latter fact was something which the back cover made clear. The copy written across a full-length color photograph of five Warriors seen from the rear said of the protagonists' activities on the "hot and ominous" Fourth of July in question, "They would rape and kill. But above all, they would stick together." The tagline at the bottom declared, "The terrifying thriller you'll never forget!" All of this was also consistent with the tone of men's mass-market paperbacks of the era. The Seventies was a boom time for exploitative action-based prose (a boom that was short-lived, soon to be wiped out by the video-cassette market). Yet while the exclamatory tone and tacky design of the Dell book would not have been out of place on contemporary spinner racks, it was a far cry from the respectable literary origins of *The Warriors*' first hardcover edition.

Over in the UK, the movie tie-in was published by Star, probably the country's most "downmarket" paperback publisher of the period and certainly a stark contrast to the reputable mien of the novel's British hard-back publisher, W. H. Allen. Its designer had clearly seen the Dell cover, for it used the same motifs of a New York skyline and running figures, even if not the same drawings. Said motifs sandwiched within a minimal-ist layout the Warriors logo as seen in the film poster. The cover copy read, "The classic novel of urban youth. Remember it next time you're on the streets alone."

The arrival of the film saw Yurick's book break out of the English language for, other than the Japanese edition, the first time. As well as a Japanese version in a new translation, *The Warriors* was now published in France, Germany, Italy, Portugal, and Spain.

More promotional cross-fertilization came in the form of a poster magazine, although this one would seem to have been a belated release judging by the tagline at the bottom of the front cover: "The Inside Story of the Film That Shook the Nation!" Poster magazines were a glossy format all the rage at the time. Their back covers, unusually for magazines, contained editorial. Opening its letter-sized pages revealed two further pages of editorial, which when themselves opened out exposed two editorial pages of double size. Opening the item out once more yielded a massive poster suitable for tacking to a bedroom wall, in this instance a huge detail from the Armies of the Night one-sheet (which also adorned the front cover). As their format suggests, poster magazine were usually devoted to pop stars, sports teams, TV shows, and youth-oriented movies. However, it's not as strange as it might first appear that Paramount licensed a poster magazine for *The Warriors*. The horror-movie and Bruce Lee poster magazines that had already done well in the decade so far had clearly racked up many sales from youngsters who were legally unable to see the films they discussed.

The features this publication offered were "The Warriors Production File" (detailing the film's making), "Meet the Warriors" (a profile of each of the movie's characters), and "War in the Streets of NYC". The latter was a full recounting of the movie's plot, something very handy for under-seventeens who would otherwise not be able to become conversant with it until the achingly distant, abstract point in time when they came of age. Although the poster magazine was also produced in the UK (with the cover picture replaced by the photo on the British film poster), judging by their comparatively infrequent sightings on the likes of eBay neither edition was given a large print run.

The Warriors: The Original Motion Picture Soundtrack (A&M Records) was also a belated release. That it appeared the month after the movie came out seems unwise dawdling for in those days such artefacts could be key pieces of merchandising and promotional cross-fertilization. With no disrespect intended to John Williams' talents, the major reason that he made the charts with a soundtrack album of a non-musical like *Star Wars* was because, in an era before VHS, DVD, or streaming, a soundtrack was one of the only ways by which the public could readily revisit a motion picture.

The front cover of the *Warriors* album featured the illustration from the one-sheet, with its reverse proffering the photograph seen on the British poster. In the days of vinyl, a one-disc album was limited to a maximum playing time of around forty minutes before sound quality suffered. As such, not everything from the movie soundtrack could be included on the LP. The album featured the six songs produced by Kenny Vance and four parts of the DeVorzon soundtrack ("Theme from 'The Warriors'", "The Fight," "In the City," and "Baseball Furies Chase"). "I listened to the score and I picked out the pieces that I thought would work inside of the soundtrack album," Vance says. "I can't remember if I remixed it." DeVorzon was unhappy with the record. "They had a lot of source music that the DJ was playing and, because of that, it didn't really sound like a soundtrack album," he says. "I thought they could have included more of the underscore. But I guess they can convince the record company that the more songs you had on it, the better off you were." "The goal of it was to stand on its own first and also for it to complement the movie," says Vance. "I think it does both of those things."

Vance notes, "I did the same thing I did in *Animal House*, which I think might have been a first: I incorporated things from the movie. Little pieces of dialogue that tie the whole thing together." Samples of dialogue from *The Warriors* included on its soundtrack album are the DJ saying, "The Baseball Furies dropped the ball," New Cyrus insisting "I want all those Warriors!", and Luther's taunt "Warriors come out to pla-a-ay." In this regard, Vance was remiss only in failing to include Cyrus' "Can you dig it?" line. "Yeah, you're right," Vance concedes with a chuckle. In his defense, he says, "I never really got to see the whole thing until they put it together. I only saw little pieces of it. So I just was on the fly. I never realized that that was going to be the iconic line."

For those inclined to read anything into the track sequencing, "In the City" did not close proceedings the way it did the movie but opened side two; the final track instead was "Last of an Ancient Breed."

Nor was "In the City" issued as a single. "Theme from 'The Warriors'" backed with "Baseball Furies' Chase" was chosen instead—although that had nothing to do with Vance. "Joe [Walsh] had a string of hits," says De-Vorzon of his co-composer. "To be frank with you, I was a little disappointed that he didn't release it." Although "In The City" becoming a hit single would have been perfect promotion for the movie, for DeVorzon's finances the fact that it wasn't given the opportunity so to do may ultimately have been for the best. In September 1979, the Eagles would include a new recording of "In the City" on their LP *The Long Run*, something that might not have occurred if the band thought it had already had too wide an exposure. *The Long Run* topped the *Billboard* album chart for nine weeks.

Another controversial omission from the soundtrack was the sinister, glittering snippet of DeVorzon music heard behind the Wonder Wheel at the film's start. In fairness, though, it's an omission DeVorzon made himself with the single, which he supervised. "In retrospect, I'm sorry I didn't use it on the record," he says. "Their point was they were trying to get something that was radio-friendly and you could get right into the theme. The Wonder Wheel kind of set everything up. But of course you had the visuals to work with that. And now, after the fact, everyone wants to hear that Wonder Wheel music." Not present on either the single or album version is the dialogue with which "Theme from 'The Warriors'" was peppered in the film. In apparent contradiction of his previous comments, DeVorzon says he feels the theme worked as a piece of music on its own.

DeVorzon doesn't hold with the idea that instrumentals from films don't make for big hits. "I've had two very unlikely but giant instrumentals: 'Theme from SWAT,' which was number one, and 'Nadia's Theme,' which was from a motion picture called *Bless the Beasts and Children*, and that was a giant hit. I thought the *Warriors* main title had a shot because synthesizers were relatively new and it's rock 'n' roll and it just had a great vibe and a feel, and especially people related the theme to the movie: just sounding tough and city."

SOL YURICK SAID he only became aware of the imminent release of the *Warriors* film when he saw subway posters and TV spots advertising it and that only when he telephoned the Paramount publicity department was an invitation extended to him to view it.

Yurick termed the screening he attended a "premiere." However, Lawrence Gordon insists "There was no premiere. They just opened the movie. They weren't gonna have a premiere for a movie that did what we did in Long Beach." As Yurick said he saw Hill at this event, he would seem to have been referring to a New York promotional preview just prior to the picture's formal opening night. Hill didn't attend the latter because the Friday *The Warriors* opened found him in London where he'd gone to look at the first cut of *Alien*, the Ridley Scott-directed film of which he was a producer. The latter mission dovetailed with his standard "defensive maneuver." He explains, "Once you've sent them out there, there's nothing you can do so I try to focus on what's ahead rather than what's behind."

"We had one of those previews via a radio station that had invited a lot of kids down into Times Square," explains Hill. "It must have been Wednesday night." Yurick later wrote that he found Hill in the lobby "trembling," because his last picture (clearly a reference to *The Driver*) had been a flop and his reputation was riding on this one. "Oh, that's bullshit," says Hill. "I've never shaken at a fucking preview in my life. I remember I was in quite a good mood, as a matter of fact… We blew the roof off the place. They were yelling and cheering and roaring. It was a happy audience… I remember calling back to LA to Larry saying, 'Jesus. I know that the studio is not exactly too keen on us, but if they can get this audience into a theatre we're gonna do fine.' It had a sensational reaction."

Symptomatic of the rollercoaster ride that the reception to *The Warriors* would consist of, however, was a review Hill read on the craft that took him across the Atlantic. "As I was getting on the plane to London, I bought a paper. I guess it was the *Post*, I can't remember. The movie was not reviewed with everybody else 'cause they hadn't shown it to the critics, but one critic had seen it, [possibly] the late screening. I opened the paper, I saw the review. It said I had made three movies and this was strike three and out, it was terrible. I remember going to the sports page or something and thinking 'Well, on to the next' or whatever we say to ourselves." Surely behind the bravado lay a dread that if *The Warriors* flopped, no studio would ever let him helm another film? "Oh, it might have, but the truth about it is all these things have to do with what the project is and who's going to be in it. They certainly wouldn't have sought me out, but if I'd have showed up with a action script with Steve McQueen or something, I'm sure they'd let me direct it."

Although *The Warriors* was given a "wide" release—in this case, placed in 670 theatres—there still seemed a certain half-heartedness about Paramount's attitude toward selling it. "We did not do a lot of promotion," says Michael Beck. "There were no press junkets and stuff like that. We might have had some local—we were all in New York—interviews and things. More papers—I don't remember doing a lot of radio promotion for this movie." "They didn't spend much money at all," says Gordon. However, the amount the studio did spend was a lot more than what at one point he feared it might be. "I assumed we were going to have a huge fight over pulling the movie. They were going to pull the marketing, do something ridiculous, 'cause they didn't expect anything. And neither did we."

Perhaps what might be termed Paramount's final insult was not granting advance press screenings. As this is a studio tactic that is traditionally perceived as betraying a complete lack of confidence in the product, it's often a kiss of commercial death. The media seemed to take its cue from Paramount's coyness and deemed *The Warriors* of no importance. The February 9, 1979 front page of the *New York Times'* "Weekend" section carried the headline "Six Films Open with a Galaxy of Stars." It excitedly listed *Agatha, Hardcore, In Praise of Older Women, Murder By Decree, Quintet,* and *When You Comin' Back, Red Ryder?* It made no mention of *The Warriors.*

When the reviews did start coming in, they weren't exactly a counterblast to the one Hill had seen. "The daily papers were almost entirely negative," says Hill. A case in point is the write-up on February 10 by Ernest Leogrande of the New York *Daily News.* Noting that its use of Yurick's novel as a jumping-off point was "a jump of Olympic proportions," he adjudged the film to be "both surrealistic pop art and sentimentalized pandering to the attitude of 'us against them,' the have-nots against the haves." The kindest thing he could bring himself to say was that "the movie is so perversely fascinating in a variety of ways that it's too bad the imagination demonstrated wasn't used for something better than what turns out to be one more exploitation film in which the audience is encouraged to cheer the sights and sounds of mayhem." Also on February 10, Gary Arnold of the *Washington Post* said, "None of Hill's dynamism will save *The Warriors* from impressing most neutral observers as a ghastly folly. It seems a little demented to choose gang warfare as a pretext for showing off virtuoso technique."

The verdict of Roger Ebert of the *Chicago Sun-Times* arrived on February 13. He felt that the movie was of a peculiar piece with Hill's previous entries. Noting that Hill liked to deal with characters who took on a "mythic stature" within "urban tableaux," he said the film was a "ballet of stylized male violence" which never sought to be believable. He found "great vitality and energy (and choreography and stunt coordination)" in the gang fights and run-ins with cops but felt the film to be dominated by a "stiff stylization." The dialogue of the characters bore no relation to the way people interact in real life: "Three members of a street gang are lined up in a row. The camera regards the first one. He speaks. The camera pans to the second, and he speaks. The camera pans to the third. He speaks. Because the movement of the camera dictates the order and timing of the speeches, there can be no illusion that the characters are talking as their words occur to them." The same artifice afflicted the way the participants squared up to each other: "People move into their symbolic places with such perfectly timed choreography that they must be telepathic." He questioned whether Hill's singular style was suited to the violent action-picture demographic at which Paramount's advertising was pitching the film: "Action audiences, I suspect, will find it either incomprehensible or laughable."

It transpired that such brickbats mattered little to what Terry Michos terms "Mr. and Mrs. Front Porch." Asked what kind of business he thought the picture might do, Hill says, "I didn't think I had much of an idea." James Remar says, "I just thought that we made a good movie and it was going to be a success." Van Valkenburgh offers, "Well, on the one hand you always hope that something really cool's gonna happen. It's your first job and you're making a movie and you have fantasies, but that's just a really personal feeling. Other than that, I really had no idea." Lawrence Gordon—shaken by the preview and Paramount's attitude—wasn't optimistic. "We were very nervous about it," says the producer.

Things changed on Gordon's part when he took in the opening night in Westwood, California. "We were very shocked by the massive response," he says. "The audience started cheering when the Wonder Wheel is trolling around. Even before the credits, they started cheering." It was a harbinger of great things. As Hill notes, "It turned out from out of nowhere we were the number-one box office film."

"You got a movie that was in its opening weekend the top grossing movie, even without a lot of promotion," observes Beck. In its first three days on release in the "Domestic Theatrical Market" (the United States, Canada, Puerto Rico, and Guam), *The Warriors* grossed $3,478,000 million. By the two-week mark, it had surpassed $10 million in receipts, which meant it had already taken two-and-a-half times its generally theorized production budget (or more than three times the one Hill recalls). By its sixth week of release, *The Warriors* had grossed $16.4 million. As with all box-office statistics, there is some question of exactitude. For instance, while contemporaneous reports claimed that the film opened in 670 cinemas, other reputable sources cite 551. Moreover, some might point out that during the month of *The Warriors*' release, domestic box-office receipts—partly because of snowbound conditions—had declined for the first time in two years, i.e. the film wasn't up against much competition. However, *The Warriors* did the only thing that could be asked of a film in the commercial arena: beat out all the competition. Moreover, that competition included *The Great Train Robbery*, a Sean Connery-starring project based on a Michael Crichton novel.

Of *The Warriors*' Westwood, CA. screening, Gordon says, "The big shots didn't even come. Only a couple of distribution guys, and a marketing guy. I think Don Simpson may have come, but none of the big executives came. And they were shocked that we opened the way we opened. They couldn't believe it. We sold out every show." The edgy relationship between the *Warriors* camp and Paramount suddenly softened. "After the movie came out and it did well, everybody was sort of friends," Hill would later note.

"It became an utter shock when the film was released and the lines were wrapped around the blocks and it was just turning into this gigantic smash surprise," recalls Van Valkenburgh. Remar notes, "It blew us all away... That was a journey of discovery—to actually go to the newsstand and pick up a *Variety* and look at our position in the box office. That was something I'd never done before. I was really not educated in that aspect of the business 'cause I was on the side of the show. That was pretty exciting."

"I didn't think it was going to be for young people," says David Patrick Kelly. "I had no idea about [the sort of] youth demographics that became huge in the Eighties. I just knew it was a kind of genre fiction. To be number one like it was, that was a huge surprise.... I think it was the Bronson/Clint Eastwood [crowd]. These are not cineastes. It's a particular thing. Now it's all mixed, of course. In the post-Tarantino universe, it's high art and it's crowd-pleasers. Back then... there was this deep divide between arthouse movies or regular mainstream Hollywood movies and action movies, which were considered just a sub-genre."

Dorsey Wright feels that New Yorkers perceived *The Warriors* differently to the rest of the country. Simply by dint of their familiarity with the backdrops, denizens of the Big Apple were able to grasp more readily the picture's fable/metaphor nature. "We got that in New York immediately. The moment you start showing make-up and high hats... you could almost lose a New York City audience." NYC residents could have also been alienated by the topographical and geographical inconsistencies. "New Yorkers look at the movie and go, 'That is not 86th Street. That's 72nd'... They didn't take advantage of a lot of backgrounds, because we didn't shoot in a lot of places that they said, 'This is the location.' They never went to the Bronx, at that time your idea of what the decay in New York looked like. They shot places in Brooklyn, so they captured a little bit of the feel. But through osmosis it actually got in there. A lot of the bombed-out buildings and stuff aren't in the movie. You don't see a lot of it, you just feel it." The potentially risible elements proved of little import. "It was like, 'You know what, I'm gonna root for this film'... By the time that the film was over, they loved the film. We know all the sets are wrong, half the dialogue is wrong. Interracial gang—not happening... But New Yorkers let it go because they actually got into this whole gang fantasy and the characters. It was a character-driven movie. Ajax really carried this thing for a lot of people. They got into him and then when he got… arrested… it was like, 'Damn—he's gone.' So it became one of those movies: who's gonna survive? I get a lot of people who come up to me even today and go, 'All the best people got killed off. What happened to Ajax?' I have no idea. One guy told me that he believed that Cleon and Ajax both wound up in the same jail cell."

The Warriors' turnabout in fortunes continued into the critical arena. The next wave of reviews proved as enthusiastic as the public had shown itself to be. Janet Maslin had been alone among the first tranche of reviewers in her positivity. Her review in the February 10 *New York Times* was fairly small in terms of space—about a sixth of one of the paper's oversize pages—but expansive praise-wise. She was another critic amused by the extreme dramatic license that dictated the Warriors so often speak sequentially. Also in common with many critics, she didn't consider the film one that gave much leeway for great performance. None of this, though, detracted too much from her enjoyment. "Mr. Hill stages some wonderful-looking encounters," she raved of Swan and Mercy's subterranean kiss and the set-tos with the Baseball Furies and the Punks. "The film is as handsome to watch as it is preposterous to listen to, full of gorgeous nocturnal city images that splash blaring neon colors against filthy, rain-slicked gray." Maslin's newspaper verdict prefigured the favorable tone of the magazine reviews.

"It was the magazines that followed up the next week that turned it," says Hill. "The reviews [of] Kael and any number of others were terrifically positive, and they were in theory the harder reviews to get. So it had this odd pedigree and reception." Michos: "I think people were saying to themselves, 'Why are so many people enjoying this? What is actually happening?' The ones that took the time to think about that examined why the film was successful."

While Sol Yurick was phlegmatic about the fact that the film possessed only what he termed the "skeleton" of his novel, he was convinced that the central conceit of his book was what lay behind much of the critical respect the movie acquired. At the screening he was asked by what he took to be a public-TV reporter about the film's classical source, of which the man had vaguely heard. When Yurick explained the parallels with *The Anabasis*, he recalled that he saw the man's eyes light up as if he now had a reason to give a good review to a movie he had already vouchsafed to Yurick he didn't care for. Yurick recalled having a similar experience when telephoned by Pauline Kael prior to the appearance of—and implicitly when she was in the process of writing—her *New Yorker* review.

Film-criticism doyen Kael—just coming up to her sixtieth birthday—had been analyzing motion pictures for the *New Yorker* since 1968 with a prolixity and solemnity that made it clear that she considered the medium to be no less credible than literature, a stance not as common then as it is today. Not only was Kael renowned, she was also notoriously hard to please. One major star went so far as to publicly claim that her critiques were less about what she was watching than her own self-hatred. The cast and crew of *The Warriors* found themselves the subject of probably the closest thing to a rave of which Kael was capable.

Her assessment of *The Warriors* was her swansong in the magazine prior to her departure for a new post as consultant at (interestingly enough) Paramount Pictures. It was a 2,800-word, multi-page review that ran under the heading "Rumbling" in the magazine's "Current Cinema" strand. Although it's remembered impressionistically as glowing, it was actually balanced and nuanced, but the serious, lengthy consideration it granted the film unquestionably served to confer gravitas on it.

One of several things about which Kael was negative was what she felt to be *The Warriors'* flatness of both emotion and atmosphere. She said its characters stood in stark contrast to the passionate types previously found in juvenile delinquency movies: "He cools them out... they seem almost redundant—it's as if Hill's vision were complete without them." She found the depiction of New York sterile: "The performances seem to be taking place in the void of a studio." She had several problems with the script, from the plot device of a previously unseen witness conveniently materializing to tell the Riffs who it was that really killed Cyrus to her idiosyncratic feeling that the park-bench policewoman initially seems a man in drag. "The dialogue has the effect of inserts," she opined. She even took issue with the much-loved prom-couples scene, scoffing at the "sentimentalized confrontation of the haves and the have-nots." This was evidently related to the fact that, unlike Hill, she was an NYC native: "Prom kids wouldn't make eye contact with street punks," she claimed.

However, she also admitted, "Maybe it's partly because Hill isn't a New Yorker that he is able to sustain the jumping excitement of this vision." She celebrated the fact that *The Warriors* took movies "back to their socially conscious role of expressing the anger of the dispossessed," although she didn't confuse giving a voice to the dispossessed with creating gritty realism. Pointing out that in the source novel (to which she made several references), the youngest of the gang carried a comic-book recounting of Xenophon's beleaguered trek, she said, "The movie is that comic book seen through the young reader's eyes: it's a slum kid's vivid fantasy of the hardships and adventures of a group of boys who have to prove their courage, their discipline, and their fighting skill to survive the night." She insisted that "the literate shouldn't miss out" on *The Warriors* just because its TV commercial promoted the picture as an exploitation film. She said, "*The Warriors* is a real moviemaker's movie: it has *in visual terms* the kind of impact that 'Rock Around the Clock' did behind the titles of *Blackboard Jungle*."

She enjoyed the stylized, cartoonish physical action, which she found redolent of Peckinpah and Kurosawa's *Yojimbo* and the higher-grade kung-fu movies. She also noticed that "each battle is different —spatially and kinetically—and tops the one before..." She thought the conclave scene reminiscent of D.W. Griffith's *Intolerance* and the film's atmosphere suggestive of the decadent feeling of Vienna in Carol Reed's *The Third Man*.

She was entranced by *The Warriors'* palette. "The purplish cheap-thrill color is as deep and strong as what cinematographers used to get when Technicolor was still Technicolor. And it gives off a hot glow against the darkness... There's a night-blooming, psychedelic shine to the whole baroque movie."

Although pointing out that at the 11:15 p.m. Broadway theatre show she attended the audience was attentive and hushed, Kael almost made a virtue of the somewhat different atmosphere at other screenings. "There have been violent incidents in theatres showing *The Warriors*, as there were in the Fifties at *Blackboard Jungle*, and as there frequently are at theatres that run action movies... If there's one immutable law about movies, it may be that middle-class people get hot and bothered whenever there's a movie that the underclass really responds to."

"That was a gigantic event," remembers Van Valkenburgh of Kael's review. A veritably misty-eyed Kelly says, "I'd read her books and reviews since I was a teenager, so for her to champion the film..." Tom McKitterick: "I was opposed to her opinions on many directors such as Alfred Hitchcock, and she was very opinionated, but she was the hot critic." "Pauline Kael wasn't just a reviewer, she was a real film critic," says Michos. "We were getting panned. Jeffrey Lyons panned it and all these reviewers on TV, and she came out and said, '*The Warriors* is a social commentary that people are not understanding.' When that review came out, I think it changed a lot about the way people looked at the film. Not immediately, but it changed people's understanding that it was more than just a gang film."

New York Magazine (not to be confused with the *New Yorker*) featured across one-and-a-third pages of its issue cover-dated March 5 the judgment of the also-esteemed David Denby. He found *The Warriors* "funny and volatile and mock ferocious—a cross between a kung fu battle epic and a friendly Broadway musical." He cautioned that there was "hardly a believable minute in the film," pointing out that the gangs arriving for the conclave were so outlandishly dressed, and so clearly matched to their costumes that it was "like a gathering of chorus boys for a big Broadway production number..." He said "no one ever seems to get badly hurt... The violence... represents moral rather than physical strength." Stating that "*The Warriors* is an ecstatic fantasy of a city wholly dangerous and wholly glamorous, a city empty and free at night..." he asserted that the fantasy was in danger of giving way to mundane reality at Swan's line about how unprepossessing their holy grail of Coney Island is. However, he admitted that "the swaggering menace of teenage toughs can be great fun (from a distance)" and that he found the film "exhilarating." The main reason for the latter was because "it really *moves*." Of Hill, Denby opined, "He may be one of those rare American directors with a choreographical sense" and admired the "brilliant-looking nighttime landscape" of "spray-paint purples and reds against black background" created by him and Laszlo (he took the trouble to credit both men). Despite such high-falutin' comments, in his summary he made a quasi-pugnacious comment that almost gave ammunition to those who would come to consider *The Warriors* a malign influence: "The movie will never win any awards for intelligence, but it sends you out feeling happy and alive, ready to knock someone's hat off."

These reviews added another element to the film's audience: the arthouse crowd. Hill: "They showed up later. The first weekend was all kids." Of course, wonderful though the commercial and critical success was, it could also be said to be a vindication of Paramount's belief that the post-production touches for which Hill had unsuccessfully petitioned were unnecessary. Does that not prove that sometimes the compromises directors have to make to get a picture to the screen can result in a better product? Hill: "I was clearly wrong about that in that the film certainly worked and got through to an audience." Baxley in fact thinks it's fortunate that Hill didn't get his way on the comic-book panels. "Back then it would have been awful, 'cause I don't think they were capable of doing what needed to be done to carry that concept off," he says. Hill does add, "Do I think that sometimes the push and pull of the studio system and all that kind of business and finance can make films a little better? Yeah, I do. I think that occasionally can happen. I'm obviously mostly on the side of the director, but directors are not perfect." However, Hill soon had far greater issues on his plate than the embarrassment of arguably being shown to have lost an argument.

A clue to it lies in a thread running through the second wave of reviews, one noting that the film had started attracting bad publicity that was nothing to do with its aesthetics. Most critics dismissed the legitimacy of this bad publicity, even ones dubious about the film's qualities. On March 12, New York counterculture weekly *The Village Voice* published a column by Andrew Sarris which reviewed *The Warriors* in tandem with *Richard Pryor — Live in Concert*. Watching *The Warriors* with a companion in the presence of "a conspicuously posted security guard with an intensely watchful expression on his face," Sarris found he couldn't get worked up about the social-menace qualities that were being attributed to the Hill picture: "I have been told that children find *Watership Down* more frightening, and I can believe it." He thought the film's gangs to be pussycats compared to the people he daily saw walking the Gotham streets. "Hence, there is no point in banning *The Warriors*. One might well wish instead for some way to ban many of the viewers of *The Warriors*."

It wasn't only the film critics who were providing an alternate narrative to the idea of *The Warriors* as a malign influence. Kelly remembers an episode of *Saturday Night Live* which addressed the *Warriors* controversy in its Weekend Update spoof news section presented by Jane Curtin. "She did a little report on screenings of *The Warriors*. 'The audience breaks out into bubblegum and hula-hoop events.' They were just saying, 'What is all the fuss about?'"

Despite such derision, though, the bad publicity was becoming a groundswell, one that was working to transform *The Warriors'* triumph astonishingly quickly into a tragedy.

CONTROVERSY

WHEN LAWRENCE GORDON had taken in the February 9 Westwood opening of *The Warriors*, the pleasure he obtained from the audience reaction was soured somewhat. While he might have been astonished by the evident keen anticipation for the film and the ecstatic response to it, he was equally astounded by the trouble that erupted in the theatre. Sadly, Westwood did not transpire to be a one-off, but a portent of terrible things to come. Within a week of the film's release, three young men in separate areas of the United States had been killed in incidents that were being directly blamed on screenings of *The Warriors*.

"Westwood is an area of LA where all the UCLA kids and all the kids go to school," explains Gordon. "It was a huge market. Big theatres. My mother, my wife, and my two little sons were coming to the screening, and my brother and his wife. I got there earlier than everybody... Opening night in Westwood was something I've never seen before or since... There was this giant line around this block. I couldn't believe it." That was just the paying customers. "People were trying to break into the theatre. You know by the screen they have two exit doors? People were coming in from those doors, banging those doors. They went nuts."

Gordon met the manager of the Westwood Theater in the lobby. "The manager said to me, 'I've never seen these people in Westwood before. Who are all these people in line?' We had car clubs, we had gangs, we had everything in line... One person I saw there was a giant guy, he was a member of a bike club, a car club. He was about six-seven or eight. He had a little derby... I saw him in line with a bunch of his guys... They had colors like the Warriors, vests and so on. Not the same logo but their own logo."

Gordon's good mood took a dip shortly after the cheer that went up at the sight of the Wonder Wheel (an odd reaction from Angelinos to this New York landmark). "There were almost two or three fights in the theatre of different groups yelling at each other," he recalls. "I broke one of them up in the lobby. They all walked down the aisle together like they were going to fight and I convinced them not to fight, to go back in and watch the movie. I told them my wife and my children were in the theatre, my mother, and if they started a fight everybody was going to go to jail. Just using a little bluff. They calmed down. They went back in. But it was like a heavyweight championship fight."

Gordon's good mood now returned and lasted the weekend and slightly beyond. "We sold out every theatre around the country. All I could think about was, 'We have this gigantic hit'... When I came to my office on Monday, there was a message to come see Mr. Eisner and Mr. Diller." When he got to the office where the meeting had been called, Gordon found that the subject of discussion was not the exceptional business *The Warriors* was doing. "It was about the violence that happened in theatres. They were scared to death for the studio. Don't forget Paramount was owned by a gigantic conglomerate. Paramount was thinking about pulling the movie out of distribution."

The reports of violence not only continued to filter in from across the country but got incrementally worse. That very Monday—February 12—several friends attended a drive-in showing of *The Warriors* in Palm Springs, California. Among them was nineteen-year-old roofer Kenny Eller, a father of a one-year-old son. Eller got into an argument with a youth who was blocking the path to the facility's toilets. Amidst a tumult that involved flying garbage cans, bullets were fired from a small-caliber handgun that Eller's assailant had brought to the screening. One of the bullets went through Eller's skull. Taken to hospital, Eller was put on the critical list.

The same night, 165 miles across state, eighteen-year-old Ventura construction worker and prospective law-college student Tim Gitchel, his brother, and two friends caught a one-dollar 10:10 *Warriors* showing at the Esplanade triplex theatre in Oxnard. Just as the film started, the quartet got into a battle with fifteen people suspected through the previous screening of drinking and smoking grass. The fight spilled into a walkway. Three of Gitchel's party were stabbed, with Gitchel himself receiving a fatal knife wound to the heart. An eyewitness said, "They were caught up in a battle fever. They just had the look of crazy in their eyes."

The death three nights later of sixteen-year-old high school sopho-more Marty Yakubowicz wasn't at a *Warriors* screening but supposedly was linked to one. The Boston resident had left the job he held placing bindings on skis half an hour early to surprise his mother with a gift. On the subway home, he encountered six youths who had just seen *The War-riors.* Two of them were said to be friends of his and they left the subway together. However, as Yakubowicz headed for a bus a fight broke out. He was stabbed to death. Meanwhile, the following day in California, Eller succumbed to his injuries.

The California movie houses where the fatal incidents had occurred cancelled the film. Gitchel's family quickly announced that they were to file civil suits against both Paramount and the theatre complex. There were reports of picketing outside cinemas. There were also reports of theatres hiring extra security. Frank Melatti, director of operations at the Translux Theater in Stamford, Connecticut, revealed that he had engaged an off-duty policeman to stand watch following a fight at the theatre on February 14. "We've had quite a problem," Melatti said.

"When I was over in London, the firestorm hit," reflects Hill. "We went from one of the most obscure movies to the most notorious film in the United States." Newspapers, magazines, and television pundits had in recent years taken to claiming that growing societal violence was to a large part at-tributable to what might be termed Hollywood's pornography of violence. *The Warriors* was considered to supply grist to their mill. The apportioning of blame wasn't restricted to grieving parents, media commentators, nor conservatives. Tony Bill, a Hollywood producer then most famous for *The Sting,* opined, "It makes sense that a movie that basically glorifies violence would attract violence." It so happened that Bill was the executive producer of *Boulevard Nights,* one of the cluster of gang-related films that had gone into production at broadly the same time as *The Warriors.* He insisted that his own film was antiviolent. Meanwhile when Roger Ebert went to view *Boulevard Nights,* he reported that he was handed a leaflet by a group that linked the movie with *The Warriors* and other current and violent films as part of a plot by the "fascist ruling class" to "poison the minds of thousands."

"Surprised, dismayed, and very upset," is Lawrence Gordon's sum-mary of the reaction in the *Warriors* camp to these stories. "I am a father and I don't like anybody getting hurt at any level." James Remar says, "I was completely shocked that that sort of thing became an issue."

The issue, of course, had the potential to seem a bigger one than it was. With the commentariat latching onto a story, it can rapidly turn from a news report into a crusade, and once something has been designated a social ill by the Fourth Estate it is in their interests to emphasize and even magnify it. "It's the old journalistic phrase: 'If it bleeds, it leads,'" says Michael Beck. Walter Hill also seems to be of this view, as did Sol Yurick. While the director concedes, "There were some terrible incidents that happened," he also insists, "It wasn't quite the apocalyptical event." "There were not that much," said Yurick of the movie-house violence. "That was vastly overblown. It spread an alarm very quickly, but I think it was only one killing."

The cast now found themselves thrust into the glare of hostile scrutiny. It was an unnerving experience for them, partly because they were young, partly because it had been the veritable five minutes since they were Goliath-toppling box-office heroes. Van Valkenburgh reflects, "The other extreme of it went so far that it became a hazard."

"I think all of us were initially feeling some sense of guilt and responsibility for being in a picture that would cause that," muses Beck. "I had to go through my own sense of, 'God, did we do something that was morally wrong and that caused all this stuff to happen?' You second-guess yourself." It seems reasonable to assume that Beck's agonizing was informed by a recent change in his perspective, even his morality. Beck doesn't make reference to his Christianity as freely as does Michos ("He was a very strong witnesser," Beck amusedly notes of Michos' on-set proselytizing). However, around three weeks before the movie's opening night, Beck was Born Again. "I had been a child of the Sixties: drugs, sex, rock 'n' roll, you name it," he says. "Raised in a kind of culturally Christian family, the Episcopal Church, but I didn't have any kind of relationship with God. I just had gone to church and things like that, and once I got to university I gave up what cultural trappings of church I carried. So when I came to a realization of Jesus being who He said He is, it was like scales falling from my eyes."

Even protestations of innocence could just make the actors feel guilty. "We got a few more interviews after all the brouhaha happened with the movie," wryly notes Beck, and on that point Van Valkenburgh says, "I would do these interviews and I would try and defend the film and what we were doing and somehow that made me part and parcel."

Sol Yurick experienced no dark nighttime of the soul. "My phone rang constantly for 24 hours and I was asked did I feel responsible," he said. "Well, no, I don't feel responsible. I don't think that what you see necessarily drives you into a frenzy... There was a killing at a showing of *The Sound of Music* too in New York, so what can I tell you? People bump into each other, they get angry and it doesn't matter what they're seeing." (It's interesting that the novel on which the film was based did not attract criticism for its far more real and revolting violence. Literature having a cultural free pass that cinema is not granted, it seems fair to assume that Yurick received no phone calls from the press when his book was first published.) "If someone comes to a movie with a gun, who's at fault?" David Holden—one of the film's editors—reasoned to the media. Paramount Vice President Gordon Weaver was also contacted for comment. He pointed out that the violence was "the sort of thing that happens at rock concerts, high school basketball games, and any place where diverse groups meet. It could have happened anywhere."

Dorsey Wright doesn't seem to agree with that perspective. "That line on that poster alone sent chills through people," the film's Cleon says. "I was like, 'Holy shit, they have lost their fucking mind.' So when things started happening in movie theatres, I was like, 'They brought that on themselves.' I blame the Hollywood elites because you really didn't know what you were doing from beginning to end with this movie. You had something that's very explosive. You put those lines on there—'We could take over the city.' Are you fucking crazy? You can't put shit up there and not have the police department go, 'I hope these idiots aren't reading that shit and taking it for being true.' I think they should have had a little bit more foresight. This is not LA This is not the 'burbs. You don't say, 'There's 60,000 of you and only 20,000 cops' or whatever. And 'Armies of the Night.' You don't do that shit. You wet down the street and you put these guys in these vests and then you get a bunch of hyped-up kids in a movie theatre with this music going? Oh yeah, there's going to be problems. Gang members would come to the theatre. You can't go in and go, 'Excuse me gentlemen, there's no smoking in this section.' It's not that type of party... So you got that element... So when a fight broke out, a fight broke out. Became just a street brawl."

"That's a big controversy," muses Larry Gordon. "You're opening up a very big area here: do movies really cause this or not? There's many, many, many, many articles written about that. Hundreds of hours of discussion about that... That happened, but that's happened to many people who make movies." "I am a believer from a young age in that kind of magical identification," says David Patrick Kelly. "You'd come out of the movie feeling, 'This is who I am.' But I don't know... I don't know if you can definitively say that this provoked people." Hill is more certain about his view. "Movies don't cause murder. Murderers cause murder." He recalls,

"Sigourney Weaver and I had gone to a party. She was giving an Academy Award. This was a few years later and it was right after President Reagan had been shot and wounded and there was this comment about Scorsese's movie [*Taxi Driver*] inspiring the incident. A reporter from the *Los Angeles Times* kind of came out of nowhere, introduced himself, and asked me what I thought about it. They thought that I was a particularly good person to ask because of all the problems on *The Warriors*. I said, 'Well, why don't you find out what movie the guy that shot [Abraham Lincoln] saw?' The phenomena is not related to movies. But the deeper question is, 'If it could be proved that it was and ninety-nine and nine tenths of your audience was moved in an aesthetic way by the thing and one one-hundredth or one one-millionth went out and did a bad thing, is that a reason not to have the film?' What price are we willing to pay for freedom of expression? There's obviously copycat behavior. There's vastly more as a result of the news than anything else and I don't think anybody really believes that we should curtail newscasts."

Whatever his initial discomfiture, Beck now feels the same way as Hill. "Every Western that you've ever seen that's any good has violence in it," he reasons. "Shakespeare was pretty bloody. Movies—especially action movies—tend toward having physical conflict between the protagonist and the antagonists throughout [the] history of drama."

All of which is fine on a philosophical level but raises the question of why people—however few in number—were getting involved in violence at *Warriors* screenings rather than those of other pictures, Yurick's comment about a *Sound of Music* slaying notwithstanding. Hill: "The film obviously supplied an arena where certain disparate people showed up who didn't like each other and trouble began. I do not believe there's any evidence that the film itself inspired this kind of desperately bad behavior." Remar says, "There was violence in Oxnard. I think a Hell's Angel was stabbed. These were guys who were already gang members and there was some kind of rival gang there. And some slashings in Brooklyn, and that was a pretty common occurrence anyway." Beck: "I investigated the who-what-when-whys of it all. In every instance where there was violence, it was between existing gangs who had gone to see this movie and had a confrontation. A kid was killed in a drive-in in Southern California. One gang member shot by another gang member. *The Warriors* didn't make that gang member who shot that other gang member put a gun on his person prior to going to the movie. I don't think that the movie caused people who were already predisposed to that kind of behavior to do that kind of behavior, but it gave them a venue to meet simply because it was a movie about them." Van Valkenburgh: "The incidences I heard about happened outside and they hadn't even seen the film, so I think it's circumstances. Just who was attracted to coming to the theatre and how they affected each other. It's not what they were looking at that created the upset." She also says, "Our film was pulled out of one theatre and replaced with *Midnight Express* and I thought that was a fascinating exchange. What makes *Midnight Express* more palatable and insightful?"

In the context of the raging debate, it was difficult for the *Warriors* cast to get a perspective on their (in most cases) movie debuts, although of course they tried. In late February, a few weeks after the movie opened, Michael Beck, David Harris, and Terry Michos attended a *Warriors* screening together. Michos recalls, "The place was packed and they were going crazy in there and this gang were saying, 'Man, I know I can fight but I can't fight like that.' It's almost like they bought into it. We were walking out. Somebody saw Michael (I pulled my hat down over my face) and they said, 'You look like that guy in the film.' And Michael said, 'Oh, yeah, lots of people tell me that. Yeah, yeah, that's why I came. I wanted to see.' And he got the heck out of there." Having taken his mother to the Times Square sneak, Marcelino Sánchez accompanied the whole family to another showing. "In our neighborhood, there was this big theatre right underneath the train and we went there to see the movie together," says sister Mayra. "The line was around the corner. He was very proud to show us and for us to go all together." However with almost crushing predictability, the stain affecting the *Warriors* story rears its head when she appends, "Some fights broke out in that movie theatre and he wasn't happy about that."

Dorsey Wright first saw the completed movie at a much later point in '79. "I was off filming, doing work," he says. "I didn't even pay attention to what *Hair* was doing. I'm not reading the trade papers or anything… I seen some of the early reviews and it was like, 'Okay, 'nuff of that. Heck with the critics.' The people that I listen to are people that go to movies. The paying public." He also says, "I don't really like looking at myself on screen, because then you start saying, 'I should have did this, I should have did that.'" He was at least aware of all the controversy surrounding the movie. "My mother kept me up on that. She's like, 'Oh, the paper and on the news.' I'm like, 'Ma, I had nothing to do with that. I can't do a damn thing, Ma. I did the movie, I'm gone.'" Friends finally persuaded him to take in the picture. "It was playing in a multiplex… It was like close to the undercard... I told them, 'I only seen like the first few minutes.' 'Are you kidding me?' They're my same friends I have today because they kept me grounded. By the time me and my friends went to go see it, [the audience reaction] had calmed down a lot. Because I'd have never went to a movie theatre with that shit going on and have anybody recognize me."

Contrary to the misgivings he felt when he left the set, he enjoyed what he saw, finding that he finally "got" it. "I thought it was a damn good film, and that I missed out on the fun. It was like, 'Okay, Mr. Actor, the movie didn't get good until you died.' I love the movie after Cleon is gone... Once my character is killed off, it becomes a lot of colors and flashy one-liners... It's Saturday-afternoon action. It was something I always wanted to do. And it was like, 'Well, you were in it. You didn't get to do a lot of it, but you were in it.' I can see why it's a cult."

The gainsayers to the idea of *The Warriors* being responsible for violence were not restricted to movie-industry figures. William Glazer, a spokesman for the Sacks Theaters Corporation, said the stabbing of Yakubowicz would not affect the film's Boston engagement. "An unfortunate fellow was stabbed by someone who happened to have seen the movie and everybody's blaming the movie," he told Robin Herman of the *New York Times*. Glazer might have had a theoretical vested interest, but Herman's report also quoted Sergeant Bob Cooper of Palm Springs Police as saying that he did not believe there was any connection between the film and the death of Eller in that locale ("It was just a big coincidence"). The story also noted that Lieutenant Edward Conroy, the city's Police Department's youth aid division gang coordinator, had said, "There has been no increase in gang activity that we know of because of the movie."

Yet a feeling persisted that a "Who, me?" attitude from the *Warriors* camp was disingenuous. This, after all, was a film in which the "heroes" (to use Gordon's own term) were a stripe of people who, to say the least, are hardly associated with either high morals or pacifism. The Cyrus speech would have legitimized for some the idea that the forces of authority, particularly law and order, are worthy of contempt, while of course the Warriors are seen battling with the cops who chase them, however self-protectively. Moreover, the schematic manner in which the stylish-looking Warriors go toe-to-toe with other sharply dressed gangs couldn't help but glamorize the notion of physical conflict. Ditto the way instructions are often conveyed not by untidy dialog but the stylish likes of jerks of the head and fingersnaps. Gary Arnold of *The Washington Post* summed up the feelings of many when he said, "While it's impossible to pin a definitive rap on *The Warriors*, it's also difficult to shake the feeling that the movie is socially irresponsible in some respect."

There were also glimmers of active ill intent surrounding the project, ones which though not completely the responsibility of the filmmakers were generated by their vision. For instance, a shocking publicity photograph was prepared showing the Warriors on a subway train surrounding a seated old woman, pulling at her bags and menacing her with a bottle as she grimaces in terror. The aim in releasing the photo—which bears no relation to anything in the film—seemed to be to glorify youth violence and provoke controversy, all of course in the pursuit of audiences/money. "Never seen this before," Walter Hill says when shown it. "Looks Photoshopped." However, the participants remember it.

That said, they all remember the background to the staging of the photo as being perfectly innocent. "Every movie has a still photographer," says David Harris. "That's all his job is—to be on the set every day taking a thousand pictures. I remember him shooting that picture." "All the trains were occupied by extras," says Tom McKitterick. "There was an elderly extra on the movie who was charming and we did some goofy shots with her. That was a spontaneous thing. She was having a good time." Indeed, another picture from the session shows the entire Warriors gang smilingly posing, some with spread arms, in front of the similarly happy-looking woman. With regard to the more sinister variant, McKitterick says, "I don't think there was any intent to create publicity by that sole image. No one came up and staged the picture for us." Nonetheless, somebody took the decision to release it, even if it's not clear how widely circulated it was.

Things that most certainly were widely circulated were the ads—which the *Washington Post*'s Arnold adjudged "ominously" descriptive—and that infamous one-sheet. The phrase "Armies of the night" is closer to superlative than pejorative. In conjunction with that, the statistic claiming that said armies outnumber the cops by five to one could convey the idea of approval of the numerical disadvantage supposedly facing the forces of law and order. Moreover, Gordon is happy to defend a poster he may not have commissioned but championed the deployment of. "You'd have to be a much better marketing man than I am to [conclude], 'This is going to bring in a whole bunch of bad people who are going to hurt people,'" he says. "That's like putting a poster up for a heavyweight boxing match with two mugs on it and say, 'This is going to make people go out and kill each other.'"

Then there is the fact that outfitting the protagonists and antagonists like athletes crossed with superheroes/supervillains could be interpreted as sending out a message that street violence is as glamorous and consequence-free as the clashes in contact sports or the brawls in comic books. "It was more like a character thing," Bobbie Mannix insists of her costumes. "It never occurred to me that I was glamorizing anything. My whole point of view was dividing things by the color and character and names of the gangs." With regard to the reports of violence and death, she says, "I was horrified, of course, like everyone else at the time." She says of *A Clockwork Orange*, which has been bracketed with *The Warriors* for more than one reason, "I recall walking out of the theatre 'cause I couldn't handle it." Some might find her squeamishness odd in the context of the *Warriors* controversy, but she says, "Listen, I've designed *Texas Chainsaw Massacre* [2003 version]. I walked out of that premiere too. When I work on a film, it's different than actually seeing it put together. Way different." Does she feel that what happens in real life can be attributed to what appears on screen? "No. It's like today, with school shootings and everything else. Just a sign of the times, I guess." Did the *Warriors* storm make her hesitant about projects that she took on afterwards? "Not at all."

Another layer to this debate is the fact that in movie history people like the Warriors had previously almost always been villains. As mentioned earlier, Hill takes pride in the fact that *The Warriors* portrayed gangs from their own point of view. However, he rejects the idea that the film is non-judgmental in nature and therefore liable to legitimize to audiences the values endemic to gang culture. "That's way too sweeping," he says. "It is non-judgmental in that it does not have an overview. It examines it from within. But it doesn't say that there isn't good and bad conduct from within. It is absolutely judgmental about conduct and codes of honor and all of that. It's just that they're not hierarchical and imposed from above."

For Britain, there was a sense of déjà vu about the whole controversy, for it was very similar to a furor dating back eight years. *A Clockwork Orange* and *The Warriors* share a remarkable number of similarities. Both are Seventies movies about what it was by now becoming passé to call juvenile delinquents. Both feature a street gang with a uniform. Both set their protagonists in a slightly surreal, implicitly futuristic setting. Both feature ultra-macho types in incongruous face make-up. Both have a soundtrack dominated by doomy synthesizer music. Both, too, were condemned as a social menace.

Hill admires Anthony Burgess' 1962 source novel and states "We're all influenced to some degree by films we've seen. We stand on each other's shoulders." However, he also says that he took no cues from either the *Clockwork Orange* book or its film adaptation. ("Nobody in their right mind sets out to copy something. You know that there's no high ground there.") Yet, like it or not, Hill's adaptation of *The Warriors* will forever be bracketed with Stanley Kubrick's 1971 adaptation of Burgess' teen-violence novel, and for alleged offences far more heinous than imitation. A homeless man was kicked to death in Buckinghamshire, England in an incident similar to a scene in *A Clockwork Orange*. The evidence in a British rape trial suggested that the defendants' actions were incited by another scene in the picture. British newspaper editorials and politicians raged. Defenders of the still-very-young permissive society countered that wrongdoers would naturally lay the blame elsewhere in order to get themselves off the hook, but such was the public opprobrium that in 1973 Kubrick—in fear for his family's safety after direct threats—voluntarily withdrew the film from UK distribution, a situation that lasted until beyond his death 26 years later.

Little of this controversy seems to have filtered back to Kubrick's native America. Told by this author that the director had taken *A Clockwork Orange* off the UK market, Gordon, Hill, and Remar stated that they hadn't been aware of this. (David Patrick Kelly knew that it had been taken out of UK distribution, but—like many have down the years—interpreted this to mean that it had been banned.) Beck, though, was fully acquainted with the events. "I was in the UK when *Clockwork Orange* opened and when all of that went down," he says. "We'd inevitably be having a pint in the pub talking about that very thing as students in drama school." Which makes it somewhat surprising that Beck was taken aback at the scandal that followed in the wake of *The Warriors'* release. "Well it just was not something on my radar at the time," he says. "Perhaps I was naïve." "I would love to be compared to Stanley Kubrick in any small way you can ever come up with, but I don't think our movie had anything to do with *Clockwork Orange*," says Gordon. "I don't think our characters were as violent. *Clockwork Orange* was a very scary movie. It was a brilliant movie, but it was scary... *The Warriors* is very interesting. If you look at the movie, there's no blood. There's one little speck of blood on somebody's mouth after a fight. It would have in reality left the whole place bloody. We chose to do it that way. In fact, we thought if we had done anything, we felt we had made it too soft." Even before the film's release, in fact, Gordon had an interesting observation to make about the action in it. "It has a kind of pop-gun violence," he told *Film Bulletin*. "This movie is basically an adventure film. I like to describe it as the difference between war movies and a picture like *The Guns of Navarone*, which was an adventure film set against a background of the war."

Largely bloodless *The Warriors* may be, but there's much violence in it, whether it be Cyrus being slain or one of the Lizzies having a chair smashed over her head (the latter, furthermore, depicted in almost salacious slow motion). Moreover, everything in it seems to endorse confrontation. The endless tableaux of squaring-up extends even to the inter-gang dialog and the romantic sequences. However, there is no denying that *The Warriors* is not a gorefest even by Seventies standards, let alone today's. As David Shaber said at the time, "[It's] like *Sesame Street* compared to a film by Sam Peckinpah." Not only is there little blood or gore, but the stylized physical confrontations are sometimes closer to *West Side Story* than *The Wild Bunch*. The men's room incident in which Vermin literally flies through the air is closer to a Road Runner cartoon than anything else, while the way Luther's refusal to pay for a candy bar is presented almost as grand villainy is approaching the level of laugh-worthy teenage-delinquency movies like *Reefer Madness*. "It would be PG-13 now," says Beck of *The Warriors*. "I always said at the time this movie's more like a musical than it is a super-violent exercise," says Hill. "I've made movies that are much more violent that *The Warriors*." Certainly *The Warriors* included nothing as chilling as the cold-blooded murder of the Ronee Blakley character in Hill's previous film, *The Driver*. Michos says, "A lot of people have said to me, 'I don't know what the big to-do is over this. It's a good film but it's not violent like we thought.'" These days, with ratings boards—and indeed society—much more lenient and with moral ambiguity far more prevalent in art, *The Warriors* would almost certainly be made nastier. However, that paradoxical innocence is possibly another reason for the film's wide and enduring appeal.

There had been one voice in the *Warriors* camp sounding the warnings all along. At least part of the reason Thomas Waites had been kicked off the project was his objections to *The Warriors'* violence, even if perhaps more for the way he voiced them than for his message. His anxious counsel about what Hill was creating had now seemed to come horrifically true. Did he have a feeling of I Told You So? "I did not," Waites says solemnly. "I wish I were that clever. I was just appalled that there were riots in San Diego, riots in Detroit. I was just consumed with the shock. The horror."

Yet he doesn't blame the violence on the movie or Hill. "It's just that we, as a society, haven't figured out certain questions. We haven't figured out how to educate or nurture our young people. So they erupt, they explode. It's about responsibility as a society. It's an observation. If you look at his other movies, they all have this recurring theme. They're all almost like Westerns. The good collides with the bad and there's violence that erupts. He is entitled to make the kind of movie he wants to make. That's his God-given right as an artist. What I think is sad is poverty and conditions that cause the violence."

Some might say that *The Warriors* is too exploitative a vehicle to merit the description "observation." "I don't know how to respond. I guess we're all exploiters. Everybody's trying to do something to get attention. Everybody's trying to exploit their talent. Why should he be any [more] guilty than I or you or anybody else that's trying to make a name for themselves or sell their wares? That's what it is: it's exploitation in the medium of the film genre. Pauline Kael loved the movie. Look at the movies Clint Eastwood had made. Why is he an artist and Walter Hill is not? Why is Clint Eastwood not accused of exploitation?"

Waites estimates that he never saw the finalized theatrical cut until the year 2000. "When I did happen to revisit it, I thought it was a much better picture than I originally experienced," he says. "It was pretty good. I especially liked the use of the music in the film. I thought that James Remar did a really, really nice job. And I thought the cinematography was excellent." Was the violence as bad as he remembered? "It probably pales by comparison."

"WE WERE DISAPPOINTED as heck because the film was the top-grossing film," says Michos. "The first three or four weeks it was killing it, just killing it. And then it just died."

The metaphorical death the Vermin actor mentions was the result of an extraordinary piece of damage limitation by Paramount Pictures. Regardless of the justice or otherwise of the accusations being levelled at the picture, as the scandal engulfed the studio it could hardly just brazen out the bad publicity and be seen to be doing nothing. When its initial protestations of innocence failed to quell the storm, Paramount ramped up the defense maneuvers. Radio and TV advertising was cancelled. The arguably provocative press-ad campaign was halted—there was a six-day hiatus in print advertising—and then substituted by something more subtle. The revised advertising simply provided the times and places of the shows *sans* artwork. Paramount offered to pay for extra security at any of the theatres screening the film and pledged to release exhibitors from their contractual obligation to show the picture if they thought doing so would pose a risk to persons or property. The studio, of course, also ensured that the media were made aware of these measures. Gordon could be forgiven for a response of grim amusement. He says that at the opening night at Westwood, he had spoken to those Paramount people who had deigned to attend. "Afterwards I said to them, 'I'm a little concerned. You think we need some security?' And they said, 'Absolutely not. Don't be ridiculous. No.' Their distribution people didn't take that seriously at all. I got scared shitless because it really was very, very close to a big fight in the lobby that I broke up."

In any case, none of these measures proved enough. "They had to pull it from all the theatres," says Van Valkenburgh. "I can't imagine how long it might run if there hadn't been any violence." "I was a 24-year-old actor getting my first big break," says Remar. "It was very exciting that it was a successful, cool movie. And then they fucking took it off the marquee. What kind of imbeciles think that this is destroying the fabric of society? It was so stupid. It was a movie, for God's sakes. I still don't see it. I just don't see it. We bit the bullet hard. The media got a little excited and ran with it and really screwed us." "It was pulled after I think two weeks or ten days... at most two weekends," says Lawrence Gordon. An absolute blanket absence of screenings? "Yes. Pulled out of distribution in the United States. For many years. It was gone. it was out... The movie would have been a huge hit had it been allowed to play."

"They didn't pull the movie out of the theatres here," demurs Walter Hill. "They pulled the advertising. There were probably certain exhibitors that might have thought the movie was dangerous and dumped it... When Paramount pulled the ads, that was such a admission of defeat by their part. That was a tough moment." Tough not least, he says, because it "wrecked the business of the thing, or certainly severely limited it." Beck: "They stopped publicizing it. That's all. If you don't get the publicity, a movie will usually die. I never was under the impression they pulled it from distribution. They're not going to do that—come on! They still got to make money." Hill: "They didn't pull the movie because that would have been intellectual cowardice of monumental proportions and they knew that. So they took this halfway step."

"Walter's wrong," insists Gordon. "They pulled the movie. Not the first weekend. We had a huge fight and I said, 'You got to give us one more week. You can't just pull the movie. You got to see what we do.' And all week long we had problems in theatres across the country. Little things, bigger things. And then the next weekend we had problems in the theatre again. That was it. They pulled it. We hoped against hope—me and Paramount and so forth—that the second weekend it would all die down. It did business all week but things were happening in theatres. They were being vilified by people in the industry, the other studios trying to knock us out of the box, and also by Gulf + Western. Their parent company already had a bunch of Wall Street problems and things going on, and they didn't want the bad publicity."

Does Gordon remember a specific meeting with Paramount in which he was told that *The Warriors* was henceforth not going to be made available to any domestic theatre? "Yes, of course I remember. 'We're pulling the picture.' Listen, in all due respect—I love Walter—this is my area. Fighting with the studio is my area. I don't tell him how to direct and my job is to protect the movie and to protect the director. Especially when it's somebody like Walter, who's my dear friend and also a great director. I go to war. And I could not win this war. They pulled the movie. By the way, that means they pulled the marketing too. They're not going to spend marketing for a movie that's not going to be in the theatres. Maybe that's what's confusing Walter. But no, they pulled the marketing, they pulled the movie, they pulled everything... You're a studio. You're gonna get sued by those people who were injured or killed or whatever. So they're not gonna leave that out there to take a chance on more incidents and get more lawsuits."

While Gordon's forcefulness on this point is persuasive, it's undermined a little by the implausibility of his timeframe. "I think it played two weekends," he offers. "Maybe there was some dribs and drabs around the country, I don't know." Yet contemporaneous media coverage suggests the film was playing in the States at much later dates than late February. Theaters—as opposed to Paramount—certainly hadn't exhibited any lack of willingness to carry on with *Warriors* screenings. Although around 200 movie houses took up Paramount's offer of paid-for security, it was reported a month after the opening that only ten had opted for the other proposition of a no-penalty cancellation. In its issue cover-dated March 12, 1979 the weekly *People* magazine was told by the assistant manager at Boston's Saxon Theatre of *The Warriors* engagement that his venue hadn't, "done such good business since *My Fair Lady* [1964]." Then there is Wright's recollection of first seeing the film in its entirety in New York several months after it came out. However, the possibility of the producer being confused about the precise dates doesn't mean that *The Warriors* wasn't at some point withdrawn.

As noted, the pulling of the advertising was initially limited to six days. It should be noted that after around two weeks in which no incidents were alleged at *Warriors* screenings, it was reported that Paramount was expanding the display ads, not to reinstate the original menacing tone but to draw attention to some of the recent favorable reviews from critical heavyweights. There was an odd aspect to the new approach, though: one advertisement reproduced a Janet Maslin quote in which the *New York Times* writer criticized the original advertisements for being misleading. Her review had noted, "What a surprise they'll be for anyone who's misled by the ads for *The Warriors*... and goes to the film expecting good old-fashioned headbashing on a grand scale."

IF *THE WARRIORS* was indeed withdrawn from the American market, that didn't mean Paramount was unable to show it in other countries.

"After the violence in the theatres, we had a very hard time getting to play anywhere else," recalls Gordon. "Luckily a couple of guys at UIP, Paramount's foreign distribution, were able to finally get it into Europe. And it was a big hit all over the countries. That's where the profits in the movie came from."

Simply by dint of a shared language and culture, the United Kingdom is considered by Hollywood to be the most important film market outside of North America. *The Warriors* was released there on May 10, 1979. It was passed as Certificate "X" by what was then called the British Board of Film Censors (renamed in 1984 the British Board of Film Classification). This rating was more stringent than the closest American equivalent, the "R". It barred entry to under-18s with or without an accompanying adult. (Moreover, anecdotal evidence suggests that American culture was less strict about actually enforcing its ratings code.) Instead of the North American "Armies of the Night" one-sheet of hostile, staring gang members stretching to the nocturnal horizon, Britain's movie houses ("the pictures" in native parlance) displayed a fairly undramatic landscape-format film poster featuring a color still from the final section of the movie showing six bedraggled Warriors along with Mercy walking the early-morning streets of Coney Island, the Wonder Wheel looming behind them. There were also necessary territory-related changes such as "Read the Star paperback" and "Distributed by Cinema International

Corporation." Unusually, the poster had no tagline, possibly because by this point the film's notoriety meant it didn't need one.

Time Out was mightily impressed by the film. "Hill has elevated his story of a novice gang on the run into a heroic epic of Arthurian dimensions, with sex as sorcery and the flick-knife as sword," the listings magazine said. "Mixing ironic humor, good music, and beautifully photographed suspense, it's one of the best of 1979." In contrast, Richard Combs of the highbrow cinema publication *Sight & Sound* was scathing. He described the film as a "compromise between old Hollywood genres and new Hollywood pretensions" and "*West Side Story* without the songs." Conversant with Hill's growing oeuvre, Combs felt that the director was predominantly interested in "ambience" but failed in his objectives because of shorthand methods. The reviewer felt the film contained plenty of plot but all of it of a banal nature. He seemed to detest the very things that so endear multiple generations to *The Warriors*. "The sequence in which the messianic Cyrus imposes himself remarkably easily on the assembled gangs before being shot is… perfunctory… unconvincing… and… pointless;" "The use of the largely unseen disc jockey as omniscient commentator is a relentlessly trivial device;" "The street scenes are directed with numbing lack of vigor…" Whether the UK reviews were good or bad, business was healthy. *The Warriors* topped the country's weekend box-office charts in its first three weeks of release.

British, American, or anything else, anyone who went to see *The Warriors* understandably expecting a bloodbath would be severely disappointed. Britons in particular, though, were likely to find the film laughably tame. Although cinema censorship in Britain was roughly the same as that to be found in the States, British television was far more permissive than its American counterpart and graphic violence was common on the country's small screens, as was a moral ambivalence attached to authority-figure protagonists like police officers. *Starsky & Hutch* was the edgiest American cop show of the time but was still sentimental and broadly clean-cut; the UK's police drama *The Sweeney* was frequently callous, profane, and grisly. Meanwhile, the BBC police drama *Target* had, within the last two years, shown gruesome sights only just beyond the 9 p.m. adult-viewing watershed like teenage criminals having holes blown in their torsos by rivals' shotguns. The only thing in *The Warriors* that could not be found (and in more concentrated doses) on British airwaves was f-words, and it was this alone that made the film's UK "X" certificate appropriate.

Nonetheless, some were determined to prevent the British public seeing the picture. In the UK, local authorities have the power to ban films even after they have been passed for general release. The power is rarely exercised but in 1979 the Licensing Sub-Committee of northern English city Leeds took the step of forbidding screenings of *The Warriors* on the grounds of its violent content. ('Seventy-nine, in fact, was quite a big year for censorship in the country: several local authorities would shortly ban *Monty Python's Life of Brian*, albeit for very different reasons.) However, a loophole in the law meant that a banned film could still be shown in private-member cinemas. This ambiguity was usually exploited to show sex films. Leeds' Tatler Cinema, in fact, dispensed with its usual erotic menu to start showing *The Warriors* four times daily.

ALTHOUGH SOMETHING in the zeitgeist had created the flurry of synchronicity that saw several other street-gang movies go into production at the same time as *The Warriors*, few are widely remembered. The one real exception is *The Wanderers*.

The Wanderers made it to the screen on July 13, 1979. It achieved reasonable commercial success and had a wonderful early-Sixties soundtrack but secured mixed reviews. Philip Kaufman's film was based on a 1974 novel by Richard Price. Although Sol Yurick once met Price, he hadn't read his book when this author spoke to him in 2009 so couldn't comment on it beyond offering, "I think he was looking at a different set of people than I knew." The *Wanderers* film is set in New York City in the first half of the 1960s and revolves around the titular Italian American street gang. Its title (deriving from the Dion hit of that name) and the fact that it's based on a literary work are not the only likenesses with *The Warriors*. The two films are similar in subject and New-York setting. Another link is the suggestion that has been made that *The Wanderers* obtained limited exposure in the domestic market because, after the *Warriors* experience, exhibitors were nervous about screening another youth-gang movie.

Such are the similarities that one suspects that many minds conflate the two pictures. Van Valkenburgh: "You can't technically confuse them but some people... Yeah, we could think of it as a *faux pas*." Remar, though, is skeptical. "They're so unrelated. I can't understand why anybody would confuse them." He certainly seems to feel that Kaufman's film doesn't deserve to be mentioned in the same breath as Hill's picture. "I don't know really what it was striving for," he says of *The Wanderers*. Did he like it as a film? "I'm not going to get into that." Michos offers of *The*

Wanderers, "It was a little more real." However, he points out that only one of the two movies under discussion sustains a convention circuit four decades on. "*The Wanderers* was good, but it just did not have the cult impact of *The Warriors*."

Meanwhile, when *Boulevard Nights* opened in March 1979, Tony Bill found himself accused of pretty much the same offences he had alleged of Walter Hill two months previously. The Michael Pressman-directed film depicted a pair of Mexican American brothers, one of whom leads a straight life while the other deals drugs and battles rival street toughs. There were some good notices. However, Roger Ebert's review ("a sensitive and thoughtful film about the tragedy of gang warfare in the barrio… with none of the pseudo-romantic posturing *The Warriors* employed to make killing look great") illustrated that to some extent *The Warriors* had queered Bill's pitch: in the wake of the Hill movie's problems, Warner Bros. displayed public nervousness by putting out preemptive statements insisting that the film was a "family story" merely "set in a gang environment." Even so, the city of Los Angeles expressed anxiety about the possibility of violence if rival gangs attended the same screening. The controversy in which the picture was quickly embroiled was remarkably similar to that which had afflicted Hill's film. Incidents involving weapons occurred on opening night in Ontario and San Francisco, leading to the relevant venues pulling the film. On March 24, a fifteen-year-old girl named Jocelyn Vargas, heading for a bus home after seeing the San Francisco premiere, was shot in the neck when caught in the crossfire between two rival gangs who had also been in the theatre. The withdrawal from the San Francisco Alhambra Theatre seemed to be a direct result of pressure from the city's Mayor, Dianne Feinstein. Hill could be forgiven a bitter smile at the publicly expressed fury of Bill, who fumed, "She might as well close down Candlestick Park because there are fights there, or the taco stands in the Mission District because there are fights there too… I refuse to accept the contention that a movie is the cause rather than a reflection of what is happening in society."

Over the Edge was released on May 18, 1979. Directed by Jonathan Kaplan, the Charles S. Haas/Tim Hunter script was inspired by true events in Foster City, California, a planned community with a remarkably high level of teenage crime due to the absence of any facilities for that age group. The film was unusual for the time in the way its adolescent protagonists were genuinely depicted by actors of the same age (fourteen-year-old Matt Dillon made his debut). While the film got good reviews, once again *The Warriors* to some extent appears to have done for it commercially. In 2009,

Hunter told Mike Sacks of *Vice* that, in the wake of *The Warriors, Boulevard Nights,* and *The Wanderers,* Orion Pictures didn't want his movie tarred with a gang connection. "So they marketed it as a horror film. And then they just dropped it. It wasn't shown anywhere. They were afraid of copycat violence. It was hugely disappointing."

June 15, 1979 brought *Walk Proud,* directed by Robert L. Collins. Interestingly, it was written by Evan Hunter, who could be said to have inadvertently kicked off the whole teen-violence movie genre by writing the novel *The Blackboard Jungle,* whose movie adaptation was arguably the first motion picture to enable teenagers to define themselves as a distinct social group and inarguably was sometimes screened against a backdrop of movie-house violence. The story is a little reminiscent of David Shaber's vision of *The Warriors.* Just as Hinton was ambivalent about gang membership, seventeen-year-old El Barrio resident and Chicano gangbanger Emilio Mendez meets a nice middle-class girl and decides he wants out of his violent environment. There weren't many reports of violence at the film's showings but there were anecdotes about forcefully expressed outrage at alleged racism: some Chicanos were weary of people from their culture being depicted in films as gang members, while not only was Mendez's romantic salvation white, but blue-eyed leading man Robby Benson appeared in "brownface."

A similar theme of love-trumps-violence informed *Sunnyside,* released on June 1, 1979. Directed by Timothy Galfas and written by Galfas and Jeff King from a story by King and Robert L. Schaffel, it starred Joey Travolta. The latter played Nick Martin, leader of a Queens gang named the Nightcrawlers but aspiring to something better. It was suspected that Travolta (a recording artist by vocation) had been cast to cash in on the popularity of his actor brother. The press-related anecdotes about New York location shooting being saved from sabotage by the act of moviemakers befriending local youth and the fact that Janet Maslin's (unfavorable) *New York Times* review complained of crowd disruption at her screening only added to the impression that *Sunnyside* was almost designed as a faux *Warriors.* TV film critic Gene Siskel—who found it "a weak imitation of *Saturday Night Fever*"—named it his Dog of the Week.

ALTHOUGH TONY BILL had insisted *Boulevard Nights* was responsible and *The Warriors* irresponsible, it didn't prevent his movie being, like Hill's, on the end of a civil action. In fact, it was one far worse than *The Warriors* legal case. Whereas the father of Marty Yakubowicz, as administrator of his son's estate, brought a wrongful death action against Paramount Pictures and exhibitors the Saxon Theatre Corporation, Jocelyn Vargas and her mother brought lawsuits against the executive producer, producer, director, and production company behind *Boulevard Nights*.

The *Yakubowicz v. Paramount Pictures* suit reached the courts on December 29, 1981. It provided further details about the Boston tragedy. Marty Yakubowicz had arrived at the subway station at around the same time as Michael Barrett and two friends who had all seen two consecutive Saxon-Theatre screenings of *The Warriors*. While waiting for his train, Yakubowicz recognized some other friends and went over to join them. The two separate groups had a history of arguments and tension. On the subway, an intoxicated Barrett tried to provoke Yakubowicz, saying, "I want you. I'm going to get you." As Yakubowicz left the train, Barrett stabbed him.

Count one of Yakubowicz' father's suit alleged that the way Paramount produced, distributed, and advertised *The Warriors* induced viewers to commit violent acts in imitation of the violence in the film. Counts two and four alleged that both Paramount and the Saxon Theater caused his son's death by continuing to show *The Warriors* even after learning of violent acts at or near other theatres exhibiting the film. The third count alleged that Paramount failed to warn theatres and public officials of the danger of violence and to take reasonable steps to protect persons at or near the Saxon Theatre.

The plaintiff argued that the deaths near theatres showing the film in Palm Springs and Oxnard had apprised Paramount of the fact that *The Warriors* could spark violence, pointing out that, after those incidents, a Paramount executive had telegrammed district and branch managers with the instruction to advise all theatres screening the picture to hire security guards at Paramount's expense. The Boston theatre where Yakubowicz's killer saw *The Warriors* accepted this offer, although Paramount didn't receive notice of this until after Yakubowicz's death.

The case was on shaky ground from the start. It was suggested in the media that Barrett's words came directly from *The Warriors*. The lines "I want you. I'm going to get you" don't appear in the film. New Cyrus exhorts the Riffs, "I want them all, I want all those Warriors. I want them alive if possible, if not—wasted. But I want them." At the conclave an anonymous gang member yells of Cleon, "Kill him!", while in the men's-room scene Mercy exhorts Swan to "Kill that bastard!" These lines, though, are all at best only vaguely reminiscent of what Barrett said. Moreover, none of them can reasonably be accused of being either irresponsible or inflammatory, let alone unusual in motion pictures.

The trial court, which granted summary judgment for the defendants, and the Supreme Judicial Court of Massachusetts, which affirmed it in 1989, were interested in matters other than accurate reportage of dialogue. Although it was found that Paramount and Saxon Theatres owed a duty of reasonable care to members of the public, it also concluded that the defendants had not violated that duty. It was also held that "[a] fatal assault occurring miles from the theatre… could not be attributed to a failure to 'protect [people] at or near the theatre' or a failure to warn Saxon or public officials of the dangers of film-related violence." The court pointed out that because the fracas that led to Yakubowicz's death had not occurred at the theatre but a nearby subway station, the plaintiff had not proven proximate cause. Regardless of any security measures Paramount had taken, it could not be expected to provide security throughout the surrounding neighborhood. Similar reasoning was used when the courts upheld summary judgment for the defendants in the *Boulevard Nights* case (*Bill v. Superior Court*).

Walter Hill was gratified that one public figure at least didn't join the *Warriors* pile-on. New York's mayor Ed Koch was a frequently controversial figure and, like all politicians, wasn't averse to posturing. In the case of *The Warriors*, he refused to join in the excoriation of a film that could be said to be in danger of placing his city at an even lower point in the nation's esteem than the lamentable one it already occupied. "I am eternally grateful to New York City and Mayor Koch," Hill says. "He dismissed all that and the city of New York was always very sophisticated about it." On a related note, the director said to journalist Jennifer M. Wood, "Koch was very sophisticated and generous in his attitudes, as I've always found New Yorkers to be. I even married one!"

BARRY DEVORZON AVERS that it wasn't only the fortunes of the movie that were affected by the controversies surrounding *The Warriors*.

He says US radio "very definitely" stopped playing the film's single because of the uproar. "'Theme from "The Warriors"' became fairly popular in Europe, but in the United States, everyone backed off," he recalls. The release failed to chart in the US. Meanwhile, despite being granted a full-page ad in *Billboard* that sought to capitalize on the film's notoriety ("The pulsating soundtrack from the most controversial film of the year"), the album reached just #125 in the States. The single didn't make the UK charts either but the album obtained a placing of #53 there.

The ancillary products aside we'll never know whether, had its exposure not been seriously circumscribed, *The Warriors* would have vied with *Superman: The Movie*, *The Amityville Horror*, *Rocky II*, *Star Trek: The Motion Picture*, and *Alien* for highest domestic gross of 1979. However, Hill points out that—notwithstanding his comments earlier in this text— "It was quite a profitable film." The picture finished in a respectable position of 32 in the end-of-year table. Its annual grosses were $22,490,000 on sold tickets of 8,960,159. For what it's worth, *The Wanderers* and *Boulevard Nights* didn't feature in the chart, and *The Great Train Robbery* came in at 61. As for those six films that opened on the same weekend as *The Warriors*—edging the latter completely out of the frame in terms of media profile—*Agatha* did reasonably in making #49 and is aesthetically quite well-regarded. The others didn't make the table, and none are much remembered, let alone do they enjoy the status in the culture subsequently achieved by *The Warriors*.

DEMOBILIZATION

AFTER *THE WARRIORS*, David Shaber's so-far stuttering screenwriting career truly took off, although not necessarily because of it.

Last Embrace—a noir thriller that saw his script directed by Jonathan Demme—was released three months after *The Warriors* and was therefore in production at the same time as Walter Hill's movie. It was succeeded by *Those Lips, Those Eyes*, a 1980 romance starring Frank Langella, the Alan J. Pakula-directed political thriller *Rollover* (1981) starring Jane Fonda and Kris Kristofferson, and 1981's Sylvester Stallone-featured actioner *Nighthawks*. Shaber also received a co-writing credit on John Milius' Vietnam picture *Flight of the Intruder* (1991) and contributed an uncredited production polish to the 1990 Sean Connery cold-war submarine-based thriller *The Hunt for Red October*.

He remained true to his history as an artist comfortable at both ends of the culture. In 1987 his first play, *Bunker Memories*, hit the boards of New York's Roundabout Theater. He also wrote short stories which were printed in O. Henry Prize Collections and in *Cosmopolitan, Life*, and *Esquire* magazines.

In 1987, aged 70, Shaber died of complications from a stroke suffered about two hours after teaching his last class at Columbia University's film school, where he was a professor of screenwriting. At the time of his death, he was working on a musical based on Theodore Dreiser's *American Tragedy*, as well as an original movie script.

The unfortunate consequence of Shaber handing over the reins of *The Warriors* to someone with the hyphenate role of writer-director—with all the auteur/omnipotence public perceptions attached to it—is that he rarely gets mentioned in discussion of the film. Story-wise, however, his contribution is actually more significant than that of Walter Hill. Not only did Shaber give the film a classic three-act structure not found in the book, but several of the now-iconic elements of the finished *Warriors* picture were present in his first screenplay draft, including "Can you dig it?", Mercy's live-for-today discourse, the simmering class warfare of the prom-couples scene, and the downcast return to Coney Island. While it can't be denied that Hill improved on Shaber's vision, neither can it be gainsaid that the director was provided by Shaber a more-than-substantial head start. One wonders what a Hill script for *The Warriors* would have been like if he'd had to adapt the Yurick book from scratch.

"I only met David Shaber one time," says Hill. "We shook hands. He was visiting Larry Gordon about something. He was very pleasant. It was after the movie had been shot... When I met him, he said something to the effect that the blueprint and the layout he felt very much was his but the tone and the approach and all that was very much mine. I remember thinking at the time that was a fair assessment... When the screenplay credit was determined and I shared it with David, I certainly thought that was just. I didn't have any problem with it."

Sol Yurick also did well out of the *Warriors* film, albeit partly by accident. Asked how he felt about the merchandise industry that ultimately resulted from his book, he said, "I might have resented it if there wasn't a mistake made in the contract which has brought me money since the movie has come out. That never happens to any writer who is not a movie writer. You sell the rights and that's all you get." Yurick found that he became an accidental beneficiary of a putative legal action by the film's producer. "Because Lawrence Gordon threatened to sue Paramount, they made a settlement and I've been getting a piece of the action all the way through," he happily relayed. "It had to do with some promise they must have made to him. I never saw the reason why exactly. My agent, Georges Borchardt, who is a big agent, said he has never had a case like this where the writer's made money."

Although Yurick was happy to take the money that flowed from the industry that grew up around *The Warriors*, weren't the likes of video games, figurines, and comic books taking things further and further away from the book he wrote, which he presumably felt should be appreciated on a somewhat higher plane? "Yeah, sure. But look, the book has been reissued here in the States two more times. I've written an introduction to it, [in] which I tell what was in my mind when I wrote it and how it came to be and my comments about this becoming a movie and the effect this has had on people… What can I tell you? This is the real world. If I've been in the position where I don't have to compromise my writing, that's terrific. And if I can get enough money to keep on going, that's terrific too. That's the best I can do."

Yet it could be suggested that Yurick didn't quite manage to keep on going as a writer. *The Bag* (1968) completed what became known as his Sixties New York trilogy. It was followed by short-story collection *Someone Just Like You* (1972), the novels *An Island Death* (1976), and *Richard A* (1981), and the essay collection *Behold Metatron, The Recording Angel* (1985). Yurick also compiled *Voices of Brooklyn* (1973), an anthology of unpublished writers. Unfortunately, that latter description could be said to apply to himself in his later years. It was no doubt gratifyingly lucrative that *Fertig* was adapted into the 1999 film *The Confession* starring Alec Baldwin and Ben Kingsley, but in close to the last three decades of his life Yurick had no new books published. He was reputed by 1987 to have taken a Brooklyn office job. His stock, though, remained significant. Critic John Fuegi said of him, "He is an extreme rarity: a social critic with broad theoretical and 'street level' experience. Yet, he is at the same time an erudite novelist with solid historical knowledge of the genre and great skill in handling the form." Yurick died in 2013 aged 87 from complications of lung cancer.

Both the producer and director of *The Warriors* enjoyed great fortune in Hollywood, often together.

A list of some of the films Lawrence Gordon produced subsequent to *The Warriors* provides an indication of his golden touch: *48 Hrs., Streets of Fire, Brewster's Millions, Hellboy, Predator, Die Hard, Field of Dreams*, and *Watchmen*. "It goes on and on," he cheerfully says. However, a glimmer of dissatisfaction is evident when he talks about the anonymity of even the most successful producer. "A lot of times they don't interview the producers 'cause I don't think they think we have anything to do with these movies," he says. "That they magically appear. Being a producer's a very bizarre profession. Especially today when everybody's a producer, including Prince Harry."

Gordon produced seven films for Walter Hill before their professional relationship ended. "I went in another direction," says Gordon. "We never had a discussion about let's go our separate ways." Both men say they remain good friends.

Numbered among Hill's subsequent directorial credits are *The Long Riders, Southern Comfort, 48 Hrs., Brewster's Millions*, and *Red Heat*. He was a writer on all those pictures except *The Long Riders*. On occasion he had a triple-hyphenate role: *Alien* was the start of his own move into production.

Tonally, Hill's career is in some senses surprising. Four decades on from his third directing effort, the Walter Hill style can now be definitively adjudged to be man's-man stuff: films in which macho characters need little provocation to square up to each other, and furthermore in ways that facilitate the throwing of mythic shapes. "You never see a woman in any of his movies," says Craig Baxley. "I never got that. He was just a sweet guy, but his movies, they've always been like *Geronimo* and *Hard Times*." This fact is almost astonishing. Thomas Waites' assessment of Hill as a "gentleman" is not isolated. Asked whether Hill engages in the confrontationalism that his characters do, Michael Beck says, "No. Steady as a rock. I've never seen Walter raise his voice." David Patrick Kelly, who knows Hill perhaps better than any other *Warriors* actor, offers some insight: "He's a really literary fellow—he really reads and reads—but he's also that sports kind of guy, USC. His best pal is Allan Graf, who's this Rose Bowl linebacker. He's that combination." Says Gordon, "Walter is extremely well-read. Extremely. And he's a real gentleman. And no, he's not confrontational. He can be confrontational if somebody is messing up his movie, but not in the way Sam Peckinpah would be confrontational. He's very smart and great at handling people. People respect him when they work with him. I don't think we ever had a real fight. Maybe the closest we ever came to an argument was about the music under the [Baseball Furies] fight." James Remar has also worked extensively with Hill. "It isn't peculiar at all," he says of the apparent contradiction. "Macho, hairy-chested guys don't necessarily make macho, hairy-chested movies. He's an artist and you have to understand cinema and the making of films. A lot of guys that make what appear to be extraordinarily violent films are very quiet, gentle individuals. They express violence that all human beings have inside them through their art."

The one that got away for both Gordon and Hill may be *Last Gun*. "*Last Gun* is about the last bounty hunter," says Gordon. "It could get made. It's a good script… Walter and I talk about it every time we talk. But we're both getting a little long in the tooth. [It's] not quite the kind of movie they're making today, although it'd be a really good streaming movie. We just need to get an actor. We were going to make it with Tommy Lee Jones when he was kind of a youngster. I never count any good script out. Scripts recycle. Right now with all these streaming movies they're making, I'm digging out all my old material because people are coming to me all the time. I got a call two days ago: they want to remake *Hard Times*."

The career of *The Warriors'* stunt coordinator went from strength to strength. Craig Baxley's credits in that field include Warren Beatty's *Reds* and the Arnold Schwarzenegger vehicle *Predator*. As with *The Warriors*, both projects found him adopting roles he feels amounted to more than the one for which he was formally acknowledged. Indeed, after cutting his teeth behind the camera on TV series *The A-Team*, he officially graduated to the position of director with *Action Jackson* (1988). Even so, he went on to become president of Stunts Unlimited, a company that continues to this day and on the books of which can be found his son, Craig, Jr. Baxley *père* says that whether it's Baxley *fils* or anyone else, stunt performers today are a different breed. "The fights are very different now, with the green screen and wirework and the type of fights, MMA [mixed martial arts] stuff." Those elderly stuntmen who he felt weren't right for *The Warriors* might be relieved to know that the profession has been made infinitely safer by the advent of CGI.

THE SURVIVING MAIN cast of *The Warriors* have had mixed fortunes that their onetime prominence in no way augured. "We were big stars," David Harris says. The Warriors' Cochise recalls an incident wherein he was approached by Bianca Jagger at New York's Studio 54 nightclub, an epicenter of popular culture in the period straddling the end of the Seventies and the beginning of the Eighties. "She gave me the biggest hug in the world. She goes, 'I can't get enough of you'... We were big stars at 54. We got in all the time. Carte blanche. Everybody was watching the film. Mick Jagger was a major fan."

Marcelino Sánchez was less happy about such fame. "He felt the fans were very invasive," says sister Mayra. "He couldn't really do what he was normally doing in New York, especially when he came home to Brooklyn... Everywhere he went, people knew him... There were stories about fans sometimes chasing him and just really being very overt in their excitement. He was taken aback by that. He was not expecting the movie to make such a difference for people's lives." Although he could do nothing about his distinctive lips, Sánchez dispensed with his bushy hairstyle shortly after the film came out. "It didn't matter," says Mayra. "People always recognized [him]. It was so weird for me. I was young. I was like, ''What's happening here? Why are these strangers talking to you?'" She adds, "But then he made very good relationships with some fans. People sent him paintings and he wrote letters to fans. He really honored his fans. He really valued any kind of attention that he got from that movie."

Whether its actors liked or loathed their recognizability, *The Warriors* proved the wisdom of the adage/cliché about one minute being hot, the next not. Not a single one of the *Warriors* actors has become a household name. Some felt compelled to drop out of the industry completely, while the fortunes of those who continued as working thespians have been seriously mixed. Deborah Van Valkenburgh—one of those who remained in the game—says, "People make choices... If acting isn't your greatest passion or it's not working... some people are very practical. 'If this isn't working, I need to find responsible ways to live my life.'" Thomas Waites notes, "This is a tough way to make your living. There's a hundred thousand people that come to New York every year that want to be actors and a few of us manage to keep going after ten years, twenty years, thirty years. There's not just a question of talent. There's also a question of business acumen, savvy, guts, drive, all those things." He could have added "luck" and "fashionability," as well as the observation that nothing proves all this better than how the *Warriors* cast has fared.

By dint of being the finished movie's lead, Michael Beck was the obvious candidate for superstardom. "We all thought that Michael was going to be the breakout movie star 'cause he was good-looking, young, could act," recalls Harris. "Hollywood's going to jump all over this guy... That was a talk back in the day." "Oh, *The Warriors* certainly helped my career," insists Beck. "It was my big break. Even though it was low-budget, it was still a major studio movie." The fact is, though, that few moviegoers today would recognize Beck's name or face.

His long list of credits demonstrates that he has carved out a reasonably successful career as a working actor, but much of his résumé is made up of television shows, while those entries that are motion pictures seem rather low-rent for someone of his talents. (Hands up anyone who remembers, let alone cherishes, *Battletruck*, *Megaforce*, or *Forest Warrior*?) That he has become the first choice as the voice of John Grisham audiobook releases can be scant compensation. "We can always look back and go, 'If I'd done this', 'If I'd taken this role and not that role,'" Beck says. He adds, "Not that I was getting all that many choices." He partly attributes the latter to his next big picture after *The Warriors*. *Xanadu* (1980) has gone down in history as one of the classically bad movies and is reputed to be one of the films that directly led to the creation of the Golden Raspberry Awards, an annual ceremony which mocks aesthetic awfulness in cinema. That Beck surprisingly chose to line up alongside Olivia Newton-John and Gene Kelly in this modern musical—soundtracked by Newton-John and Electric Light Orchestra—was partly down to the persuasive powers of its producer, Lawrence Gordon. "I actually turned it down two or three times," Beck says. "Intuitively I knew I was miscast, but they made it attractive for me to do it as a young actor. I don't regret doing it in the sense that I still have friends from that picture, but it's just not the thing that I do best, playing that kind of light romantic comedy-musical character. Since that was my first picture out after *The Warriors*, I think what promise was created by my performance in *The Warriors* certainly was affected in a negative way by my performance in *Xanadu*. If you have to do over again, maybe I would have turned it down a fourth time, but I didn't, so you just live with it."

However, Beck admits that there was another impediment to his achieving mainstream Hollywood success. "I was letting people know that this conversion had happened in my life, and Hollywood has never been Christian-friendly in my time." He also confesses that it wasn't merely anti-Christian sentiment at work. "I was pretty vocal and obnoxious. I wasn't being discreet... I was not a mature Christian. I didn't handle this newfound faith in the way I would handle it ten years later." Additionally, he says, "It also had an effect on the choice of material that I would do... I didn't go to the audition with Larry Kasdan for *Body Heat*. There were two or three movies like that which I may have looked at differently down the line but at that point, because it was all within that first year, I just went, 'I just don't feel that I can do this movie so I'm not gonna waste your time.' And that's not to say I would have been offered it over Bill Hurt, but I just took myself off the playing board... Once the dust settled, I could go, 'It's fine for me as a Christian to play a heinous role 'cause there are heinous real people in this world'... But I have no regrets about it. I am, forty years on, still following Jesus and that to me is much more important than where my erstwhile career might have gone."

Beck is interested in branching out into other areas of artistic endeavor. "I have a couple of novels. That's where my artistic juices are flowing now. Trying to tell stories in other ways. Since I got past the required reading list in high school to where I actually enjoyed literature, I've been just an avid reader of classics to beach novels. I love the written word and we will see if I have enough of a gift at writing to actually get published." However, he admits, "The things that I've written have not been to the level that I want to put them out there yet."

Household name or not, James Remar has a post-*Warriors* professional record that more than one of the *Warriors* cast cites as a success story. "Jamie did just phenomenal work throughout the film," says McKitterick. "His work ethic was terrific. His energy was just amazing. I knew that that energy would sustain him... He's had a long and very respected career in films."

The year after *The Warriors*, Remar appeared with Al Pacino in *Cruising*, a film that could be said in its own way to be as controversial as *The Warriors*. "They blamed us for everything under the sun," reflects Remar. "It's a murder mystery set against the backdrop of the rough trade of Greenwich Village back then and it's a neat concept. But some people that were mad that wrote for newspapers, said, 'This is horrible.' But it's kind of a beloved film in the gay community now, so go figure." Since then, Remar has appeared in a formidable list of films and TV shows. Significant motion pictures include, *The Long Riders, 48 Hrs., The Cotton Club, Judge Dredd, What Lies Beneath, X-Men: First Class, Transformers: Dark of the Moon, Django Unchained*, and *Once Upon a Time in Hollywood*. He was a mainstay in television shows *The Huntress, Dexter*, and *Black Lightning*, and racked up a good run on *Sex and the City*. "I'm not like any character I have ever played," Remar says of his long list of roles. As for his role as Ajax, he says, "It's very much a part of my career. It helped a lot. *The Warriors* was a great experience and a great education and a real blessing. I'm real grateful that I got to do it." Has he been surprised that the picture didn't confer the same good fortune on his ex-colleagues? "No. I started out about the same time as all of them and I didn't really have any preconceived notion. If I expected something and something else happened, then I would be surprised. Certainly there's been surprises as people's lives have developed. But we were all just doing our best."

The case of Thomas Waites is more complicated. Ironically, his act of removing his name from the *Warriors* credits seems to have had the opposite effect to its objective of avoiding professional damage. "That really upset Walter and Paramount and didn't do much for my career either," he says. "You got to be really lucky to come back from getting fired from a major motion [picture] and then pissing them off even further by taking your name off it."

Some people mitigated the full extent of the potential damage. "I had an amazing agent, and his belief in me did not waver one iota," he notes. Moreover, "Al Pacino sort of rescued me." Waites is referring to being offered the role in the 1979 Norman Jewison-directed courtroom drama

And Justice For All in which A-list thespian Pacino played idealistic law-yer Arthur Kirkland. "Always great," Waites says of his relationship with Pacino. "From the minute we met, we were the same kind of actor. We just understand each other. He's been very good to me and very generous and opened up his home to my family and friends and had the greatest parties over at his place. He's a great guy. He's very intense. I'm not sure that he and someone like Walter Hill would ever get along, because Al has to have the scene a certain way. He's an actor's actor. He's a very complex man be-cause he's an artist and he keeps working things. Most people don't know this, but you do a play and it opens on opening night and you don't really rehearse anymore unless you have to rehearse a replacement. But with Al, he makes you comes into rehearsal every day." Waites found out the latter fact when in 1981 he, Pacino, and Clifton James appeared on Broadway in David Mamet's three-hander *American Buffalo*. "I actually recommended that he do it. It was a huge hit. We had lines from Thompson Street out to Sixth Avenue and around the block."

Waites is also able to say, "I was lucky enough to have someone like John Carpenter believe in me and give me a chance with *The Thing*." As Waites points out, said Antarctica-set 1982 picture is "considered one of the great horror movies of all time." Waites also appeared in Broadway show *Teaneck Tanzi—The Venus Flytrap* which, though extremely short-lived, featured Deborah Harry when Blondie had only just split up. However, these pieces of good fortune—assisted naturally by his own dedication and talents—were not enough to put Waites back to where he had been.

It could almost be said that this rising star had been doing as much a favor to the producers of *The Warriors* by accepting a role in it as the producer and director were doing to him by casting him. "If you were a betting man you would have bet that I was going to be the next Robert De Niro, Al Pacino," he says. Although he is able to make the proud-ish boast, "I've always been a working actor, I've always worked," Waites is obliged to also point out, "I've never become a big, big star." Whatever successes he racked up under the aegis of Hill, Pacino, or Carpenter, Waites gradu-ally began noticing that plum roles were slipping through his fingers. He explains, "You get a reputation." Yet although he states that *The Warriors* was pivotal to his damaged-goods aura, he admits it wasn't the beginning of it. "I had quit a Broadway play before I auditioned for *The Warriors*. A full year before. I was going to play Renfield in *Dracula* with Frank Lan-gella and I didn't want to wear bat sneakers with wings on them. 'This is being designed by Edward Gorey, darling. He's the artist.' And I was like,

'Well, what the fuck am I? A construction worker?' and I walked out of a Broadway contract at 21 with absolutely no money in my pocket out of sheer arrogance."

The fact that Hollywood's film industry is effectively a small village played its part in this bad-reputation process. At one point, he was a candidate for the Sylvester Stallone prison drama *Lock Up*. His readings were powerful ("I'm good," he is comfortable asserting), so much so that its once-bitten producer Lawrence Gordon allowed things to proceed. "I was called back once, I was called back twice, I was called back three times. It looked like I was going to get it. I really needed the money. I had a wife, a child by this point." However, Gordon finally lost his nerve. "Larry didn't let it happen. It was like, 'I just can't take the chance of having you and Sly on the same set. From past experience, I can't do it.'" Said past experience was not even recent. "Ten years afterwards," Waites notes. Yet Waites says that neither then nor at any other time did he regret choosing *The Warriors* over *The Wanderers*. "I think *The Warriors* is a seminal moment in film history. My only regret is my terrible behavior on set."

By this point, Waites had changed his professional name to Thomas G. Waites. "I met the other Tom Waits, who I admire greatly." He adjudges the singer-songwriter responsible for semi-*avant garde* works like *Swordfishtrombones* "a musical genius." Waites is himself a songwriter and singer, albeit at the Spotify rather than record-label level. He says, "We got the occasion to hang out several times. He came over to my loft when I lived in the Village [and] very generously sat and listened to my not-very-good songs and taught me 'Jersey Girl' on the guitar. I was like, 'Tom, you're getting so big, what are we gonna do about this?' and we actually sat and talked about it. He's like, 'Well, if you ever make a record, I'm sure my record company is going to ask you to change your name because you can't use Tom Waites.' So we sat there like in pure frivolity going, 'Well, how about Tommy G?' 'How about TG Waites?' 'How about just Thomas Waites?' 'Well, that's what I've been using and they still confuse the two of us.' So I added my middle initial, actually my confirmation name: Gerard."

In Waites's character—intense, self-confident ("I have a huge ego"), and sometimes prickly—can be discerned the ghost of the rambunctious young man who infuriated a preternaturally patient character like Walter Hill. However, he is without question contrite about his past behavior. He now says of his remonstrations to Hill, "I had no business proffering those opinions because no one asked me. It was an amazing lesson for me because I learned that the way that you express your opinions can be either constructive or destructive and, in my case, it was the latter. I tried to make amends to Walter many years later, saying, 'Listen I'm really sorry.'"

Crucially, Waites has been able to wrest some lessons from his downfall. "I came away, I think, a better person, a better actor, a better guy for it," he says. "I've learned how to be slightly more diplomatic. I read a quote somewhere: 'If you really need to say something, you probably shouldn't.'" He says of Hill, "When I went to apologize to him, I don't think he minded so much that somebody had a different point of view creatively. What he really didn't like—and where I feel like I went out of bounds—is by removing my name from the credits. It was an error in judgement by a kid who had way too much success way too quickly and didn't know how to handle it. In many ways, that's why I'm also an acting teacher. I feel like I can help a lot of young people not to make the same mistakes that I made, where you make judgements based upon the egoistic part of your nature rather than the creative part, which is what got you the job to begin with." "He's in a much better place now," confirms Gordon of Waites. "I've seen him. He's a very nice man."

Waites credits his stage hinterland with his success at negotiating a living in the reduced circumstances in which he found himself post-*Warriors*. "I had such extensive theatre training at Julliard, I'm still able to do plays, though now more often as a director than just as an actor. Because of that solid theatre training, I developed a technique that enabled me to last. I always keep the fires burning because I'm talented to a certain extent and I work hard, I go after it."

In the first half of 2004 Waites finally beat the demon drink that had aggravated the egotism that had adversely affected his career. "I'm a recovered alcoholic, thank God," he says, before quickly appending the ex-alcoholic's vigilance-conscious mantra, "One day at a time." He explains, "I honestly didn't know I was alcoholic until I was in my thirties. It wasn't until I was married and had children. My wife was like, 'You have a big problem.' I wish I addressed it much sooner. It upsets me that I've caused harm to others as a result of my alcoholism."

"Who knows?" reflects Waites of the alternative reality that might have resulted had he not been fired from *The Warriors*. "Maybe I would have become super-successful and drank myself to death by the age of thirty. Maybe it all happened because the universe is looking out for me."

As early as its opening night, Terry Michos saw the beneficial effect of *The Warriors* on his acting career. "I had a couple of agents that I didn't know come up to me after that and want to take me on," he recalls.

Having spent '75-'79 in the Big Apple, he relocated to LA in 1980. "I did a miniseries called *The Contender* for CBS Universal Pictures. I played a middleweight boxer. That had some depth to it and people said it was a really fine performance… I did *Simon and Simon, Maclean's Law, Grease* on Broadway, but no big thing." He reflects, "I was successful in that I made my living acting. There were periods where I wasn't working. I just sort of got out of it and got into other things."

Michos moved into factual television in the Hudson Valley Region of New York State. "I was a news director and a television news anchor for eighteen years." Programs of his were nominated for awards and *Meet the Leaders*, which he produced, won the New England Cable Television Award for Best Public Affairs Show. "Then I worked for Congresswoman Nan Hayworth on Capitol Hill as her press secretary and communications director. They pulled me out from the news over to there. So it's been an interesting ride. The acting part of it was maybe seven years."

"I think it helped me," David "Cochise" Harris says of *The Warriors*. "I've done nineteen movies now." He has also notched up half-a-dozen television movies and multiple TV episodes. "I was in *Brubaker* with Robert Redford and Yaphet Kotto and Jane Alexander and Keith David and all these people. Wonderful actors." Harris also played opposite Denzel Washington in *A Soldier's Story* (1984). "We should have won the Academy Award," he insists. "We lost out to *The Killing Fields*." He adds, "I was never going to be Denzel Washington. I'm a character guy." Not that he has a problem with this: "They last longer, and they get the best roles."

"It wasn't a help nor a hinder," says Dorsey Wright of the effect of *The Warriors* on his career. "Most of the jobs that I went to afterwards was really more interested in why I was hired by Miloš Forman for *Hair*." The man who played Cleon says his subsequent acting career "went very well." He was certainly on a roll in '77/'78, proceeding almost on a conveyor belt from *Hair* to *The Warriors* to *Hotel New Hampshire*. However, his acting "went" not just well but very quickly, as in was over. "It was not long after *Hotel New Hampshire*. My son was born during that. I had to fly in from that for the birth. I think I stuck around for a year more. Did a couple of Broadway things and then it was like, 'You know what, I gotta get a regular job.' Acting is 'Sometimes.' It's catch-and-catch-can. I really wanted stuff to be a lot different for my kid. My agent thought that, 'You are fucking insane.' But I don't like to sit around. It was cool when I was a kid, but I got responsibilities now. It didn't bother me. I left from it and that was the end of that."

Wright took up a day job with the New York Transit Authority—the very same organization responsible for maintaining and running the subway trains that were such an integral part of the Warriors' adventures. "You're not the first person to see the irony in that," he laughs. He does, however, have a toe in his old industry via voiceover work. The latter came about by him lending his voice to the 2005 Rockstar *Warriors* video game. "I said, 'Look, I got two days off, so I can give you one day.' They were like, 'I don't think it can be done in one day.' I did it in one day... That's how I got my agent that I have now for voiceovers, because he was impressed... I do plenty of voiceovers. They don't take a lot of time, they're very easy to do, and it keeps me plugged into the business. Once I retire, I'll see where it's going as a full-time basis. But my thing is, I will have a pension."

After playing Cowboy, Tom McKitterick never appeared on screen again. "I was out of the profession two-and-a-half years later," he notes. He considers this fact to stem from the same place as the decision he recalls he made during the *Warriors* shoot to turn down the male lead. That memories differ on this is less important than the fact that in such a situation 99% of other actors would have bitten Walter Hill's hand off and brushed aside any apprehension that this was not a logical plot turn. "That's why I left the profession," McKitterick says of his lack of confidence and ambition.

"I don't know that I went to the premiere," McKitterick says of *The Warriors*. "The rough cut—I don't remember much about that. Once the movie was over, I quickly got a job at the Public Theatre." McKitterick's role in Thomas Babe's *Fathers and Sons* as Jack McCall, Wild Bill Hickok's real-life killer, involved many more lines than the 21 he delivered as Cowboy in *The Warriors*. "I thought, 'Wow, here's where I get to prove myself,'" he says. "I was playing a leading role opposite Richard Chamberlain and Dixie Carter and I was at work immediately. I just didn't think much about the movie. I went forward in life." He admits he may have felt "ambivalent" about *The Warriors* after shooting wrapped. "It was exhausting and I didn't know what to make of it really. I spent three months with this crew. I didn't really think the film would advance my career. I don't know why." He also says of his *Warriors* performance, "I should have been more aggressive in trying to define the character. Cowboy didn't seem to have verbally any place where I could assert myself. It did seem that the part was underwritten... If Tony Danza had played Cowboy, I think just his physicality, his size and whatnot, would have inspired some sort of development... And I think there were physical expectations of me in that role that I didn't meet very well. I'm short. I've never thrown a punch in my life. When I was ever in fights, I wrestled, and that wasn't called for. Looking back on it immediately afterwards, I said, 'Gee, I sort of blew that.'" He also says something which hints at a deeper uncertainty. "I didn't know what my career was. I was ambivalent about being an actor—and yet I was getting success. I was trying to figure out, 'Do I like doing this?'"

Not that he, at least initially, wasn't having a good time. "*Fathers and Sons* was great... It was a huge challenge and I was very happy to have the opportunity to do the play again with the same director, with the same designer, with Richard Chamberlain and Dixie Carter, in Los Angeles. I felt it was a unique opportunity because I could correct faults that I felt I made in my first attempt at the part. I love to work on what I do and make it better... I got phenomenal reviews for that in Los Angeles."

However, his enthusiasm wanes incrementally as he recounts the rest of his career. "I did a play with John Lithgow and Fred Gwynne called *Salt Lake City Skyline* at the Public Theatre. That was sort of okay. I did a show called *Say Goodnight, Gracie*. Austin Pendleton directed that. I hated doing that. I really thought, 'What the hell? Why am I doing this?' Then I went to Hollywood, because *Fathers and Sons* took me out there. I read for a lot of people and basically I just thought, 'I'm not in control of any these situations.' I'm given four pages to read it, or not even a side, and I just felt like, 'If you're going to be selling yourself, you should know what you're selling.' I didn't have a defined product. I felt I should have had a personality that I went in the door with and pretended that that's who I was.

"My agent—and I had a good agent at the time—said, 'We want to make you the next John Ritter.' I didn't want to be the next anything. And in Hollywood, if you go up and you audition for a TV series, you have to obligate yourself to seven years. That spooked me. I like my freedom."

A psychologist would instantly pounce on the fact that when McKitterick departed the acting profession, it was for a career as a photographer: moving from in front of the camera to behind it. "Oh yeah," allows McKitterick. "This is the truth about me. I'm an observer." In his new career, McKitterick alternated between sports and hard-hitting current affairs. "I was working as a tennis photographer at the US Open and Davis Cup. I shot for an agency called Impact Visuals and we did progressive news issues. You don't make a lot of money as a photojournalist, but I was successful in the sense I produced images that I think are really important and, on certain issues, I made my mark. I'm included in books, I'm included in retrospective shows about the topics that I was able to really connect with and do something for." Unfortunately, the print-media outlets for his work shriveled under the onslaught of digital technology. "*Newsweek* went from a thick book to a [thin one] and photographers on the mastheads were fired left and right. I thought, 'I gotta get out of this. This is not working.' That's when I started producing."

In this new role, he has successfully brought two shows to the West-End stage. He says that returning to the theatre world after so long didn't feel strange. "It felt like coming home. And a more appropriate role for my personality." His 2006 revival of Tennessee Williams' *Period of Adjustment* was directed by Howard Davies and starred Benedict Cumberbatch, Lisa Dillon, and Jared Harris. He followed it in 2011 with a production of Terence Rattigan's World War II RAF drama *Flare Path*, directed by Trevor Nunn and starring James Purefoy, Sienna Miller, and Sheridan Smith. *Flare Path* received two Olivier nominations, one for Best Revival and one for Best Supporting Actress, which Smith won. "There were shows in between that I researched and I worked on for a year and then things fall apart," McKitterick points out. "It's risky, but my last show recouped and made 80% profit."

Paramount's *Warriors* press book—already shown as not accurate in its reporting of McKitterick's age—claimed that the movie's Snow was, even as the film was set for release, planning to return to school to study engineering. "Well, close," says Brian Tyler, who after *The Warriors* would secure no further roles on either stage or screen. "I went to auditions after that and you got to make a decision whether or not are you going to stick with this and I decided to go into college… I started school with architecture and the school I went to, they actually closed it down. So I had to switch schools and I ended up graduating with a sociology degree. Then I went to John Jay College and got my Master's in Public Administration." From there, he became a trooper with the New York state police. "I've worked all around the state of New York. I didn't deal as much with individuals as I did, let's say, accidents. My state police work involved mostly work on the highways." Although now retired, he says, "I still work for the state police in a part-time capacity. Basically, I'm a private investigator, a contractor." Asked if at any point he regretted leaving acting behind, he says, "No. I enjoyed my career." He laughingly adds what amounts to his mantra, "You gotta be flexible."

The main supporting cast of *The Warriors* have had fortunes as varied as those of the principal actors. Asked whether the film has been a help or hindrance, David Patrick Kelly initially says, "I think both," but then instantaneously changes his mind: "Nah, I think it's only been good." The film's Luther has subsequently appeared in, among others, *Commando, Wild at Heart, Malcolm X, The Crow,* and *K-PAX.* He can also be seen in two further Walter Hill movies, *48 Hrs.* and *Last Man Standing.* The first saw him play another low-life named Luther ("I think it was an homage. I think we even vaguely talked about it"), the second a neo-noir project starring Bruce Willis that he talks of with particular fondness. Television-wise, he can be seen in episodes of *Twin Peaks, Miami Vice, Moonlighting, Spenser: For Hire, Law & Order,* and *Gossip Girl.* He has also maintained a presence on the boards. "My favorite things—along with Walter's films—are the stage things that I've done [with] this avant-garde theatre director, Richard Foreman." Theatre has kept Kelly in New York. "I love going to LA but I never lived there. I've done all these bizarre things because of the accessibility of theatre. Everybody wants to be on Broadway and I've managed to do that a dozen times now, and it keeps going." He muses, "I've had a really varied career," but adds, "Most people know just that one." The come-out-to-play catchphrase in "that one" has to his pleasure followed him around. "Nearly every day for thirty years, someone has said that phrase to me on the street. I appreciate that." He also adds, "I finally read Sol Yurick's original. There was no gang called the Warriors in the book. History would have been so much different if I had chanted, 'Coney Island Dominators come out to play.'"

Kelly declines to participate in the *Warriors*-related activities by which most of the cast members now make a tidy adjunct to their living or pension. "I've never done the autograph thing, the conventions or the comic con or any of those things, but I have always appreciated the fact it's constantly brought to me."

"I thought Deborah would have a bigger career," says McKitterick. "She's incredibly photogenic and just a joy to work with." At first, Van Valkenburgh was probably more famous than any of her *Warriors* colleagues courtesy of her prominent role in the first five seasons of *Too Close For Comfort,* a sitcom starring Ted Knight that began airing on ABC in 1980. "Deb was a household name at that time to a degree," notes Michos. However, that was the peak of Van Valkenburgh's fame, even though she has also racked up multiple one-off television-episode appearances, a clutch of TV movies, and a dozen-and-a-half films, including Walter Hill's *Streets of Fire.* "I've been in and out," says Van Valkenburgh, "but I keep doing it. I'm tenacious if nothing else. And sometimes we do parallel careers. You do your acting when you get to do your acting, but you also do other things at the same time." And those other things? "I'm an artist and I have a card business and I make art."

"He was amazing. I don't know why he chose not to pursue a movie career," says James Remar of Roger Hill, the man whose performance as Cyrus was for so many the highlight of the picture. Hill's son reveals that Roger was initially happy to follow that professional avenue. "After *The Warriors*, he decided to go after more roles in film and television because he had a really good experience on that film and really liked Walter Hill," explains Chris W. Hill. "I don't think he did that much more theatre after that." The family relocated to Los Angeles. At first, Hill experienced something of a cycle of excitement and disappointment. Chris: "There were a number of pilots that he shot for networks in the early Eighties that didn't go to series. The pilots were not broadcast either." However, Hill then secured the role of Alec Lowndes in longstanding ABC soap opera *One Life to Live* (ironically filmed in New York). "He was a regular on *One Life To Live* from around 1981 to 1986," says Chris. Hill was almost unrecognizable on the show from his stint as Cyrus, looking far more conventionally black. Chris notes of his hair, "He teased it on *One Life to Live* to create more of an afro."

Although the role was hard work, necessitating shooting five episodes a week, Chris says, "Those were good times. He made great money… He was having the time of his life. For him, for our family, that was a bigger deal than *The Warriors* because it was a steady job and he got to work with some incredible actors like Phylicia Rashad, who went on to do *The Cosby Show*. She played his girlfriend on *One Life to Live* for quite a while. Debbie Allen. Al Freeman, Jr. He was thrilled to be a part of that show."

Many outside the States won't even have heard of *One Life To Live*, but Alec Lowndes made Chris' dad a celebrity. "As a six-year-old, seven-year-old… I didn't quite understand what fame was, but I understood that all my friends' moms knew who he was. I remember one time we were at a boat show at the Coliseum Convention Centre. He was thinking about buying a boat and I was like, 'This would be so cool' and I wanted to explore all the boats, but we had to make a run for it because the crowd realized he was there and wanted to get autographs and he got nervous… I understood he was on a TV show. I would go to the set and I spent a number of years just sitting in this big communal makeup room where all the actors would get their hair and makeup done. They had these monitors in the makeup room and I would watch them film the scenes. It just seemed like normal, as like, 'This is what my dad does for a living.' My mom was an art director at the *Village Voice*, so both my parents were creative."

The good times came to an end when the show changed formats. "It was a thirty-minute show when he was on it and then they switched it to a one-hour show and they recast a lot of the show. He was among the people who were not renewed." It was also the end of the road for Hill's career. "After *One Life to Live*, he quit acting," says Chris. "He was disappointed in the business." Aside from *The Warriors*, Hill made no films and, *One Life to Live* aside, only appeared in a handful of TV shows, among them *Once Upon a Classic*, *American Playhouse*, and *The Leatherstocking Tales*. "The business is tough, especially for mixed ethnicity [people]," says Chris. "People had a hard time figuring out what we are in the Eighties. It's not as big of a deal now, but in the Eighties if you were mixed African American and white— especially in Hollywood—they were like, 'Well, we can't cast you, because nobody writes parts like that.' People write types... And a lot of the things he auditioned for were like getting arrested, playing the perp. He got sick of that, and he wanted to do other things. It's never easy for any actor and I get that—I grew up around a lot of actors. I think at a certain point, he felt, 'This isn't healthy for me to continue to try to do this'... At one point we were going to move to LA because he had a show on a network that they wanted him to star in and it looked like it was about to get a green light. So we had packed up our apartment in New York and then the network decided not to move forward with the series. At moments like that, you have to be incredibly strong, incredibly grounded as a person, to deal with that excitement and then rejection, that up and that down. He was a really sensitive person and after fifteen years just didn't want to do that anymore."

Did his father ever regret leaving acting behind? "I did ask him that, and he didn't. In the Nineties I was like, 'Why don't you get back into it? I mean, you look good.' But other things took over his life, particularly trying to be well. His mental health really consumed the 1990s for him and trying to get to a good place and he just didn't want to be in that world. I don't think that he really liked that I got into the entertainment business, although I'm not an actor... He went back to school. I lived with him in upstate New York in the late Eighties when he was going to get his master's. He was really into reading and literature in English and wanted to teach."

Part of Hill's mental-health issues may have been due to his complicated familial hinterland. Chris: "The man who raised him in the house turned out not to actually be his dad, which is why he changed his name later in life to Wilkinson. He found that man Wilkinson who was his actual father, but he wasn't interested in being family… He only met his dad once and his dad did not want to talk with him."

Roger Hill's absolute lack of interest in returning to the acting profession persisted even in the face of extraordinary hardship a universe removed from his recent stardom and riches. "He was homeless for a few years," says Chris. "We fell out of touch in the early 2000s. He disappeared and I couldn't find him. He was sleeping on a park bench somewhere. We finally got back in touch and I was sending him money for a while and trying to help him get back on his feet and get a place to live… He remarried in around 2006 for a little while. I think that marriage lasted five years."

In the years before Roger Hill's death in 2014, media reports tended to say that he had taken a day job in a Manhattan business library and wrote poetry in his spare time. "That was probably accurate for a month or two," says Chris. "He didn't work in a library up until his death." However, Hill was certainly immersed in writing. "It was poetry. It was also philosophy. He was really into ruminating on the meaning of life. Like I said, he was a very intense man." This writing was not something Roger Hill envisaged as a way to make a living. "I think it was an outlet for his mind. It was about organizing his thoughts and putting down what he was feeling. It was therapy for him."

With one person, it's impossible to determine whether or not he would have used *The Warriors* as a springboard to spectacular success. The youngest of the Warriors was the first to pass away, Marcelino Sánchez dying in 1986, aged just 28.

The Warriors' Rembrandt made one other movie, appearing in Walter Hill's *48 Hrs* (1982) "I wanted very much to use him again," explains Hill. "I had wanted to involve him in the plot to a greater extent, but the story got very complicated." David Patrick Kelly also renewed his professional relationship with Sánchez in *48 Hrs*. "I thought he was great," he says. "In the Seventies, I was directed by Sal Mineo in Michigan. Marcelino reminds me of Sal Mineo. I think a lot of people have said that. He had the similar kind of look and he had that kind of function from *Rebel Without a Cause* in [*The Warriors*] as well… He was the good-looking fellow so, depending on the parts, he had the ability to go far and do a lot of other things." "He could have become the next Raul Julia," says Waites. "I think he would have soared. He was very talented. He could sing. He could dance."

Mayra Sánchez's says of her brother's role in *The Warriors*, "He was very happy that he had gotten such a big opportunity. Now, I will say that I believe that he found it difficult to then go to smaller roles from that major role. So I think it was a little bit of a rollercoaster adjustment for him, because that was his very first real role and it was quite significant. But he was still very happy to be working at all. That was always his goal—to be working at all. He just was very focused on that. His joy was when he was working... He had an incredible work ethic... Marcelino developed a great desire for success in the hopes of giving our Mom a better life."

Acting-wise, Sánchez felt himself to be blessed by his youthful looks and cursed by his ethnicity. Mayra: "He did a lot of TV work and had opportunities that were for parts for someone younger, but because he just looked so young he was able to do those things... His biggest issue with acting was that he was pigeonholed, because he looked so Latin and he was very disappointed about the kinds of roles that he could go for based on the fact that there were limited roles for a minority at that time... Another thing [was] that the roles that he played were counter to what his nature was. He was unhappy that he had to play gang members or garage attendants. Things that are typical minorities, or at least was at that time. He felt that he was capable of so much more." Mayra suspects that the pigeonholing issue is what lay behind her brother discontinuing use of the family name. "He changed his performer name to 'James Marcelino,'" she says.

Sánchez was acutely aware that the limitations imposed on him would not apply to his sister if she entered his field. "He and I actually physically look very different. I was blonde and I had very fair skin. He had great desire for me to be an actress. He was trying to push me in that direction and he would constantly tell me that he was limited but I would not be limited. When we lived together, he made it a point that I take lessons and take pictures and do the whole thing, but I personally never really desired to be in that industry. I had a difficult time with that. Even though I didn't want to disappoint him, I just was not as [interested as] he was."

Regardless of his work ethic, like most actors Sánchez had dry periods. "My mom helped him during some of those times, and he worked with other friends and people in his community that he could trade with in order to continue forward," says Mayra. "He used to paint backdrops for friends who were in the business so that he could trade dancing classes and voice lessons and things like that." Because of his recognizability, the career-lulls could lead to humiliating scenarios. "My mom told me a story he told her about trying to get a regular job. When he went up to ask for an application, the person who was there recognized him and made such a big fuss of it that he ended up going home without the application."

Sánchez appeared in television series *3-2-1 Contact*, *CHiPs*, *Hill Street Blues*, and *CBS Schoolbreak Special*. He also landed a role in the TV movie *Death Penalty*. Additionally, he did plenty of theatre work, his résumé featuring stage productions like *Sidewalkin*, *The Coolest Cat in Town*, *The Blind Junkie*, *The Adventures of Professor Pennywhistle*, *Gingerbread*, and *Jeremy and the Thinking Machine*. "He did it all, actually," says Mayra. "I'm always amazed because every now and then some fan will bring something into Facebook or send me something I've never seen before. I'm quite amazed at the body of work that he left behind."

That body of work is only substantial, however, when taking into account Sánchez's brief lifespan. As with so many homosexual men's deaths in that period, his passing was AIDS-related. When Auto Immune Deficiency Syndrome raised its head in the early 1980s, it sent a chill through the gay community. "I think he was worried about it," says Mayra. "He didn't say so to me, but I definitely sensed changes in his patterns and in his behavior." Mayra estimates the point when her brother began displaying visible signs of illness to be 1983, when she was fifteen. In those days, with no known cure, a diagnosis of AIDS was a slow death sentence. Mayra lived with Sánchez for the last two years of his life, during which time she says of his impending mortality, "He resolved himself. He accepted that."

Sánchez's idols included Bette Davis, James Dean, Marilyn Monroe, Barbra Streisand, and Elizabeth Taylor. "He liked glamour," Mayra laughs. Another performer that Sánchez greatly admired was Cher. In 1985, the singer welcomed him into her home. "He had painted her various times and brought her one for that visit," says Mayra.

Mayra asserts of her sibling, "I think he'd still be acting… I think that the only reason he's not acting is because he died. I really believe that." She describes Sánchez as "the most amazing brother and just an incredible mentor. He made a huge difference in my life… He and I were extremely close… He had faults, but they were so little. He was an overachiever and sometimes a little too protectionistic. He would get anxious, and it was hard to connect with him when he was overly anxious. But in general, he was private and he was friendly, and he was very, very principled. He valued his friendships and valued his family and he was always trying to reach for ideals, always trying to do his best."

While that may seem the biased viewpoint of an adoring little sister, Sánchez also seems to be universally fondly remembered by his *Warriors* colleagues. "He was joyful," recalls McKitterick. Walter Hill says, "He was good-tempered, very sweet-natured, and there was an innocence about him. A kind of pervasive innocence and sense of wonder. Made everybody smile."

"He was the most beautiful kid," says Waites. "He never had a negative thing to say about anyone, ever. Even when things got really tense, he was just like, 'Come on you guys, it's okay.' You couldn't invent it. He made everyone laugh, all the time. He lifted everyone's spirits up with his smile. He was just a lovely person to be around. He was a riot. He could copy any one of us on the spot and do it exactly letter perfect. That's really the tragedy of this story. Me and my behavior, Walter firing me—it's my fault. The tragedy is losing that kid. He was a gem. He was a jewel. He made every place he went a little bit better, just by his presence."

"All of us adored Marcelino, and I think all of us felt protective of him," says Beck. "Certainly Swan's looking out for him in a nonverbal way in the movie. Some of that was just character and some of it was just how I felt about Marcy... We were all devastated when he died. He was just a prince of a man."

Part of the sadness surrounding Sánchez's death stems from him not having lived long enough to see the revival in *The Warriors'* fortunes. Mayra: "I often think to myself that if he had lived, he would be shocked at how much attention this movie has accrued... He was unhappy that it had been pulled... He was disappointed because he had put that effort in and he wanted the movie to be successful. I guess in his mind it meant that it was not getting a chance to be successful and we would never really know the success it could have been. But of course, all these years later people still talk about *The Warriors*, and that's one of the things that I often wish he had stayed alive to [see]. I think it would have been very, very meaningful for him that he really was able to make a mark... It's been very helpful in my grief process to be able to connect with my brother in unexpected places and remember him and know that people remember him fondly. And it was a good project. I really wish he would have known that before he died. I wish he had known that it was going to be so epic, so memorable."

"He would have loved it more than any of us," Beck says. "He would have loved being in a cult classic movie."

AFTERBURN

THE WORLD HAS MOVED on since 1979 in many unexpected ways. The advent of digital technology, for instance, has made the old movie synonym "celluloid" almost redundant. Chris W. Hill notes, "I have enormous respect for editors who cut actual film on an upright Moviola or Steenbeck. It was much harder to make an edit and keep things in sync and keep the footage in your mind when you had to go and find it in a bin. It's a lot easier on a computer to do that. So I have great respect for Walter Hill and the entire cast and crew." The old Gulf + Western building on Columbus Circle that was the center of much *Warriors* activity is now called Trump Tower, owned by a man then only known as a businessman, not a TV celebrity, let alone a president. The studio system that gave rise to many disputes on the *Warriors* production is now all but defunct, with film titles now routinely preceded by an almost comical procession of production-company logos that bespeak a different, more diffuse, type of dependency, although not necessarily a better one. "Every one of those logos means the director had to go pitch the movie to five different [people] and to get five different people to say yes probably means that she or he had to see fifty more," observes Walter Hill. Meanwhile, the New York City seen in the film has disappeared into the realms of folklore.

Although *The Warriors* was never realistic, it not only impressionistically conveyed issues of its time but ones that in particular were dismayingly familiar to residents of the graffiti-bedecked, violence-simmering, stench-filled Big Apple. "I think the movie is very much of New York in the late Seventies," says Walter Hill. "Even though it's kind of timeless in its approach—there's a nameless future to it—there is also something about it that's very much of the time and place where it was made." "I

239

think it did capture the decadence of New York in the Seventies," says Thomas Waites. "But he did it with flair. He did it with a sense of style. The wet streets. The choreographed fights. The music." As a Californian and a Pennsylvanian respectively, Hill and Waites could be accused of not being experts on the subject, but NYC-raised Mayra Sánchez agrees with them. "It was more gritty than that, but yes, absolutely," she says. "Even today, if I watch that movie it just brings me right back to how we experienced New York at that time. I think it really did create a good snapshot of the vibe of New York."

That vibe was almost apocalyptical. In his *Village Voice* review of *The Warriors*, Andrew Sarris summed up the feelings of many when he wrote, "It's possible… that what is most frightening about the movie is the essential truth of its basic premise: that the streets already belong to the violently and criminally inclined. The city is dying, block by block, from fear, loathing, fire, and desertion."

For Sol Yurick, things never really changed. "I don't think it was much," he said in 2009 of the reduction in crime rates that the city had exponentially experienced since the early 1990s. "I mean, you're talking small numbers. Let's say your murder rate dropped by twenty dead bodies. That's not much, but propaganda-wise that's very big… In a city of seven million people where there may be like 50,000 crimes total, that's nothing… I've lived here all my life. It's a question of percentage about you encountering any danger whatsoever." As was his wont, Yurick strayed from the sociological into the political: "I grew up in a sense always being wary. When I was growing up during the Depression, what you had in fact was a different kind of violence, which was political violence. My father would engage in strikes and get into fights with police and beat up police and get beaten by police. And then there were the conflicts between organized crime and union leaders and what have you." In fact, Yurick felt that real life was possibly more horrific than anything that either a writer like him or Hollywood could portray and that part of the reason was the blossoming of the type of criminals he portrayed in *The Warriors*. "Since gangs have taken on a more international flavor, they're really part of the global economy in a very big way. They have their class structures within them."

Yurick was in a minority. For most, the city has achieved a miraculous rebirth. "It showed a part of the city that you'll never see again because New York City's cleaned up and beautiful now," says Terry Michos of the movie of Yurick's book. "It's really like Disneyland now compared to what it was," says David Patrick Kelly. James Remar notes, "People that lived it don't forget it... There were plenty of places in Manhattan you shouldn't go, especially at night... There are still areas you shouldn't go if you're not from there. But the vast majority of Manhattan is a very safe place."

For most New Yorkers, within two decades of the release of *The Warriors* the markedly better quality of life in the city could be measured objectively by the plummeting crime statistics or impressionistically in such things as the fact that the graffiti-adorned trains that are a signature of *The Warriors* are now a thing of history. There is much debate about why these changes occurred. Some cite the shaming and peer pressure that resulted from publicity campaigns and public service announcements about anti-social behavior. Some point to "zero-tolerance" crime policies practiced by Mayor Rudolph W. Giuliani and police chief Bill Bratton. Some theorize that it was an unexpected legacy of the reduction in use by motorists of leaded gasoline, which is theorized to have adversely affected behavior, particularly of adolescents. Some claim that the abortion legislation resulting from the Roe vs. Wade judgment had an unintended effect in that ethnic groups associated with higher levels of crime began having fewer children. Others point to the trend of the lower-waged being priced out of the locale. Some claim that the trend is a consequence of some or all of these things.

"Subway stations are there but they've been redone," says Dorsey Wright of the post-1979 alterations to the topography seen in *The Warriors*. "Where the candy-girl thing was, that's a whole different neighborhood now. If you go on a sightseeing tour, it's just basically looking at regentrification. Brand new buildings." Also long gone, says Wright, are street gangs. "What we have here now are offshoots of LA gangs. There are a few Bloods and a few Crips, but it's nothing like it was in the late Sixties, early Seventies." For him, New York's street-gang era was already dying even as *The Warriors* was being shot, peaking with the city's 1977 blackout. "The [blackout] brought in the era of hip hop because all the gangs became what we call crews. The Peacemakers, which was a gang, became the PM Fun City Crew. The Black Spades, the gang I was part of, became Afrika Bambaataa and the Soul Sonic Force, otherwise known as the Zulu Nation. After people had vandalized stores and stole a lot of turntables and speakers, they all became DJs. And that was basically the end of gangs. It was really weird to see these guys who less than two weeks ago would run up on you and rob you and now they're trying to get you to pay five dollars to come to a party."

Also reborn is the reputation of *The Warriors*. Period piece it may now be, but *The Warriors* has exponentially come to be perceived as a cinematic milestone. On that score, U.S. President Ronald Reagan got in early. "It was a year or so after the picture had opened," recalls Michael Beck. His timeline might be hazy (Reagan entered the Oval Office in January '81), but Beck remembers the events vividly. "His press secretary called when my wife and I were living in New York," he says. "I was out walking our dog and getting some ice cream and when I came back to our studio apartment, she had a Cheshire grin on her face and said, 'Guess who just phoned? The White House.' I said, 'Get out of here!' She said, 'No, really.' Because when they called she thought somebody was putting her on, so she was giving them some lip about it. I don't know whether it was the main press secretary, but it was someone in his press corps who called to simply say that the President had screened the movie at Camp David and wanted to send his congratulations." A more direct endorsement came a few weeks later: "I received a note from the White House, a little handwritten note, expressing those same sentiments." What would arch-conservative, pro-law-and-order Ronald Reagan have got out of an "alternative" picture like *The Warriors*? "I have no idea. I was stunned at the time and am still taken aback that President Reagan watched the movie and responded in a complimentary way to me."

Of course, as an ex-thespian Reagan could simply have been operating on a level of collegiate courtesy. However, down the years admiration for the film has proven not uncommon, both among the prominent and the obscure. Some had always sung its praises, of course, but that can be said of many movies that are now barely remembered. "When I became aware that maybe the movie was going to hang on in people's minds was in the 1980s," says Walter Hill. "As I was travelling about making films and everything, I was always asked about *The Warriors*. And they never asked me about violence. They always would ask me about certain scenes and people would talk about whether or not Ajax should have been able to break away from the police and be there at the end and things like [that]. They weren't film people or anything. They'd just be people you would run into. I was moving houses once and the guy that was loading the truck saw a little poster thing for *The Warriors*. He said, 'You saw that movie?' I said, 'Well, I directed it.' 'God—really? Jeez.' And this was fifteen, twenty years after the movie had come out."

The long tail of *The Warriors'* impact was partly down to revivals at cinemas. In 2017, Beck explained to the *New Musical Express'* Leonie

Cooper, "In the early to mid-1980s I had a friend who had been on vacation to Paris. When he returned, he said, 'You won't believe this. When I was in Paris, there was a midnight screening of *The Warriors* and it was like *The Rocky Horror Picture Show*: all the people were dressed up as the characters.' That was the first inkling. I went, 'Wow, something else is happening with this movie.'"

Something else that occurred during the Eighties was that video cassette recorders turned from a luxury item into something that most homes could afford. In 1981, *The Warriors* was one of the then-select films given a new lease of life by the nascent VCR market. The leisurely and repeated revisiting of the picture enabled by that medium caused a reassessment—or confirmation, for those already enamored—of its qualities. As the home-entertainment market developed, *The Warriors* was subject to Laserdisc (also 1981) and DVD (2001) releases. "Once it was on DVD, it had terrific sales for an old movie, so you could see that something was percolating," Hill reflects.

In addition, the film was circulating on television, albeit usually in versions significantly different to the theatrical release. One version has swearing (and possibly some violence) deleted. Another starts with Coney Island daytime footage. A third contains the deleted sections to be found on the *Ultimate Director's Cut* DVD. In addition, down the years there seem to have been screenings of cuts with swearing reduced further. Hill has had nothing to do with these variations and was shocked to be told of the reinsertion of the Coney Island scenes that he, with considerable deliberation, jettisoned.

Regardless of their fealty to the director's vision, TV broadcasts enabled its actors to give their children a *Warriors* baptism. In the late Nineties, Beck permitted his eleven-year-old daughter to watch a broadcast, one of the few times he himself had viewed the film in its entirety. "I thought, 'Well, this is the sanitized version of it, so she won't see Dad dropping the f-bomb too many times,'" he explains. "It was fun, 'cause she'd look at the screen, she'd look at me, and she went, 'Dad! You used to be a hunk. What happened?'"

It, of course, wasn't just the actors' own children who were apprised of the film's virtues. One day in the late 1990s, Michael Beck's teenaged son arrived back from school with a group of friends. "One of his buddies went, 'Oh man! You're the dude that played Swan in *The Warriors*!'" recalls Beck. "I'm sitting there thinking, 'How does this fifteen-year-old even know about this movie?' This was before video games came out about it or before 25th anniversary stuff. It was just a movie that, if they found it, they either saw it on TV or they found it at Blockbuster. That was when I knew for the first time this was a cult movie, because it had now skipped generations. I don't think any of us had any idea we were making a movie that would still have legs thirty years later."

Michos had his own version of this revelation on the day in 1995 that he walked into a television studio in his home state to start a job as anchor for News Center 6. "All these young people, probably in their twenties, were staring at me and talking and I just didn't understand it. Finally someone said, 'I can't believe it,' and they were all talking about, 'That's the guy in *The Warriors*.' Then they started quoting lines, and said, 'It went on HBO and we used to have parties and we'd dress up as characters.' I would hear this over and over."

Gareth Jones first saw *The Warriors* in 2002 when it was broadcast on BBC One in the UK. He was nineteen, which meant he hadn't been born when the film was released. He found himself immediately captivated by the grimy urban cityscapes of 1970s New York, the characters and outfits of the different gangs, and the rapport and the cooperation between the Warrior members as they fought their way home. He quickly ordered the VHS cassette in order to watch it again and went online to find out all he could about the film. His enthusiasm led him to build the Warriors Movie Site (http://warriorsmovie.co.uk) to share his thoughts on the picture. The site's forum has become home to a community of thousands of *Warriors* fans from across the world, manifestations of whose love for the film include creating costumes, artwork, and fan fiction, and visiting the production's filming locations.

In the Zeroes, inchoate, fragmented adoration developed into organized fandom involving both congregation and monetization. Conventions—both as fringe events at comic-book conventions (comic cons) and gatherings solely based around *The Warriors*—have been staged regularly since. They have snowballed in terms of attendance of both audience numbers and *Warriors* personnel.

"We were in Coney Island in 2015," recalls Michos. "They just did a one-day show of a *Warriors* reunion: Back to Coney. There were, they said, six, seven thousand. I'm telling you there were more than that. There were probably eight to ten thousand people there waiting in line, and some of them didn't even get to the line. It started at eight o'clock and by the time we ended at nine, they didn't get in to get the signature. And people were flying in from Europe, from everywhere. I had no idea the phenomenon." As indicated, it's a phenomenon that spans the ages. "There will be people who were in their late twenties, early thirties when the movie opened," says Beck. "They will be next in line to somebody who's nineteen years old, goes, 'God, dude, this is my favorite movie. I've watched it fifty times!'"

At the Warriors Festival on Coney Island in September 2015, tickets ranged from $15 all the way up to $400. To the actors, such numbers are a welcome addition to annual *Warriors* residuals that are more a revenue trickle than a stream. ("It's a couple of sacks of groceries," Beck says of the latter.) Michos is a "hundred percent sure" that he has made more money from *The Warriors* after the fact than he originally received for appearing in the movie. Says Beck of the convention circuit, "With us who are approaching or are in some kind of semi-retirement, I call it collecting our annuities, which is really pretty nice to have something that you did that many years ago that people still want to come and see you for."

Encouraged by Dorsey Wright, Bobbie Mannix attended her first Warriors convention in approximately 2018. "I think the boys have been doing it on and off for ten years," she says. "It's a whole new world for me to meet these people and sign autographs... The *Warriors* fans are just incredible. Everybody's so nice... So many people—oh, so many people—come up to us and say, 'Oh my gosh, oh my gosh, you changed my life.' But it seems for the best instead of the worst. It seems like a lot of the people at these conventions would say, 'You know, I was bullied as a kid and after I saw *The Warriors*, I took my life into my own hands. I wasn't bullied anymore. *The Warriors* actually helped me.'"

In this day and age of "cosplay," the convention scene is particularly gratifying for Mannix as she observes people walking around in the signature styles of the Baseball Furies, the Rogues, and, of course, the Warriors. "Everybody shows up in their vest. They have all their Warriors signs and they get autographs on the vests, which look fabulous." However, the pleasure must be bitter-sweet, because she has no proprietorial rights, and therefore income, from such replication of her craft. "I do own all my sketches 'cause that was in my contract. That and *Xanadu*, my agent said that all the sketches revert back to me. But in those days, there was no merchandise contracts and no design contracts and that's why it's a free-for-all now. Everybody that is at these comic cons sells Warriors pins, Warriors hats, Warriors vests, this, that, blah, blah blah, because Paramount doesn't have a contract on any of that. Forty years ago, they didn't have this marketing and merchandising thing like Marvel has, for instance, today… It's a lot different today… I would get part of the merchandising rights and have a percentage for my designs."

Michos estimates he does around four conventions per year. "Maybe some of the guys do more. Some do less… We all do different ones because they invite sometimes just the big names, like just Michael and Debbie. Sometimes they invite all of us, sometimes me and David Harris and Michael go alone." "When we go to these conventions, people are sometimes shaking when they come up to us," says Michos. "I say, 'Look, if you guys don't come here for these conventions, we're sitting in these chairs like a bump on a log. It's a two-way love affair.' The *Warriors* fans, they're rabid. Some of them watch it every week. It touched the chord of something in a lot of these young men and women. It was women also because it wasn't that violent a film… It was a multicultural gang before multicultural was really in. It was ahead of its time because people from all different cultures loved that we were all bonded together. That's what they would tell us a lot. It brought a different feel to the film because it had a social commentary to it that was underlying, that people didn't really understand is why they were drawn to it. I don't think the women would flock to a *Warriors* remake because they would make it so violent. Even the young women, they just love the fact that there was this camaraderie and this sort of chivalrous fighting and a sense of honor somehow in the midst of a dishonorable backdrop… The *Warriors* has been this awesome gift that has just made me feel like, 'Hey, I remember I was an actor and it was [a] really good thing because we're good at these things.' The fans just love us and treat us like stars for that short period of time and then you go back to your life."

Waites is in an odd situation in that he takes part in and profits from celebrations of a film that he repudiated many years ago and from which criticisms he does not resile, despite his admiration for Hill's achievement on a technical level. He accepts that this is hypocrisy. "But the other side of it is I have touched these fans' lives and they've gone to watch other things that I've done," he reasons. "I get at least two pieces of mail a week, either from *The Thing* or *The Warriors*. The way I justify it in my mind is it gives me a chance to be with my fans. So I don't mind. If I can bring some joy into people's lives and make them forget about their problems for a few minutes because they're watching me in this movie, then yeah, why not cash in on it? What the fuck. You'd do the same thing if you needed money. It beats pushing dirt."

For Van Valkenburgh, each of the numerous times the cast have come together over the years has underlined the unusual solidarity the project engendered among its participants all those decades ago. "We had a reunion that was the Alamo Drafthouse in Austin, Texas," she says of the first gathering devoted exclusively to *The Warriors*. "There's something called the Rolling [Roadshow] and they will take their inflatable screen around the country and they do screenings in the cities where films were shot. So they did a big event in 2006 in Coney Island and it was the first time that we had all generally seen each other in about 25 years. I think we were more thrilled to just be with our tribe members than being out there in the crowds. I think they were watching us be thrilled to be there with each other again, which was really fun. The familiarity was a riot. Dorsey said, 'You and I never worked together, we didn't know each other,' and I totally felt like I had known him the entire time, so it's a very distorted sense of camaraderie. Everybody felt familiar. I didn't feel any awkwardness at all. I think we were just completely beside ourselves that we got to hang out together again. You spend four months shooting a movie, a lot of bonding can happen." Harris says of Michael Beck, "I'm the godfather of his children, he's the godfather of my children. Guess who introduced Michael to his wife? I did. Michael's wife was a dear friend of mine. We went to acting school together. We've been this close for forty-something years." "We're all very close," says Michos. "Most of us by the grace of God have aged pretty well. We're still youthful in some ways. And it's kind of nice when we get together because we really care about each other. It's very interesting. It doesn't always happen on film."

Because of his limited role in the picture, Dorsey Wright missed out on the full extent of the camaraderie. "When people ask you questions, you feel like, 'Well, I wasn't there for a lot of that. This is the only section I know.' But later on, doing shows and stuff with these guys, we became more friends. We gelled more then. Back at the time, it was a job. You do a job, you keep it moving. A couple of them I kept touch with 'cause they were New York City actors and I would see them a lot at auditions or even around the neighborhood. Brian Tyler, me and him lived in the same building for years… We're all good friends and it's like we've known each other forever but now it's a whole different thing. You look back on it and you go, 'Okay, we were young and we were doing the whole machismo thing and now that all that shit is over with, we're grown men.'" Wright attends around four conventions per year. "They have more than that, but I'm not trying to hit all these different cities. I have to go to work. And sitting there, you greet people. I try to make sure that everybody's happy. It's a lot of work. But I attend a lot of these because I like being with the guys. We have a great time together. People look at us and go, 'Wow, y'all look like you're having fun.' Yes, we are." He adds, "It's not gonna run for ever. I don't want to be doing these signings [when I'm] seventy, eighty years old."

The convention circuit was particularly important for Roger Hill. At first, his son probably got more out of *The Warriors* than the actor did. "The robe that he wore in the movie, he kept after the film and I used to run around in that robe when I was a little kid," says Chris. He also points out, "He enjoyed doing that movie, but it was only a couple of days of work for him. Actors do a couple of days here and a couple of days there and they just keep moving forward... He appreciated it as a piece of history. I don't know if he was ever well enough to see it for what it was. I appreciate it as his son, as like he has a legacy: he has something that he accomplished that outlived him and still has meaning for people. There are not that many films or TV shows or albums that become classics, that have some staying power. But I don't think he was ever well enough to look at it with that kind of perspective. I think [he] was always a little bit sour. Even though the experience of working on *The Warriors* was something he enjoyed in the moment, his view of Hollywood was that it was a bit poison."

However, Roger Hill was certainly able to appreciate the fact that he was appreciated. "In the 2000s, he started going to the conventions and stuff like that," says Chris. "I know he enjoyed it." Hill also enjoyed being remunerated. "People put his likeness on lots of things: on T shirts, on hats, on beer cans, in commercials," says Chris. "Around 2009, 2010, companies came out of the woodwork and wanted to license his likeness. It didn't make him rich, but it gave him a revenue source so he could not be homeless. And then the licensing stuff really set him up to be able to retire... Around 2011, he was able to get himself a really nice apartment in the Bronx and be comfortable and have some dignity."

It meant ultimately that Roger Hill died a reasonably happy man. "He was 62 in the beginning of 2014," says Chris. "He didn't make it to his 63rd birthday... He was having a cocktail and some lunch and had a heart attack and passed away. It was very sudden... By the end of his life I think there was an understanding that this is the role he's known for. This was the thing that stuck. I think it was bittersweet for him, but, absolutely, he saw it differently at the end of his life than he did in the Seventies and Eighties... It was a nice coda to a difficult life... He finally found some peace."

Tom McKitterick has never been a part of the *Warriors* camaraderie. "For some reason, he don't want to have much to do with the film," says David Harris of the man who was Cowboy. "Why, I don't know. He's just away from the whole project, the whole concept, the whole thing of *The Warriors*." With what sounds like resentment, Harris says, "Tom is a part of nothing. Nothing." "It's not my thing," says McKitterick of the conventions. "I went to one in Coney Island. I didn't have any publicity pictures and they gave me a pile of pictures. About ten people asked for them. I felt awkward charging them ten dollars for signing my name. I had to go up on stage and say something about myself. I felt like a jerk. It's in no way a comment about the movie or my fellow cast mates who do that. It's not a criticism of that. It's just that I'm not comfortable doing that... I have nothing but respect for the movie and I'm always charmed when people recall it and how much it means to them. I'm proud to be part of it." He has also become more kind to himself regarding how he handled his role. "I didn't see what I was really bringing to it. In the end I said to myself, 'Well, look, I'm a certain type of guy. There must be people like me in the world and so I'm reflecting that kind of guy.'"

Another non-participant is James Remar. "I go to autograph-signing conventions sometimes and people want pictures of Ajax and I sign those for them," he says. "But I don't go to specific Warriors conventions. I've been invited but just the scheduling never worked out." "I don't go to those," says Walter Hill of the conventions and events. "I'm a filmmaker, I'm not a performer... I don't condemn anybody for these things, but... I just don't feel comfortable in that kind of situation. I don't like the idea of signing autographs for money and things like that. I get a lot of mail about *The Warriors*. People send me pictures from *The Warriors*. I always sign them. And I'm grateful to the people who are loyal to the movie."

Lynne Thigpen's attitude toward *The Warriors* was different again, and not just because her scenes as the DJ character involved no interaction with the other cast members. David Patrick Kelly remained friends with Thigpen up to her death aged 54 in 2003 from a cerebral hemorrhage. He is pleased to report that she reached an accommodation with her editing-caused sidelining: "Later she was very happy that it had become such a classic and that her performance, her voice, were a big part of that." "I ran into Lynne a number of times," says Hill. The man who denied the actress full face-exposure in *The Warriors* says she always seemed to be "quite pleased" about her role: "She told me she had the most famous lips in showbusiness." Certainly, before too long Thigpen didn't need the exposure. She racked up dozens of screen, stage, TV, and talking-book appearances and in 1997 she received a Tony for her role in *American Daughter*. An elementary school in her hometown of Joliet, Illinois is now named after her.

THE WARRIORS IS NOW deeply embedded in the culture. In addition to 1985 album *Come Out and Play* by heavy metal band Twisted Sister, popular-music references to *The Warriors* include the Wu-Tang Clan's 1993 track "Shame on a Nuh," "Can You Dig It?", a 1991 single by British indie ensemble the Mock Turtles, a Canadian rock band named after the Gramercy Riffs, and the interview effusions of New York punk group the Ramones. There have been numerous other cultural references. The year 2000 saw rapper Method Man produce an extensive line of *Warriors*-themed clothing for his Johnny Blaze brand. In 2019 Converse issued "New Warriors" sneakers "inspired by" *The Warriors*. (They retailed for $120 and looked nothing like the footwear in the movie.) Walter Hill observes, "Every time that our professional basketball champions in LA won, Shaquille O'Neal would go on a tear and he would always say, 'Can you dig it?'" Quotes from the film have been repeated and parodied in television shows and video games.

For Dorsey Wright, though, it was the news that there was to be a *Warriors* video game that apprised him of the film's pervasive and enduring popularity. "Once it was out of the theatres, that was it, it was gone," he says. "When I first got a call from Rockstar is when I start realizing. They were like, 'Hey, you don't know?' 'No, not really. I don't keep up on that. *That's* a classic?'"

The Rockstar company's *Warriors* video game for home computers was released in 2005. It created one of the supreme ironies of the entire *Warriors* saga: it was a far more brutal proposition than its parent movie yet, in contrast to the brouhaha surrounding the film's original release, this fact has gone largely unremarked on. Another irony is that most of the film's cast have made far more money from this game than they were ever given for appearing in the movie.

The Warriors, first released on the PlayStation 2 and Xbox platforms, is an example of a scrolling video-game genre known as "beat-'em-up" in which points are amassed for violent deeds. Rockstar are known for some dubious traditions, most notoriously the avatars in *Grand Theft Auto* amassing points as a reward for meting out violence to prostitutes. Accordingly, the titular gang is not depicted in the *Warriors* game in the heroic terms for which Walter Hill strove. Instead, they are the vandals, thieves, thugs, and lechers they would be in real life. They also deploy weapons like bricks, planks, knives, and bottles, with the only reason for the lack of guns being period authenticity. That the game generated nothing like the opprobrium that the film did three decades earlier was partly down to the fact that both a generational and technological shift had occurred in the interim. Adults are today often only vaguely cognizant of the entertainment their children consume: with video games requiring skillsets beyond them, as well as being much less of a communal experience than films, they are a mystery to many adults in a way that motion pictures were not to their own parents.

Yet while the Warriors Rockstar game might be part of an industry that is under the radar of much of society, its potentially deleterious effects did not pass by all of the film's now vintage cast. At first, Terry Michos was intrigued by the fact that, in Rockstar's narrative, his character's role had been significantly expanded. "In the video game, it's brought out that Cleon and Vermin started the Warriors," he says. However, he was dismayed by a lack of a moral center to the game. Although he says, "A film is a film and if a character curses, I would go do it," the game's element of reward for bad behavior disturbed him. "They have to beat up old ladies to have success and they'd be blowing away people," he notes of what he was told about the game when approached to lend his voice to it. "I just felt I couldn't do it… I was a father. I was also a part-time pastor." Consequently, he walked away from a big payday. "They used my image but they had some guy do a voice. I got paid something for my image." This non-participation was something that seemed to upset Rockstar. "David Harris was up there doing loops for the game. David is a friend of mine. He said, 'Terry, they were cursing you up and down up there, man.'" Michos suspects that Rockstar got their revenge on him. "My kids said that there's a character at the end of the Warriors video game that they named Terrance—'cause I use 'Terence' professionally now—and he gets the crap beat out of him."

"I was gonna do it at one point," says David Patrick Kelly. "Rockstar kept offering more and more dough. But then I said, 'No, I don't want to do it.'" Although Kelly isn't completely convinced that there is a causal link between movie-screen and real-life violence, he is less unsure when it comes to video games. "I really think that they've contributed to this lack of empathy and desensitizing," he says. He does admit of the Warriors game, "It was kind of exciting when it came out. They had the big cutouts of our likenesses in the subways of New York. A big rollout for that. It was a new thing at the time." He adds of Rockstar, "I respect the guys—they're very nice, respectful." He also indicates that it isn't all about moral objections. "Twisted Sister called me up and wanted me to do [Luther's catchphrase] on their record named after 'Come out to play' and I said no. It was for that character, it was for that time, and I never wanted to be that catchphrase kind of guy. I like the fact that it's only right there and that's it."

Roger Hill was furious that the game used his likeness (voice provided by Michael Potts) and filed a suit against Rockstar's owners Take-Two demanding $250,000 and a court order barring the use of his face. The suit claimed that the game had generated a minimum of $37 million. "He got in touch with me when he was talking about the lawsuit… through a friend that I didn't even know knew him," says Wright. "The personal stuff he wanted to know, I was like, 'I'm not telling you how much I got, but if you need to speak to the people'… Then it got ridiculous because it made the paper."

"My impression was he wasn't against being in the video game, it was that they couldn't agree on a price," says Chris W. Hill of his father's grievances. "That's always a battle for everyone in the entertainment industry—to try to get paid for their work… At some point, there were negotiations, but I don't know the timeline of that. I know eventually it ended up in court and they did pay him." His impression is that his father was happy with the amount of money he ultimately secured from Rockstar. "It was an amicable settlement."

Beck, no less a Christian than Michos, has retrospective qualms about his own involvement. "To be honest, probably had I done proper research on it I may have made the same decision Terry did," he says. "Not being a video gamer, I didn't do my homework." As it stands, Hill, Kelly, and Michos were the only refuseniks of the living members of the main Warriors cast. Brian Tyler and Tom McKitterick were not invited to revisit the characters of Snow and Cowboy. Tyler reflects, "They probably just couldn't get ahold of me. It's not like I had an agent or anything." "I was a bit surprised by that," McKitterick says of the fact of not being approached. "I suppose they could have found me if they wanted but they didn't, and I made not a penny from that. And there were two Cowboy action figures. I never got any money for that."

In fairness, brutal though the Rockstar game may be, it is also considered to be high-quality. Rockstar are neither amateurs nor low-rent. The Grand Theft Auto franchise is a financial phenomenon even within what is routinely a big-bucks industry, while the company's penchant for high production values suffused *The Warriors*. The game didn't require knowledge of the movie to be played or enjoyed. However, it was so finely detailed and authentic to Hill's vision that even fans of the movie who were non-gamers were inclined to seek it out.

The game was also an expansion of that vision, taking a movie of little more than an hour-and-a-half and turning it—for the most skillful players—into a twelve-hour experience. Although it opens with the conclave and the murder of Cyrus, it then jumps back in time to show the Warriors when they were still collective up-and-comers. As they go through their story missions, individual hinterlands are revealed, with information furnished on how each of the nine delegates to the conclave came to join the gang, as well as how the Warriors ensemble first came together. Detail is also filled in about rival gangs, some familiar from the film like the Baseball Furies and the High-Hats, others new inventions like the Destroyers (supposedly the Warriors' Coney Island rivals). Rockstar also created a gang based on stills of the Mongols but retitled them the Savage Huns. (The High-Hats got their name changed to the Hi-Hats, as though they were part of a drum kit.)

When cops arrest Warriors members, those of the gang still at large engage in missions to free their comrades. Monotony of gameplay is avoided, however, by the Warriors having other "tasks" that include collecting protection money, stealing car radios, looting shops, leaving a tag, exacting revenge, or fleeing other gangs.

Although the Warriors avatars are slightly Pixar-cartoonish, the overarching noir is pure Walter Hill. The presence of much of the original cast is another contributing factor to a feeling of class and authenticity, their voices used sometimes to repeat word-for-word lines from the movie. Another thing this lends is power: trained live-action actors are able to orate more powerfully than voiceover artists only familiar with restrained TV or radio spots.

"That was fascinating, trying to go back in time, trying to conjure up that voice again," says Van Valkenburgh. However, some might aver that the video game demeans the original picture by reducing it to cartoon level. James Remar dismisses this idea out of hand. Although perfectly civilized, Remar can be as combative as Ajax in conversation, as demonstrated when he responds, "Why would it?... The film was always on a storyboard level. It was a surrealistic, comic book, stylized type of film. But a comic book can be great. (I'm differentiating that from cartoon.) The video game's the video game. I did it and they gave me a few bucks for it and I appreciated that. It was fun to do. I'm really not much of a gamer, but it was an honor that people are still interested in it. I did do the voice and I don't apologize for it, but I don't really think that the two are very related."

The Rockstar payment bonanza wasn't restricted to actors. The game's faithful replication of the timbre of the movie extended to the music. "They felt it was important," says Barry DeVorzon. Initially, however, Rockstar made him what he terms a "really lowball" offer to license his score. "At that time video games didn't spend hardly any money on scores," he says. It was no doubt for this reason that a Paramount lawyer advised DeVorzon that, should he not accept their terms, Rockstar could easily and legally use a piece of original music designed to be vaguely redolent of his soundtrack. "I said, 'I don't care. If they want to do that, let them do it. If they want the original music, then they're gonna have to pay for it.' And they wound up paying for it." He doesn't mention a figure, but terms it "a considerable amount" that was "way more" than he got for the original score back in the Seventies. "And I like that because, wow, after all these years the music's still valid... I think the video-game people say it all. The score was very much a part of why that movie's hung around." Has he ever played the game? "No," DeVorzon chuckles. Like many of the cast and crew of *The Warriors*, his vintage is such that he never got into this new-fangled form of entertainment.

DeVorzon's soundtrack obtained additional life in 2013 through yet another medium that wasn't around in 1979. It was in that year that La-La Land Records issued a CD entitled *The Warriors: Music From The Motion Picture* on which the original album release was remastered and—courtesy of the longer running times of compact discs—virtually doubled in length. Not only did the CD mop up the DeVorzon contributions to the score omitted from the original LP, it also included unedited versions, outtakes, and alternates. The CD must have been desired by far more people than were able to purchase it, being a limited edition of 3,000. "It's become this cult thing, especially among the black community," says the composer. "How did that happen? My gosh, I want to impress a black musician or artist, I tell them I did *The Warriors*."

THE ROCKSTAR EFFORT was an elevated example of the video-game genre. Another Warriors game featured less thought and lower production values. *The Warriors: Street Brawl* was devised by CXTM and released in September 2009 on the Mac OS X, Microsoft Windows, and Xbox Live

Arcade. It suffered from the faults of being superficial (related to the film only by title, locations, and character names) and difficult to play (sluggish graphics). Nevertheless, it served to help extend the life of the movie further.

If *Warriors* video games are indeed part of a demeaning cultural trajectory, it could be argued that the process reached its logical end point when in the same year as the release of *Street Brawl The Warriors* became a comic book. Dabel Brothers Publishing issued a five-part adaptation of the film, followed by a quartet called *Jailbreak* which followed up the movie's storyline, depicting the Warriors plotting to spring Ajax from prison.

Another example of licensed Warriors property that some might view as debasing the film, let alone its source novel, is the lines of action figures released by Mezco Toyz. The company has released ten-inch dolls (2005) and nine-inch line figures (2008) of characters from the film, with the first set being cartoonish in the sense of disproportionately large heads. Having said that, both sets were eerie in their resemblance to the real-life prototypes. Moreover, they demonstrated deep knowledge of the subject: it wasn't just the individual Warriors who were represented, but also Cyrus, Luther, some Baseball Furies, and even—in the second set—Sully, the gauche leader of the Orphans (played in the film by Paul Greco). Despite declining to participate in Warriors conventions or computer games, David Patrick Kelly has no problem with the existence of such artefacts. "I'm a Warholian in that respect. I have the action figure and [the creator] is kind of famous. He's a Hispanic sculptor. Years ago there was a guy who just did the Warriors logo on a T shirt. He had a little t-shirt company downtown New York. If it inspires people that way, and it obviously continues to do so, I think it's okay."

Wright also has no problems with the action figures ("They were cute. I didn't hate them. My son bought two of them. People bring them to shows and I sign them"). However, he did take issue with his lack of remuneration for them. "I had just signed with Abrams Artists on that voiceover. I said, 'Look, there's these dolls out and I didn't sign a likeness agreement.' So they looked into it for me and Mezco wound up paying me."

Which raises the issue of precisely what the Warriors actors are financially entitled to in the wake of their film becoming a money-spinner in ways that simply hadn't been thought of in 1979. Take-Two publicly responded to Roger Hill's lawsuit with a statement in which they said that the company possessed "a valid third-party license for the rights to use

Roger Hill's likeness and the character of Cyrus in *The Warriors* video game and related marketing materials." From his experiences with Rockstar, David Patrick Kelly feels the issue is unresolved. "I was in talks with Paramount because we had a contract that said they owed all of us money any time they use our likeness. I think the other guys who did the voices on the games signed it away with Rockstar and stuff like that. I never did to this day. I talked to the vice president over there and it's still not resolved to my satisfaction. They never paid me anything… They claimed they didn't [have to]. I remember the Rockstar contract said, 'We now own that blah be dah blah' and Paramount claims they just licensed it." Kelly never sued, however. "They got all the money, they got all the lawyers."

Says Beck of Wright's demand for remuneration for the dolls, "Dorsey's going out and getting that done, that kind of let the rest of us know that, 'Oh, okay, we do have some rights there.'" However, having at least been remunerated by Rockstar—handsomely and voluntarily in that case—there is no current motivation on his part to mount legal actions. "We're not talking about enough money for the piddling things that are there," he says. "I mean, Paramount itself doesn't even go after the different people that make Warrior things. Who wants to get into that kind of litigation? If each of us had several million dollars' worth of stuff, we might get into a class-action suit. But we're talking about a forty-something-year-old movie."

That the action-figure accessories included such things as a switchblade (Swan), nunchucks (Cleon), and a Molotov cocktail (Cochise) gives an even greater clue than their belated years of release that these products were not aimed at the type of people who were buying action figures back in the Seventies. Kids these days are on their computer games while it's their fathers who are buying the toys. "If you call them dolls, they're going to get upset," notes Wright of the items he is asked to autograph. "They're bringing 'action figures.'" This is tied into another observation he makes about the Warriors demographic. In a comment that serves as a demurral to Michos' contention that the film is an obsession for both genders, he notes, "This whole thing to me is a sausage fest. I'm going to shows where I'm not meeting too many women. It's a guy's flick… I'm meeting grown men who say, 'When it came out, I saw it fifteen times, and I can't wait 'til my son gets of age to see the movie.' It's almost like a rite-of-passage of testosterone… But hey, if this is what makes them happy, what the heck." As for himself, Wright notes, "I don't keep any of that stuff in my house. My mother has a scrapbook full of stuff and my son has all the action figures and all of that old nonsense." Of Cleon's striking array of necklaces, he reveals, "My son chewed that up when he was teething."

DAVID PATRICK KELLY makes the observation, "Wasn't *The Warriors* a remake? There is a movie called *The Lost Patrol* that was based on Xenophon." Beck is under a similar impression. "I remember talking to Walter once," he says. "He likened the Warriors getting back to Coney Island [to] that Victor McLaglen movie *The Lost Patrol*, where they're in the desert and they're having to fight their way through different enemy factions to get back." "Well, I don't know," says Hill. "I would say that probably applies more to *Southern Comfort*."

Regardless, a remake of *The Warriors* itself has, despite intentions and rumors, remained elusive. It was first planned by Tony Scott, the director responsible for the likes of *Top Gun* and *Crimson Tide*. Scott preferred the word "retooling" to "remake." "The original doesn't stand up very well, because it was very Seventies New York, but this one I'm doing about the gang culture in LA," he said in 2009. Inevitably, the Crips and the Bloods, the notorious street gangs operating in Los Angeles, were said to be both *Warriors* fans and keen to participate. In 2005, Scott told Larry Carroll of mtv.com that the opening of his *Warriors* would begin on the Long Beach Bridge and was going to resemble the LA marathon. "You'll still get the same story, but we're reconstructing the family, reconstructing the characters... The original was in New York and everything went upwards; LA goes [length-wise]." He revealed that he intended to dispense with the outlandish likes of the Baseball Furies and the High-Hats. Having worked with real-life LA gangs on *Domino* (2005), he had secured from representatives a deal worthy of Cyrus: "They said, 'If you can get this movie on, we'll do a treaty between all the warriors, all the different gangs.'" While he said he loved Hill's original movie, he was after a very different tone and feel. In reference to his director brother Ridley's current epic, he said, "The encounters will be more like *Kingdom of Heaven*. It will be the Warriors stacking up against 3,000 gang members."

A draft of a screenplay written for Scott by Terence Winter found its way to the wider public and, despite Winter's *Sopranos* pedigree, was promptly ridiculed. Partly this was because of its similarities to the original film (simply transplanting the plot to the West Coast) and partly for the bizarre or self-conscious ways it deviated from it (depicting the Lizzies as a transsexual gang, turning the Rogues into corrupt cops, showing Cyrus rehearsing his famous speech with the aid of index cards). The

Warriors themselves bore exactly the same names, but for some reason a new member had been added to their ranks, Little Inch, although he only stayed around long enough to be murdered by a Cambodian gang as a consequence of the machinations of Luther. Winter was the fourth writer to work on the project, following in the footsteps of John Glenn & Travis Wright and Joel Wyman. This already tortuous process evidently only became more so. The picture got no closer to the screen by the time of the seriously ill Scott's suicide in 2012.

Remake or retool, back in 2009, the idea was met with almost overwhelming hostility from the original cast and crew, with their contempt for the idea apparently shot through with amusement about the inordinate amount of time it had already spent in what is known in the industry as "development hell." "I've heard that for twenty years," said Remar. "Obviously if it's in Los Angeles, it's not a remake... If it were in New York City and it was the Coney Island Warriors doing what we did, that's a remake... It's a different movie with probably the skeleton idea of what we did." Beck offered, "Remakes of most movies, especially if they were classic movies, I think, 'What a waste of time that is. Why not think up something new to do?' I know that the hardcore Warriors fans are not so happy that a remake is being made. When that question is asked of them [at conventions], they're always thumbs-down." "It's madness," said Thomas Waites. "I just think it's exploitative." Van Valkenburgh seems a bit more ambivalent about the project than her ex-colleagues. She comes out with a list of objections: "I don't understand why there would be a remake. I definitely don't want to see it being called the same thing. The fans like the movie we made. They're not interested. They're not excited about another version. They like how it was shot, they like all the lines in the movie. The specificity of the first film is what the fans like." However, she also reveals that she tried to ensure that the original actors would be a part of any new project. "I went to his office, seems like ten years ago," she said in 2009 of Scott. "Audaciously, I thought I could just talk to him about the remake and I had this marketing idea and blah blah blah. I didn't get to see him. My whole fantasy when I went to his office was I thought it would be fun if he would just spot us somewhere in the movie. I don't know who we would be, but I just thought it would be a fun idea to have us popping up as a visual somewhere, and I thought the fans would be amused by that too."

Wright is neither for nor against. "Because if they want to do it, they're going to do it anyway. If they see a dollar in it, it'll be shot. My thing is, can be done, but you would have to do it like *Escape from New York*. Or *Escape from LA*. Because you need that same feel of old New York, that grittiness. So you could probably only do it as those apocalypse movies, that type of thing." He also agrees that an LA-set enterprise involving the Bloods and the Crips would not be *The Warriors* but "something completely different," adding, "Palm tree-lined streets are way too pretty and you got all this sun." Which fact, for David Harris, underlines unfeasibility issues. "Ain't no subway system in LA," he points out. "It's palm trees and beaches. You can't make *The Warriors* in Los Angeles. Otherwise Walter Hill would have done it. Why would he come to New York City to do it?" Yet he dismisses the idea of an NY-set new *Warriors*. "You can't remake. New York City's not that anymore." He summarizes, "Leave *The Warriors* alone. It's a classic movie. You don't try and remake *The Godfather*. You don't try and remake certain movies. If it ain't broke, don't fix it."

"I like Tony, he's a good guy, a good director," said Lawrence Gordon back then. "Anything can be improved on." However, he now says, "They showed me a treatment of that and I went nuts. That was like a Romeo and Juliet where the police chief's daughter is in love with the head of the Warriors so the police chief has to frame him. It was horrible." He also says, "I would hate to see anybody remake the movie, including us. We didn't make this licking our chops saying, 'Ohh, this is so commercial, let's go make this movie and make a lot of money.' We thought it was a great movie yarn. I think anybody that remade it would be making it purely for commercial purposes. We made it for the right reasons. We were excited about the idea. It's not the same thing as remaking something [and saying], 'Gosh, you know what would do a lot of business today?'"

Surprisingly, Walter Hill is not actively opposed. "Don't care," he shrugs. "I always say the same thing: good luck. I made mine. Larry always tells me that they've spent six times as much trying to get a script and develop it than we did in making the whole movie. I suspect that it may be one of those things that was of a certain time and might be hard to re-do." Like so many others, he views an LA-set project oriented around the city's real-life gangs to be such a different proposition to his picture as to make any connection meaningless. "I would say they probably ought to just make a movie, forget about calling it a *Warrior* remake."

After Scott's demise, the reins of the remake project looked briefly like being picked up by Mark Neveldine and Brian Taylor, a pair of outlandish, edgy directors known for the *Crank* films, *Gamer*, and *Jonah Hex*. In a 2015 interview with Matt Singer of screencrush.com, Neveldine said,

"It's just in rights hell at the moment. We just feel like we're the perfect guys for that job; baseball bats, roller skates, gangs, the heightened world." By 2015, the movie industry and society in general had been through a couple of cycles of opinion about the harmful effects of screen violence and he spoke of fear at some studios that a new *Warriors* would cause street gangs to act up. "You do it in *Crank* style, people are just gonna laugh and have fun," he reasoned.

Rights hell seems to have put paid to whatever ideas he and his colleague had in this direction. However, in the summer of 2016 the notion of a new Warriors project now moved on from one modern screen phenomenon—the remake—to another: the long-form television drama. It involved streaming, a broadcasting technology that didn't exist in 1979. Streaming company Hulu were to purvey it to the public, with Paramount producing. This project will seem to some automatically more intriguing than a new *Warriors* cinema venture, partly because of the unprecedentedly sophisticated level of modern TV, partly because of the involvement of directors the Russo Brothers. Joe and Anthony Russo were already Midas-touch figures, having helmed Captain America instalments of the all-conquering Marvel Cinematic Universe franchise *The Winter Soldier* and *Civil War*. They would shortly become even more acclaimed as they directed further instalments in that series in the shape of Avengers movies *Infinity War* and *Endgame*, thus giving themselves two places in the top five of history's highest-grossing films (and still one when adjusted for inflation).

Contrary to some reports, Lawrence Gordon is not the putative series' executive producer, although he has had discussions. "They did ask me to come on board one time and I did take a meeting," he says. "I'm too old to do this now, and I wouldn't want to do something that Walter hated. I've heard a bunch of ideas all these years since the movie was made and really and truly I haven't seen anything worth a damn… They wanted to go to the country Colombia and live with a gang there. I said, 'You guys will never get insurance. Are you crazy?'… The last time I talked to a studio about doing a TV series, their idea was to do a soap opera almost with the Warriors where you live with them and you slept with them and you follow them. It was ridiculous."

Gordon has successfully steered movie franchises like the Terminator movies but feels that an extended Warriors project makes no sense. "*The Warriors* is a one-shot. It's one night. That's what made it work. The pressure of getting back home before daylight. That's what made me buy the goddamn book… A lot of my stuff that I've done is being developed for television, and it's fine. *48 Hrs* can be a TV series. A lot of stuff can be a TV series. I just don't see it for *The Warriors*."

Not mentioned by any interviewee is the fact that a remake, if updated rather than a period piece, will not only have to negotiate the existing ""Why didn't they just catch a ride?" issue but also the fact of the internet, GSP, CCTV, and myraid other ways that make it nigh-on impossible in modern society to hide in the shadows and hence spin out a narrative about urban fugitives to feature length, let alone TV-series length.

It's also nigh-on impossible to predict if a *Warriors* remake would be a triumph like Peter Jackson's 2005 *King Kong* or a damp squib like Antoine Fuqua's *The Magnificent Seven* (2016), but it would seem safe to conclude that—courtesy of the goodwill engendered by the original—it would find a market. "The purists out there will scream but they will eventually wind up seeing it even out of just curiosity," says Wright.

On a related—if almost bizarrely so—note, in 2009 Yurick was talking about a project that would probably have made a lot of sense to those who thought the *Warriors* movie was not too far away from *West Side Story* in its stylized depictions of youth-culture violence. "A London playwright has optioned the book for the possibility of making a musical out of it," he said. "I can't think of his name. He had a production that was successful on Broadway. He has a collaborator named Matthew Xia. So we may now see a play, a musical. I've no idea what he's going to do with this."

Until such time as a new film or a stage musical arrives, the fans will have to make do with the existing movie, in either its original iteration or the Ultimate Director's Cut. Released as a DVD in 2005, the latter was a package that included four featurettes about the making of and reception to the film (complete with deleted film sections), and a new cut that was as close an approximation as now possible of how Hill originally conceived the film. In the latter, a Xenophon-referencing illustrated scroll was inserted at the beginning, which is also read aloud (Hill: "That's my voice, where it would have been Orson. I'm a pitiful replacement, I grant"). Rotoscoped transitions designed to resemble comic-book panels introduced seven scenes, and the freeze-frame ending was replaced by a new finale involving a shot of the Warriors jumping out of the way of waves morphing into a five-panel comic-book page facsimile of beach scenes. Nothing about the theatrical release's narrative was changed, but the picture ended up very slightly longer (around half a minute).

"I am perfectly happy with the edit of the theatrical version," Hill points out. He also says the new version is "wrongly called the Director's Cut." However, he says, "If you wanted to understand the way the picture would have been at the time, this was much closer to it. The graphics were done at a later date... It's different in the sense the artwork would have been a little different, but I wanted to clarify the comic-book intentions." The cut proved controversial, with some fans criticizing what they felt to be unnecessary changes. "Most of what I read and heard was positive," says Hill, "but there will be people for reasons of either nostalgia or reasons of wanting a more direct movie and a little less abstract movie that would prefer the original. And that's fine. I just simply say that if you want to know what I was thinking and trying to do, this is a little more in tune with that."

LEGACY

"I THINK THAT the negative vibes from the instances of violence are on the whole mercifully a thing of the past," says Walter Hill. "It's perceived to be this kind of fun youth movie and they have an endless amount of revival screenings. It's become part of the larger thing."

Maybe so, but it's unlikely that any feature has ever been published about *The Warriors* that doesn't mention the violence alleged to have been inspired by it and the status the film held, at least for a while, as a totem of what was wrong with New York and/or America and/or Western society. That being the case, has it become impossible to evaluate *The Warriors* purely and simply as a piece of cinema? "I think maybe that's the English take on it," responds Hill, perhaps thinking back to his being located in the UK when *The Warriors* was released Stateside. "Yeah, there were these incidents and they were bad things but that wasn't the framework of the movie. To me, what's kind of interesting is there was never any retraction of the positive... Pauline Kael didn't retract her review. There were some politicians that stood up and gave some speeches and all that kind of thing, but isn't there always?"

"I don't know in cinematic terms how it's even considered," says Michael Beck. "I simply know that in a continuing fanbase there are multiple generations, so it is a movie that still attracts new people to it. You don't compare *The Warriors* to *Citizen Kane*, for crying out loud. It's just what it is. It was a cult movie, like *Rocky Horror Picture Show* is a cult movie. It's attracted a fanbase that keeps replicating itself over time because newer people get introduced to it and they just dig the movie." What would the reason be? "It's very exciting, it's got a great soundtrack. It's in a lot of ways a cowboy movie more than a gang movie. I think that visually it is

263

still a really interesting picture to watch, what New York City looks like in that movie. And it's still an underdog story: with everybody out to get this one group, they get home, and that's always an appealing story, from the Greeks to now."

"It just was so crazy kitsch if you will, so outsider, that it stuck for all these different people," says David Patrick Kelly. "I guess stylized or cartoon. Corny might be another way to say it. But people loved it, people who hadn't seen anything that they were interested in on the screen. If you look at the movies that were coming out at that time, it was white upper-class marriage dramas with Meryl Streep and Dustin Hoffman. This was not the concern of the people who were having parties in the Bronx inventing hip hop. It had this symbolic effect for them that was very real to them, no matter how stylized… I remember speaking to some casting-director guy. I said, 'I'm shooting *The Warriors*,' and he said, 'What is it—the good gang versus the bad ga-a-angs?' Yeah, it was, but it lasted… I love the way it comes round full circle when it connects in that way."

Gareth Jones of the Warriors Movie Site says, "I feel that *The Warriors* has had a profound impact on a lot of people who relate to the key underlying themes of a sense of place, brotherhood, and—perhaps most importantly—belonging. In the film there's a lot of shots of a gang of friends hanging out, having fun and looking out for each other and I often think this is overlooked."

"It's a fun 88-minute romp with people dressed in costumes," simply says James Remar.

Even the two biggest naysayers about the film could perceive merit in it. "When it first came out, I found myself in the position of having to see it two or three times and commenting on it," Sol Yurick recalled. "I was irritated at it even within the context of the way Hill did it… To me, a lot of it is wooden." However, he did discern considerable positives. "That scene with the rattling bottles and 'Warriors come out and play' I thought was brilliant. And one of the things that I liked was the economy with which you got all the gangs together." He was also impressed by the almost Marxist qualities to be found in Mercy's speech about living for today and Swan's comment, "This is what we fought all night to get back to?" "I also like the touch where they encounter the people from the prom night in the subway and when she reaches up to straighten her hair and he pulls her hand back—that was brilliant," he said. While it's unlikely that Shaber, Hill, or Gordon were Marxist, could it be that, in its own way, the film was more political than his book? "Yeah, that's right. Those were good touches." The fact that so many agree with Yurick on the prom-couples scene, whether for reasons of politics or pathos, makes it interesting that both Gordon and Hill have admitted they were initially unsure about whether the scene would work. Yurick added of the film, "I've met young people who've seen it ten, twenty times. I can't imagine doing that, but okay." As if to prove that a dedicated Marxist can be just as shallow as a rampant capitalist, incidentally, Yurick admitted that what most impressed him about the film was seeing his name shooting toward him in the opening credits.

"I think it has a relevance," Thomas Waites says of *The Warriors*. "There's an excitement and a vitality to it. Even the name 'Warriors'—to a certain extent everybody has to be a warrior to survive and people do tend to cluster in groups. Musicians, actors, stick together, hang together, fight for the way home." He also thinks the film was prophetic. "In a way this is why the movie was so successful: it elicited a response in urban America and it was very glamorizing of gangs in a certain way. They weren't popular... The gang scene really hadn't become an item until after this film and I think in many ways that was the genius of Walter Hill is that he had his finger on the pulse of something that was about to happen in society. He anticipated this eruption and painted it in colors." Waites summarizes, "I think it's a fine film by a very talented guy. I think it deserves its place in film history."

As noted at the beginning of this text, the film's female lead marvels at what a ride the whole Warriors experience has been. "The whole thing has just been such a fantastical experience from shooting it to years later still riding on the rollercoaster," says Deborah Van Valkenburgh. "It just keeps on going... There's just tons of stuff about it. Philosophy teachers use that film as a tool, as an example. It's definitely got a legacy of some kind."

She also muses, "It was so short-lived in the beginning... It was something the minute it happened—and then there's all the other controversies and all the events that led to it being yanked and buried in the background, may have misdirected it into another realm... You have to talk about it a little more to make sure people realize its value. If it had had a regular run, then who's to say what would have happened, who's to say how it would have been perceived?"

Paramount's then-chairman Barry Diller and then-president Michael Eisner were approached to be interviewed for this book, but both declined. To some extent, Hill offers the mitigation for the stances the studio adopted toward *The Warriors* that those men might have. With his fights with Paramount now a thing of history (much like studios in general), Hill is a little more forgiving of them. "I'm probably a lot mellower now than I was, but I got a chance to make a movie that was a very different film and I appreciate that chance," he says. So different that he has trouble defining it. "It's very difficult to talk about *The Warriors* because it doesn't fit easily into a paragraph or something like that," he says. "It's a dystopian vision. It's a comic book. It's a analogy of a great story from Greek literature. It's many different things, but all that sounds very pretentious when you write it down. And it's an entertainment and it seems to have continued to entertain people over the years... When you said 'gang,' it was such a pejorative in Hollywood films before. This was a film that valorized the idea gangs could also be a defensive organization that protected you from the desperate perditions from the outside world and, more importantly, gave you a sense of self identity. That's what I think made the movie so popular with young people."

Of course, nothing dates faster than novelty. That innovation, therefore, would have less resonance for generations who have, partly as a consequence of *The Warriors*, grown up on a diet of more nuanced depictions of young, working-class, criminal milieux. It could well be that *The Warriors* endures simply because it is a stylish and well-crafted piece of cinema. In around 2018, Hill saw the film with an audience for the first time since it came out four decades previously. "They were doing a retrospective of films that I'd done," he says. "I got there a little early before they put me up on stage and I sat there and saw the second half of the movie and it was a full house. I was very pleased about how well it played. The audience was just with it. If you're a writer and a director, you're trying to get something that plays, that entertains at a level, that engages an audience. The film seemed to still do that."

The esteem in which *The Warriors* has come to be held is the ultimate vindication after the denunciations that destroyed its first run. "It was the source of all evil among people that were never going to go see the movie or never going to like the movie," says Hill. On this score, he continues in his vein of almost fetishizing the wisdom of youth. "The people that liked the movie never saw it that way, which was the young audience. But that audience doesn't own a lot of newspapers or magazines. They have a difficult time getting their opinions out, but they always voted for the movie vocally. It found its way."

A limited commercial success *The Warriors* may have had, but its producer has found that it has cut through culturally in a way that far more successful pictures he has helmed have not. The walls of Lawrence Gordon's office are lined with one-sheets of the films he has produced. "When people come in, they say, 'You made *The Warriors*?'" says Lawrence Gordon. "That's the first thing they say. And there's some pretty big hits up on the wall."

ACKNOWLEDGMENTS

I WOULD LIKE TO EXPRESS my grateful thanks to the following people for granting me interviews about *The Warriors*:

Craig R. Baxley
Michael Beck
Lawrence Gordon
David Harris
Chris W. Hill
Walter Hill
David Patrick Kelly
Tom McKitterick
Bobbie Mannix
Terry Michos
Frank Marshall
James Remar
Mayra Sánchez
Brian Tyler
Deborah Van Valkenburgh
Kenny Vance
Barry DeVorzon
Thomas G. Waites
Dorsey Wright
Sol Yurick

Some of the above interviewees spoke to me in 2009 for a feature for *Total Film* magazine. The majority of this material was unpublished at the time due to the inherent space limitations of a magazine feature. Some listed spoke to me more recently during the preparation of this book, and some spoke to me in both timeframes. I'm grateful to one and all for patiently putting up with my sometimes obscure questions.

It's a sadness to me that none of my 2009 interview with Sol Yurick got published before he passed away in 2013 and I am pleased to finally be able to present his thoughts herein.

I am also greatly indebted to the following for providing assistance, research material, and/or information:

Terence Denman
J. Blake Fichera
Gareth Jones
Larry McCallister
Terry Michos
Florella Orowan
Shaun Powers
Jeff Sanderson
Remy Shaber
Sam Shaber
Paramount Pictures

SELECTED REFERENCES

BOOKS
Kael, Pauline. *When the Lights Go Down*. Marion Boyars, 1980.
Laszlo, Andrew. *Every Frame a Rembrandt: Art and Practice of Cinematography*. Routledge, 2000.
Yurick, Sol. *The Warriors* (with new afterword). Grove Press, 2003.

SCREENPLAYS
Shaber, David. *The Warriors*. Undated, but probably 1977.
Hill, Walter. *The Warriors*. June 1978.
Hill, Walter. *The Warriors*. "Final Revised Screenplay" (as-filmed script). November 1978.

WEBSITES
www.dga.org/Craft/VisualHistory/Interviews/Walter-Hill.aspx?Filter=Full+Interview
www.the-numbers.com
imdb.com
aficatalog.afi.com
warriorsmovie.co.uk

Also by Sean Egan from
BearManor Media

Ponies & Rainbows:
The Life of James Kirkwood

James Kirkwood is the forgotten man of American letters.

In 1975, he had two shows playing on Broadway, while his latest novel *Some Kind of Hero* saw reviewers comparing him to Saul Bellow and Joseph Heller. One of those shows – *A Chorus Line* – won him a Pulitzer Prize for his co-writing contribution and went on to become the biggest stage phenomenon in history. Yet today his work is largely out of print and his name rarely mentioned.

Kirkwood led a life that was as gripping as any of his novels or plays. The son of silent screen stars, he grew up in Hollywood surrounded by celebrities and opulence before his parents went broke. His childhood was littered with trauma, including finding the dead body of his mother's fiancé when he was twelve. Before writing, his professional life encompassed the coast guard, stand-up comedy and soap opera acting. His private life was equally varied, involving loving sexual relationships with both men and women.

Sean Egan – author or editor of two-dozen books – took over seven years to write this definitive biography, interviewing more than sixty of Kirkwood's family, lovers, colleagues, friends and adversaries in the process. In a sweeping narrative that takes in Hollywood in the Twenties, the boom era of New York nightclubs in the Forties and the Eighties AIDS holocaust, *Ponies & Rainbows* both details a remarkable life and seeks to re-establish an even more remarkable talent.

Interviewees include: Gary Beach, Vasili Bogazianos, Ahmet Ertegun, Bill Gile, Milton Katselas, Terence Kilburn, Larry Kramer, Arthur Laurents, Baayork Lee, Jim Marrs, Vivian Matalon, Donna McKechnie, Terrence McNally, Donald Oliver, Richard Seff, Zachary Sklar, Liz Smith, David Spencer, Elaine Stritch and Robert C. Wilson.

Paperback: 576 pages
ISBN: 978-1593936808

Ponies & Rainbows
THE LIFE OF
JAMES KIRKWOOD

Sean Egan

William Goldman:
The Reluctant Storyteller

William Goldman is one of the world's most popular storytellers.

Amongst his more than two-dozen motion picture screenplays are such iconic works as *Butch Cassidy and the Sundance Kid*, *The Stepford Wives*, *All the President's Men* and *A Bridge Too Far*. His acclaimed novels include *The Temple of Gold*, *Boys and Girls Together*, *The Princess Bride* and *Marathon Man*. His non-fiction embraces *The Season* and *Adventures in the Screen Trade*, considered the definitive studies on Broadway and Hollywood respectively.

Yet despite his success, Goldman has always been a tormented man, unable to enjoy either his art or the respect it has garnered him. Convinced he is "in on a pass," he has rarely written without a profound sense of self-doubt.

In *William Goldman: The Reluctant Storyteller*, Sean Egan analyzes both Goldman's life and output, a task in which he has been assisted by Goldman himself via a series of interviews.

The result is an enthralling book that gets to the core of a man who is both supreme talent and perplexing enigma.

Paperback: 292 pages
ISBN: 978-1593935832

bearmanormedia.com

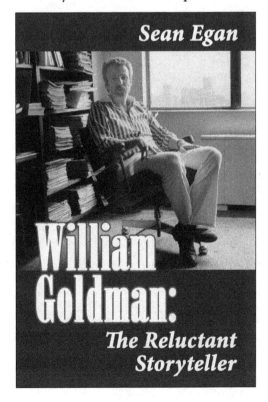

Sean Egan

William Goldman:
The Reluctant Storyteller